Some Lectures of
The Conference on
Christian Humanism

1961   1964

All art illustrations by
THE REVEREND WILLIAM C. FROST
of the Diocese of Raleigh

IMPRIMATUR ✠ VINCENT S. WATERS, D.D.
Bishop of Raleigh

Raleigh, N. C.
December 8, 1968.

The Divine

Synthesis

Some Lectures of
The Conference on
Christian Humanism

1961   1964

Mount Mary
Asheville NC

(Printed not Published)

DEDICATION

To the largest group of apostolic Catholic men in the world, working for God, Church and souls, the Knights of Columbus and their courageous leader, the Honorable John W. McDevitt, Supreme Knight, this book is fondly dedicated.

Table of Contents

Page

INTRODUCTION 1

Most Reverend John J. Wright, D.D.
Bishop of Pittsburgh

TEACHING IN THE SPIRIT OF
CHRISTIAN HUMANISM 7

Dr. Frank O'Malley, University of Notre Dame
Notre Dame, Indiana

THE AIM AND END OF EDUCATION 25

Reverend Ambrose J. McNicholl, O.P.
Collegio S. Clemente, Via Labicana
Rome, Italy

THE MATTER OF COLLEGE EDUCATION 37

Reverend Ambrose J. McNicholl, O.P.
Collegio S. Clemente, Via Labicana
Rome, Italy

THE TEACHING-LEARNING RELATIONSHIP 55

Dr. Willis D. Nutting, University of Notre Dame
Notre Dame, Indiana

EDUCATIONAL CHALLENGE OF THE SPACE AGE 71

Reverend William A. Wallace, O.P.
Massachusetts Institute of Technology

Table of Contents

Page

EDUCATION IN A PLURALIST SOCIETY 87

Reverend Francis Canavan, S.J.
Associate Editor of "America"
New York, N. Y.

SCIENCE AND THE HUMANITIES, Lectures 1 and 2... 103

Dr. Charles DeKoninck, University of Laval
Quebec, Canada

SCIENCE, EDUCATION AND THE
    CHRISTIAN PERSON 135

Sister Adrian Marie, O.P.
Siena College, Memphis, Tennessee

LITERATURE AND PERSONAL VALUES.................... 153

Dr. Paul van K. Thomson, Director
Liberal Arts Honors Program,
Providence College, Providence, R.I.

EXCELLENCE ON THE CATHOLIC CAMPUS 161

Dr. Paul van K. Thomson, Director
Liberal Arts Honors Program
Providence College, Providence, R.I.

THE SOCIAL ENCYCLICALS 175

Mrs. Anne Fremantle
New York City and Mexico City

JUSTICE AND THE SPIRIT OF SOCIAL
    RESPONSIBILITY 191

Brother Leo V. Ryan, C.S.V.
Asst. Superior General of Clerics of St. Viator
Rome, Italy

Table of Contents

Page

THE CHURCH, MANAGEMENT AND LABOR 201

Rt. Rev. Msgr. George G. Higgins, Director
Department of Social Action
United States Catholic Conference

THE CHURCH IN THE CITY 213

Reverend Joseph H. Fichter, S.J.
Department of Sociology
Loyola University, New Orleans, La.

CLERGY-LAY RELATIONS 231

Reverend Joseph H. Fichter, S.J.
Department of Sociology
Loyola University, New Orleans, La.

CHRISTIAN RESPONSIBILITY IN INTERFAITH
CONTACTS 249

Sister Joan Bland, S.N.D.
Office of Development, Trinity College
Washington, D. C.

THE END OF INNOCENCE 265

Sister M. Madeleva, C.S.C.
St. Mary's College, Notre Dame, Indiana

THE PLEROMA OF THE CHRISTIAN 275

Reverend James M. Egan, O.P.
Director, School of Sacred Theology
St. Mary's College, Notre Dame, Indiana

THE CHRISTIAN INTELLECTUAL IN THE WORLD 289

Reverend James M. Egan, O.P.
Director, School of Sacred Theology
St. Mary's College, Notre Dame, Indiana

Table of Contents

Page

THERE HAS NEVER BEEN A RED-HAIRED SAINT.. 303

Dr. Barry Ulanov, Barnard College
Columbia University, New York, N. Y.

POSTSCRIPT 319

Most Reverend Vincent S. Waters, D.D.
Bishop of Raleigh

ACKNOWLEDGMENTS 323

APPENDIX 327

FINIS

"FLAG-POLE"

iv

Introduction

Prefatory Note

Nothing seems more clear to many of us than that the prospect for faith and for every other human value, freedom included, in civilized society, depends on the kind of Humanism which will prevail in the culture slowly emerging from the intellectual and spiritual crises of the moment.

Is it to be one or another form of a heavily technological Scientific Humanism, dominated by statistics, by formulae and by rigorous planning, and relatively indifferent to classical values, to liberal arts emphases and to those philosophical and theological concepts long so intimately associated with classical learning and with liberal studies? Will it, at the other extreme, be some form of Literary Humanism, less limited by the negations of scientism, perhaps, but still only slightly more positive in its openness to those ultimate spiritual values that religious humanists, conscious of their relationship as creatures to God, have traditionally cherished? Whether the Humanism of the future be colored by scientific truth or literary insights, will it be, at least as a practical matter, agnostic or even atheist in its religious premises or its pervading spirit? Or will it be an Integral Humanism which begins and ends with a faith not only in God but in that Incarnation which links Man and God, heaven and earth, the human and the divine?

1

The Second Vatican Council ended with a recognition that all those who believe in God at all, and, above all, those who believe in the God of Jesus Christ and a consequent Christian Humanism, must prepare for dialogue with a Humanism which is skeptical about Christ and His claims and probably destined to reveal one or another form of atheism as a characteristic of its outlook on life, love, beauty and truth. I, at least, so read the themes developed and yet to be developed in the *Pastoral Constitution of the Church in the Modern World;* so also do I read most of the other major themes in the more significant Council documents. These say to me (and to many others) that the cultural debate which lies immediately ahead for mankind is between two schools of Humanism, the Humanism which sees Man as made in the image of God and God Himself as Incarnate in the Man Jesus, on the one hand, and the Humanism which sees Man as the measure of all things, not only here below but, at least for all practical purposes, exclusively and absolutely.

This stark disjunction, with the mutually exclusive overtones that it suggests, does not arise from a situation that awaited the period of Vatican Council II to be discovered. It was prophesied by Cardinal Newman, notably in his sermon at the dedication of the Birmingham seminary; it was foreseen, as if in vision, by Soloviev. Many others in the East and the West have been equally sensitive to the manner in which these polarities in modern thought have been developing.

But neither does it mean, for all the mutual exclusiveness that characterizes some of the contradictions between these two ultimate schools of Humanism, that there is neither possibility nor point to dialogue between the disciples of these opposing views of man and of the universe within which he lives. Dialogue is not merely possible; it is imperative, if only because, whatever their concepts concerning the life of the world to come, all men without exception travel together through space and time on the globe which is their present undeniable and common dwelling place. Moreover, within whatever limits, there are important validities which all who share any measure of respect for humanity and any solicitude for the person may discover that they agree in acknowledging.

Hence the need that Christians prepare themselves for the dialogue with the world of unbelieving Humanism. Nor has serious study had to wait for Vatican Council II to begin this essential work of preparation for dialogue with other Humanisms by greater appreciation of Christian Humanism. All but unknown outside a small circle of thoughtful Christians privileged to share in a project nurtured by Bishop Vincent Waters, Summer School Sessions in the foothills of Western North Carolina have been for several seasons the focal point of intense conviction, meditation and intellectual searching concerning the truths and values which constitute the heritage, the present content and the future hopes of Christian Humanism.

The undersigned has twice taken part in these summer sessions. He is thoroughly ashamed of himself that, hard-pressed by many demands arising from the Council and commitments to his diocesan and other work, he has not been able to finish the text of his own Summer School papers in time for their publication here. However, he is grateful to Bishop Waters and to Dr. Barry Ulanov for the privilege of introducing the work of the others who participated in the programs and of here recalling, with gratitude and admira-

3

tion, programs under the patronage of the zealous Bishop of Raleigh which so greatly encouraged his guests in their conviction that the final word from and about the Word Incarnate is far from having been heard in our times. That Word will echo wherever the Christian Humanist speaks with a wisdom or acts with a love born of the faith that is the ground of our best hopes for sanity here and salvation hereafter.

✠John Wright

Bishop of Pittsburgh

Teaching in the Spirit of Christian Humanism

DR. FRANK O'MALLEY

I have a text for this lecture, a statement by one of the most vital Christian personalities and prophets of our time, Léon Bloy. And the statement is:

Human personality and individuality, written and signed by God on each human countenance in so extraordinary a way, sometimes on the face of a great man, is something altogether sacred; something for the resurrection, for eternal life, for the Beatific Union. Every human face is a very special door to paradise which cannot possibly be confused with any other, and through which there will never enter but one soul.

Teaching, like everything else in the antipersonal power world of the twentieth century, is always in danger of being submitted to the process of massification. We observe this everywhere about us in the history and the society and the politics of our time; and the teachers of the ideal Catholic college—or the teachers of any college, as far as I'm concerned—who would preserve themselves and their students against the impersonal power world must find themselves somehow in agreement with the Catholic and Christian humanist and personalist thought of our day.

Teachers who want to preserve themselves and their students in our colleges against the impersonal power world have to know that they face the forces of mechanization and oppression and servitude. We wouldn't have anything like a Christian humanist or personalist thought about anything, and especially not in education, unless the facts of mechanization and oppression and servitude were very evident. If you construct the most ideal college in the world, with a plan and a program, you know that today there is always a danger of becoming ganged-up against, of a situation in which both the teachers and the students find themselves simply groaning and groping in gongs and gears. But Christian humanist and personalist thought is very great in our time—marvelous, in fact—because it rises out of a kind of spiritual underworld that forever faces the power world.

Omitting from attention those people who because of their happy vitality or warm temperaments or preconceived ideology are optimists, you know very well that there is everywhere to be encountered a deep sorrow nowadays. This sorrow is first of all concerned with political and social conditions and possibilities. It is concerned also, as we know very well, with threats of military action. But beyond these, it is also known that this sorrow involves an undeniably crucial question. Is the person, is the teacher, the professor, the student of the twentieth century still adequate to his own vocation? Is he still adequate to his own work? We know that during the last century and a half there has developed a measure of power that will grow and grow, it seems, that will grow constantly and immeasurably. Now this power is widely objectivated. We observe it in scientific perception and in institutions that in turn bring forth new problems. We observe it in political structures that are in constant movement, heading for the future. We observe it in technical works that push forward out of their own dynamism, and last but not least we observe it in the spiritual and intellectual attitudes of man.

Now, human sorrow asks whether man is still able to be masterful so that he may live in freedom and dignity and so that he may be generated and joyous. Often, I think, the conviction prevails that man as he is today is not able to be himself anymore. Activities and their effects have mastered him, and have even made themselves independent of him. They have become something which has a nonhuman, even a cosmic nature, and which cannot, it appears, be perceived and assimilated by properly human means. Now you know very well that there is at last some truth in this feeling; and confronted by it and the situation arousing it, we as creators of culture no less than as human beings, naturally want to know what we can do about it.

I have defined the Christian teacher as a creator of culture, who sees existence under the aspect of eternity, under the aspect of eternal form, of the form that delivers, at the moment that it makes sense out of the world and out of civilization, the form of Christ our Lord. We find ourselves staring, vastly startled, at the savage features of the nuclear monstrosity and at the spectacular missions into unimaginable space. Sometimes I think that as we observe these achievements we must feel the reluctance and the forlornness of those courageous and sacrificing human beings who give themselves over to speeding us on to stars that we shall never see. I think that we recognize the immense importance of the proffered solutions of political and social and economic disorders. But we, you and I, are especially concerned with the improvements of the education system. And within a context, the context of a college of Christ, we are concerned with the quality and integrity of our teaching of persons, of our teaching of men and women. We are concerned with the promotion and the sustenance through our teaching of all the arts and sciences. These are our present preoccupations.

At the very outset I think that something has to be said about the sphere whence actually and eventually all our actions are determined, the sphere of personal attitudes and judgments and decisions. Then we can deal with the educational problems and resolutions that arise therefrom. We together have to realize that the basic answer to our questions is this: that we ourselves, as men and women, as teachers and educational leaders, have to recognize and take over the full nature of our teaching responsibilities. To be able to do this, I believe we have to regain our right relations to the truth of things, to the realities of other persons, to the postulations of our inner selves, our deepest inner selves, and finally and constantly to God, to Our Lord. And our main task is this: We must make an examination of our whole attitude toward life and a change in the way in which we see and deal with men, with nature, with ideas, with things, even with animals, and particularly with our own knowledge.

As I see it, the problem for those of us who are teachers, who would try to make and maintain our teaching personal in the midst of the impersonal twentieth-century power world, rests not in matter or in method, but in our whole attitude towards life and in the examination and re-examination of this attitude. But now the really pressing questions come. Have we ever really tried to realize what happens when, say, the average teacher teaches students and main-

tains the order and the character and the discipline of learning?

It is not peculiar to teachers, of course. One can raise such
questions as this: Do you who are members of religious
orders and communities ever realize clearly what actually
happens, say, when a superior gives an order to his subordinate? Whatever really happens when a judge conducts
a trial? Whatever really happens when a priest deals with
his parishioners or penitents, or defends, as he must often,
the truths of God? What really happens when a doctor
treats a patient? What actually happens when a civil servant
or any administrative official or functionary or bureaucrat behind his desk or in a waiting room deals with the public?
What really happens when the industrialist manages his fac-
tory? When a merchant serves his customers? When an
artisan does his work, or when a farmer tills his fields? Have
we ever really perceived these actions in their concrete course,
in their determining sentiment and realized attitude, in their
immediate and in their remote effects?

Well, our question is: what happens to us when we teach
our students and maintain, as I say, the order and the discipline and the character of learning? Do we always find
respect for truth and confidence in its strength? We have
rules, but do we ever ask—is the rule always unassailably
right? Does the person dealt with always feel that there is
a personal relation established, especially one of respect?
And is the action really concerned with this relation? And is
it realized, as it should be, according to its nature? Is there a
true appeal in our courses to the animate faculty, the creative
faculty, the freedom in the student? I think we have to
understand that these are not questions of private morale
really, but of the success or failure of intellectual and cultural

11

life and of the education that would nurture this life. And I think we have to realize that everything depends for ourselves and for our students upon the activation of a true and deep respect for truth and life and personal dignity and the creative center or creative freedom of our fellow man. And I believe that if this is not done, then some kind of force will conquer and some kind of slavery will ensue.

I would like now most humbly to formulate some pedagogical suggestions, which I am impractical enough to regard as practical, as humanly realizable. Actually there is, as you will see, just one suggestion, arranged for emphasis in six parts.

First, we must renew in some measure the contemplative attitude. Emmanuel Mounier has mentioned the danger of becoming shut up in ourselves, and it is a very real one. But, he adds, of the majority of men, fond as they are of wordly solicitations, the truer description is that of the poet Paul Valéry that we are shut up outside ourselves, and from that kind of imprisonment nothing but contemplation can deliver us. And Gabriel Marcel has remarked that a civilization that denies the place of contemplation and shuts out the very possibility of contemplation, such a civilization sets us inevitably on the road toward a philosophy that is not so much a love of wisdom as a hatred of wisdom. And, he says, we ought rather to call it a misosophy. Everywhere, you know, everywhere there is action; everywhere there is activity. Everywhere there is busy-ness, everywhere there is organization. But out of what are they directed? I think from an inner self which is not quite at home or at ease with itself, but rather acts and thinks and judges from its superficial spheres, from the achievements of mere intellect or mere calculation, or from the impulses of power, possession, or pleasure. This may seem very hoity-toity, but the fact is that the depths of man have to be revived again, that man's soul has to be rediscovered; that everyone must have periods of his life and moments of his day as a permanent and constituent part when he becomes quiet, really becomes quiet and contemplates himself, and with the living heart and soul asks himself one of the innumerable questions he has suppressed during the busy day.

Now, how a particular person will do this I cannot generally state. Certainly it depends on his fundamental character, on his fundamental convictions, but equally certainly the Catholic teacher and student will do this by entering the world of worship, the world of the liturgy, the world of prayer, the world of the Mass. I recommend to my students the reading of the Short Breviary, where the great and unutterably beautiful world of the Psalms will become real and alive and closely touching to them. I also understand the suggestion of Barry Ulanov, the importance and the need for many to grasp the total meaning of the meditations that the literature of our tradition provide. They can be—as he indicated, brilliantly, movingly—a moving center in which to recompose the personality that has been disintegrated into a thousand threads. And to reweave that personality into a proper form and unity.

At any rate the person has to pull out of the daily chase; he has to become quiet and present to himself. He has to expose himself to a world of wisdom, or to the world of *pietas*. And, it seems to me, only an attitude deepened in this way can permit a person to take a strong stand against the powers of time and of the world around him. This moment or period of silence, so necessary for ourselves, is equally necessary for our students. For each of our students is capable of uttering the plaintive cry—there are times when I'd like to be alone and to be let alone. In one of his most eloquent passages, Romano Guardini has said all that we mean here in this sentence: "The soul needs that spiritual relaxation in which the convulsions of the will are stilled, the restlessness quieted, and the shrieking of desire silenced."

I also think that every college teacher and every college student in America should read and meditate upon Joseph Pieper's *Leisure, The Basis of Culture,* where he says that the tendency to overvalue hard work in the effort of doing something difficult is deep-rooted, and where he also asserts that the essence of thought does not consist in the effort for which it calls, which is great, but simply in grasping existing things and in unveiling reality. One can't help thinking of Christopher Dawson's statement, in his discussion of education and Christian culture, that education used to be the unveiling of spiritual realities, that is, in its total value. And the implication is, why can't it still be?

Just as the highest form of virtue knows nothing of difficulty, Pieper has made clear, so too the highest form of knowledge comes to man like a gift, the sudden illumination, a stroke of genius, true contemplation, comes effortlessly and without trouble. On one occasion he cites St. Thomas speaking of contemplation and play in the same breath, because of the leisure that goes with contemplation. Divine wisdom itself, holy Scripture says, is always play, playing to the whole world.

I'd like also to cite the passage, from the Book of Proverbs (8:22-36), the words of divine wisdom, which is the great context and should be the manual of a great Catholic college, a college of Christ:

The Lord made me when first He went about his work at the birth of time, before His creation began. Long, long ago, before earth was fashioned, I held my course. Already I lay in the womb, when the depths were not yet in being, when no springs of water had yet broken; when I was born, the mountains had not yet sunk on their firm foundations, and there were no hills; not yet had He made earth or the rivers or the solid framework of the world. I was there when he built the heavens, when he fenced in the waters with a vault inviolable, when he fixed the sky overhead and leveled the fountain-springs of the deep. I was there when he enclosed the sea within its confines, forbidding the waters to transgress their assigned limits, when he poised the foundations of the world. I was at his side, a master-workman, my delight increasing with each day, as I made play before him all the while; made play in this world of dust, with the sons of Adam for my play-fellows. Listen to me then, you that are my sons, that follow, to your happiness, in the paths I show you; listen to the teaching that will make you wise, instead of turning away from it. Blessed are they who listen to me, keep vigil, day by day, at my threshold, watching till I open my doors. The man who wins me, wins life, drinks deep of the Lord's favour. . . . (Ronald Knox translation)

I can only say the Christian teacher and student will have to think and meditate and act out of the divine wisdom of these scriptural words.

The second suggestion I have is that we must open ourselves again to the elementary fact of the nature of things and persons, and even a cursory examination will show how schematic or systematic we make them, how far we deal with them only on the basis of conventions, how much we handle them under external aspects of efficiency and convenience or the saving of time. And the result, I'm convinced, is not only innumerable mistakes, the effects of which eventually amount to a resistance of things and persons, but also a severe want of appreciation of reality, indeed an embezzlement of reality, giving rise to all kinds of disorder and even to catastrophe. We have to approach the essence of being again. We have to ask the truly philosophical questions. We have to commit, as Pieper would say, the genuinely philosophical act. We have to ask, what is work and what is intellectual work? as soon as it is seen in the frame of the inter-relations of life, of existence. What is learning? What is wisdom? What is thinking? What are order and discipline? What are authority and obedience? What is friendship? What is love? And I'd like here to add a footnote, which arises out of an event that occurred in the spring. A lecture by one of the most distinguished economic historians of our time was the occasion, a lecture that he gave at the invitation not of the faculty or any of the departments of the university, but at the invitation of the student government.

The lecture was titled, "What is the End of the Intellectual Life, or Is the Intellectual Life an End in Itself?" In a most moving moment, before an immense throng of students who deeply appreciated the fact that he told the story of his life as a scholar and as an educator, the lecturer declared that he had discovered many things about the intellectual life and education in the colleges and universities only in the process of having tried to live this life. And he declared that the enthusiasms of his youth were not unjustified because a number of conditions that were no merit of his, he said, led him to want not to cheat, led him to try to find out the truth. But to rest on these enthusiasms, he suggested, would not have been justified. He was beginning to find out the limitations of a search based on such enthusiasms. He said that the larger matter of historical truth—which in its turn is only a part of truth as such, and to which we human beings only have access if it is true, through Christ, that we are children of God—must always partly escape us. Historical truth and truth are both in a final sense matters of faith. We need to have a humility to know this and to breathe it, he said, into our works.

Now this is a statement of Professor John U. Nef, professor of Economic History at the University of Chicago, and chairman of the Committee on Social Thought, and certainly one of the most distinguished educators of our day. He also appealed to our students in a way not to be misunderstood. The rigorous discipline involved in the establishment of historical facts is an excellent thing, he said. The attention directed toward it during the last movements of modern civilization is a result partly of the rise of the modern natural sciences; but, he said, the danger in this quest is that persons may become so enamored of the scientific search for truth, that it will become an end in itself. He also said that some of the best intellectuals are seduced by the very honesty of their search. They delude themselves into thinking that this search absolves them from the search for truth, which is God. And so, he said, at this critical time in history, when in science the search for partial truth can produce universal disaster, what we are doing is not enough. The intellectual life can be cultivated effectively from the truths it contains only if one falls in love with it, to such an extent that it is cultivated as an end in itself, he said. And yet, and this seems at first sight a contradiction, one can only cultivate the intellectual life for all it is worth if the love it generates becomes more important than the problems that one is trying to solve or dissolve. Until love matters more than the problems, or the problems become problems of love. Until then a person is led on to see all tangible problems as part of bigger, more important problems still. Naturally, in making the intellectual life an end in itself, a person is being what he is: to be small you have only to be what you are. The road is something more than that one which merely edges an individual a little closer to truth. Is this the road towards love which has its greatest experience in the temporal world in the love of other human beings, or even in the love of one other human being?

As Professor Nef comes to the end of a great and distinguished life in the academic world, he can say that a man can grow to learn this, that one can love the intellectual life knowing that the greatest gift for man is simply to love. That will help us to take the particular intellectual problem to which one addresses himself, in whatever field, and to keep it in its place. And it can help us, without ever discouraging the search, to recognize the limitations contained even in the most perfect solution, or the most perfect dissolution, of a problem. It is not the intellectual life but love that is an end in itself. If a professor at a great secular university can say this, we in the Catholic colleges and universities certainly should be able to say it, and to understand better than anybody what it can mean, what it means to say what love is, what it means to say what is man. If those questions can be raised elsewhere, why cannot they be raised in our places, in our schools? Is there a scale of values? Which values are the more important, and which are the less important? And which are not important at all? We certainly should be able to raise the fundamental questions—what are the final aims of life, and what are the means to achieve them? We live out of these basic realities. We live for them and we live with them. We regulate them and we reform them. But do we know what they are? Do we know *what* they are? Do we know their real nature? Sometimes I think we do not. Otherwise we would not deal with them so carelessly.

And so I'm afraid that we have to learn them again, not logically, not rationally. We have learned them that way before. So it cannot be logically and rationally again. We have to learn them now *essentially,* so that we know their real nature and their real meaning, and then, after learning them ourselves, commit our students to learn them with us, so that they can realize them through all their lives.

And now a third suggestion. We have to learn the meaning of what I would like to call an asceticism of the intellect and of its lieutenant, the will. So far as our vocations as teachers are concerned, asceticism does not mean anything other than this, that we have ourselves and our minds and wills in hand, that we learn to master our knowledge and our powers and talents, that we learn to possess ourselves truly of our knowledge and to sacrifice the lesser for the greater. It means that we educate ourselves not to yield to our power or authority, but to use it with responsibility and charity and love. What I mean simply is that no form can be built or created if he who builds it is not formed himself. This is the assumption for the achievement of our greatest aims as teachers in Catholic colleges.

Our concern must be to create forms that leave room for the spirit, to create orders in which personality can exist, to create ways of discipline that allow dignity. And the asceticism I speak of should aid us in discovering what it means to command, to exercise authority, to direct and to advise as well as to obey. Nowhere is Guardini more thoroughly Catholic than when he declares that to command in the Catholic style demands humility, not only from the man who obeys but from the man who gives the command. This style rejects violence, and the more completely the more defenseless the subordinate in question. And still too often in our schools, instead of a true Catholic exercise of authority and command, we have had force. Instead of obedience, we have had complete surrender of personality. Inept ourselves in the exercise of our authority, we exact from our students not obedience but the abject submission of their persons. Nevertheless, by the manifestation of an intellectual and personal asceticism, we can encourage our students towards the development of a sane self-possession that they can maintain through all their lives.

And fourth, we must realize the importance of community, of the true relationship that must exist among ourselves and that must exist between us and our students. And I believe that Father Ambrose McNicholl has referred to that necessity, and has made it as clear to you as I could make that the community of which I speak is the unceremoniously and unofficially felt solidarity, unforced and unappointed, of those who do the same work and are in the same situation. It is the spontaneous readiness for mutual help in joint efforts, for joint intellectual creations. This attitude, involving sympathy in a sense of kinship, is essential, not only where each one of us might be concerned, but where each of our students is concerned. Out of our students, as out of ourselves, can emerge everything that we call respect, magnanimity, charity, tenderness, refinement, cordiality, sincerity and cooperation, virtues ever to be desired by our students and to be developed in their lives as citizens.

And the fifth suggestion: here I am led to emphasize the need for us to conserve and to develop the virtues of reverence and patience. The attitude of reverence—belief in God's presence, Newman called it—will keep us from committing acts of aggression against all realities and knowledge, and against those whom we would introduce into the mysteries of our realities and knowledges. And out of our reverence and respectful recognition of other persons, our students, we will be helped to avoid the dangers of instrumentalization, and depersonalization. On this point, Mounier has noted that these dangers occur whenever another person is treated as though he were not present, or simply as a repository for information for a teacher's use, or for anybody else's use, as simply an instrument to be disposed of, or whenever he is set down on a list without right of appeal. In such cases, the teacher or administrator is behaving towards him as though he were an object, a victim, which means in effect despairing of him. But if he is treated as a subject, as a person, as a presence, which is to recognize that one cannot really define him or classify him, that he is inexhaustible, filled with hopes upon which only he can act, we give him the highest credit. For we know that to despair of anybody is to make *him* desperate, whereas the credit that generally should be extended to one of the same world, which has to be extended out of generosity, can only renew a person's confidence. That really acts as the appeal that nourishes the spirit.

The sixth suggestion is simply one final and essential suggestion. We are brought to the thought, in our concern with teaching and with constructing our schools and colleges, that we have to meditate seriously about the final relation of our existence, the relation with Christ Our Lord. Man is not a being sufficient unto himself, who can acknowledge his relationship to God or reject it precisely as he thinks and decides. The nature of man is essentially determined by his relationship to Christ. Man exists only as related to God, for where there is no Lord God Jesus Christ, there is no man, and the way in which this relationship is understood, how seriously it is taken, and the consequences that are drawn from it—all this determines the nature of a teacher's life, of his work, and of his vocation. This is so. No philosopher, no historian, no politician, no man of the practical world, no poet, and especially no educator can change this unalterable fact. The maintained consciousness of this unalterable fact is our way and our students' way to personality. And above all people we have to keep remembering in the midst of the rush and the rampage of the school year, and of all our realities, Our Lord God Jesus Christ is the definite reality. And if man does not do justice to Him, his whole being will be sick, and all forms of neuroses will result. And certainly it would not have been sensible for me, in proffering these various ideas and suggestions, finally to neglect the only point at which in trying to embody them we can succeed or fail. And certainly in our meditation upon this final and eternally persisting relationship we shall realize the limitations of our little creaturey world, and we shall be put on our guard, as Marcel suggests, in our roles as teachers and as men of art and science and as men of learning altogether, against dubiousness, against unmeasured arrogance, and we may discover that all servitude and caste spirit and tin god service are defeated and dissolved.

I have not been concerned about method or matter, for the method can be different in every case, and the matter has to be serious, but the teaching in the college of Christ, in the

Christian college especially, ought to understand that there is a disposition, that there is a demeanor, that there is an attitude, that there is a spirit of approach, that there is a development, that there is a self-possession, that there is a presence, a living presence—call it what you like—that will ultimately and gradually transfuse and dynamize our actions with our students. I guess all I really mean is that we who believe that we follow in the great Christian tradition of teaching—and we have reason to believe that we do—have to be, or to be allowed to be, and to recognize ourselves as persons before we can see and treat and trust our students as the persons they are. And since at the moment in the pressure of the hour and the heat of the day I cannot develop any further what I've been saying here, I recommend only your further meditation upon these suggestions, that they may result in a profound concern for the sanctity of the person and personal life, an acute realization that personality is sacred, from a profound realization of the statement I cited at the start—that human personality and individuality, written and signed by God on each human countenance in so extraordinary a way, sometimes on the face of a great man, is something altogether sacred, something for the resurrection, for eternal life, for the Beatific Union, that every human face is a very special door to Paradise which cannot possibly be confused with any other, and through which there will never enter but one soul.

Well, this realization should provide something of a formation of an attitude or a spirit of approach to how teaching can be made personal and individual in the college of Christ, and certainly it suggests the truth of a remark by Robert Frost that there cannot be anything interesting between persons unless they are persons. It should also support the truth of another observation, that to imprison the human spirit is the unpardonable sin, the attempt to make men automatic, to force them into the same mold. No means will ever be found to induce human beings finally to surrender themselves, either body or soul, to a dictated felicity, to satisfactions chosen for them, by whatever vulgar Caesars may rule the world.

I believe the consideration of these suggestions and the absorptions of their meanings and values will fortify us all in the ministerial as well as the proper magisterial character of the action of teaching in the spirit of Christian humanism, and will strengthen us as persons, will save us from settling down into the status of functionaries of a college or university, from becoming merely business managers dealing with our consumers or credit victims, and certainly should enhance our sense of the great though still and inevitably mysterious mission of teaching in the twentieth-century power world, the teaching of the arts and sciences involving as they do human integrity and destiny and the personal and individual integrities and destinies of our students and of ourselves.

The Aim and End of Education

FR. AMBROSE J. MCNICHOLL, O.P.

Mary Queen of Scots is perhaps not altogether to be envied, but I think we may envy her her motto; what she chose as her motto is so admirable in many ways: 'In my last end is my beginning.' It's true in so many ways: when we set about anything, unless we have our last end in view, whether in life or in work, we cannot begin to move towards it, to plan our way. We begin by aiming at the end; it's the last thing we attain. And so now we come to deal with the end which has been guiding us in these conferences—the Catholic college, or Catholic education.

We have to determine what we mean by education, and the part played in it by the ideal Catholic college. We assume—we don't set out to prove—we assume that man is a rational being, with a spiritual soul—that we know by reason and by faith. We assume that man is ordained by God to a destiny that is supernatural—that we know by faith alone. Now education is a lifelong process aiming at fitting man properly to fulfill his vocation as an individual, as a social being, and as a Christian. It is a process aiming at perfecting man, at fulfilling all his powers, his capacities, at drawing out—*educare*—drawing out from his latent possibilities, the full capacities and perfection of man.

Now in this process, the primary external agents in the natural order are, as you all know, the parents, who have the God-given right to educate; the State, which comes after the family; and in the supernatural order, the Church. These are principal causes in the process of education. They have the primary right to educate; and in this fundamental sense of education, of fulfilling man's potentialities, it is evident that education applies to every aspect of human activity—moral, intellectual, physical, social, technical, cultural, supernatural. The subject himself, the human being, is the first intrinsic cause of education. Education is not a purely external thing by any means. It is primarily a work of man himself, of the student himself, because it is a natural process.

Where does the college or the school in general fit into the plan of education? We might say that the school and the college are secondary or, perhaps better still, instrumental, external causes of education. They are not by any means primary causes, because their power to educate comes from a delegation of the primary agents. The school, the college, has its power from the family, from the state, from the Church. The school is authorized by these primary agents to aid in some aspects of education. If you wish to have detailed, rather dry scholastic consideration of these various causes, I could refer you to Father Conway's recent book *Principles of Education.* It will clarify your ideas on these points.

I wish to refer now, and I will refer again many times, to a book which I cannot recommend too highly to you, called *Theology in the Catholic College.* It's right on the point that we're considering in this week. It's a work of collaboration, published by the Dominican Fathers in Dubuque. As you know, a great many of our Fathers are actually engaged in

26

this work of teaching philosophy and theology in Catholic colleges, in at least seventy colleges here in the States. These Fathers, with great experience in this work, have collaborated in this book, edited by Father Masterson, and published by the Priory Press of Dubuque in 1961. It is a series of essays on the various aspects of college education.

In the second essay, written by Father Donlan, who wrote his dissertation on theology in the Catholic college, we have some necessary precisions. On page 20 he says, "The school is not among the primary agencies of education. Its entire authority to teach is derived from that of the parents and the Church and is subject to the direction of the State in matters pertaining to good social order." Then he makes a distinction between educating and schooling. This helps us to determine more fully the function of the school. The aim of the school is not education, as such. Schooling is a part of the whole, which is education. And here quoting Pope Pius XI he says: "Schooling is a part of that whole which is education. The proper and distinctive role of the school is to train the young 'in the arts and sciences for the advantage and prosperity of civil society.' . . . " "That is to say," Father Donlan goes on, "that the inculcation of the intellectual virtues is the primary and distinctive goal attained by schooling." Now, I don't say it's the only goal. But the primary and distinctive aim of schooling, or of education in this narrow sense, is the inculcation of the intellectual virtues.

So we distinguish now between education such as is performed primarily by the family, by the state and by the Church, and schooling; the college has to do with schooling. And what is the aim of this schooling? Pope Pius XI, in his famous encyclical on education, says, "For the mere fact that a school gives some religious instruction does not bring it into accord with the rights of the Church and of the Christian family, or make it a fit place for Catholic students." The Catholic college is not just a place where Catholic doctrine is taught. To be a really Catholic college, says the Pope, it is necessary that all the teaching and the whole organization of the school, and its teachers, syllabus and textbooks in every branch be regulated by the Christian spirit under the maternal supervision of the Church, so that religion may be in very truth the foundation and crown of the youth's entire training. And this in every grade of school, not only the elementary, but the intermediate and the higher institutions of learning as well. There is the end, the aim of a Catholic college.

Father Donlan comments on this (page 31)—"The Catholic college must assist the student to habituate himself, to think, and to think as a Christian; to judge the realities of life, and to judge them by specifically Christian standards; to act and to act in a specifically Christian manner. In fine, it is the task of the Catholic college to develop the student in Christian culture, to habituate him by academic means in Christian wisdom."

And he notes that "history shows clearly that Catholicism is a culture, a specific life view, marked by definite characteristics and based upon unchanging principles." And this culture, he says, is not simply an adherence to a religious creed. It is rather a basic approach to all life.

So the inculcation of this Christian spirit, the initiation into this Christian culture, is the aim of the Catholic college. Here we have the end with which we must begin, briefly stated and put forward very clearly by the Pope.

Chesterton has a wonderful story—or perhaps it's a series of essays—called "The Well and the Truth," in which we

28

find a character, the central one, standing upon his head. He isn't doing Yogi exercises. He turns out to be a poet, one who is seeing things upside down, the way they ought to be seen. In Chesterton's inimitable way, the poet is portrayed as the only one who sees things as they really are. We, blinded by custom and biased by utilitarian approaches, don't see things as they are. The poet was upside down. He was beginning at the end.

Since we are here concerned with the role of the college and the teacher, as instrumental in aiding the student to attain the end of education, our considerations now must be centered on this instrumental activity, in the Catholic college.

In the active sense, education is an art—an art which is exercised principally under the influence of ethics and practical wisdom. And as an art it is essentially ordained to an end by which it is specified. That end as we have now seen is, in a word, to aid in the formation of the fully rounded Catholic person.

So the subject with which we are dealing is the instrumental, or ministerial activity of the college and of the teacher in forming in the student the full Catholic personality. And that means, in supernatural terms, forming Christ in the student.

This aim of the Catholic college is not that set forth nowadays generally in the world of education. What seems to be most characteristic of our age is the secularization of this Christian ideal. Many of the basic concepts which we owe to our Christian tradition and Christian philosophy are retained in the world today, at least in large portions of it. It is commonly conceded (at least in this country) that man is a person, free, destined to be happy. In countries which are not under the sway of absolute materialism these truths are retained. But often, outside Catholic or at least outside Christian circles, the faith or the philosophy which founds such truths has been lost. Our modern free civilization has retained some of the values of Christian civilization, but has lost sight of the end which bases them and which gives them meaning and value, or in other words, significance and truth.

The idea of man which is prevalent in our free societies is the Christian idea secularized, or humanized. These values are retained either because they have been handed down, or perhaps because they are obscurely felt to be true, to be in accord with reality. Now if the true end of education is not recognized explicitly, and if these values are sought for their own sake, we get the first and most radical perversion in education: mistaking means for ends. We lose sight of the end, and therefore something which is of itself a means is actually in fact regarded as an end. What does that mean in practice? It means in practice, for instance, that education will be seen as a process of fitting man to perform a function: fitting man to be a worker, to be an artist, to get rich, to get a job, and so on. All these are means. They all have their part to play; but if they're sought for their own sake, as they are when the true end is lost sight of, we get then the radical perversion of means being sought as an end. In the moral order that is what sin is. Sin is precisely making an end out of means. When we get this educational sin, or perversion in education, as a consequence the technique of education becomes all-important.

In fact we do find that education nowadays tends to be regarded as an end in itself, instead of a means. There is a quasi-religious attitude towards education, as though by it alone one could attain salvation and security. Education, which is a means, a process, is in fact regarded as an end in itself. This is an utter inconsistency, because of course no process can possibly be an end in itself, for the very simple reason that as a process it tends to something beyond itself.

Where this attitude prevails we get at once a serious conflict. On the one hand the individual strives to perfect himself according to his own desires, to go his own way; this sums up the motto of education as set forth by Pindar, which is very true, I think, in many ways: "Be what you are." It is now: "Become what you are." This is a slogan taken up by Nietzsche over and over again. It does sum up one aspect of education. On the other hand, there is the desire of politically organized society to develop and perpetuate the kind of culture it cherishes. Society wants to preserve its way of life, its conception of value; to develop its culture. Thus the aim of social conformity clashes with the intrinsic natural diversity of human beings. The human being, as different from all others, wants to develop himself in his way; society wishes to develop him in its way. This clash, which in fact renders education detestable to students, provokes resentment and rebellion. The student refuses to be molded into the social pattern which society wants.

Now these errors are normally connected with the naturalistic and materialistic view of man. If man is no more than matter, or just a stage in the evolution of the cosmos, with no supra-temporal destiny, then education will be conceived as a mere training, enabling man to use and dominate nature. That is its end, the secularization of the Christian end. Training becomes an end in itself. A means is made an end in itself. The domination of nature, the knowledge of nature, is of course very important. It has its place in education. It is made into an end, because according to naturalism, there is no end higher than nature for man.

So the ultimate aim can only be to further the progress of evolution. If there is an ultimate aim, it can only be to further this progress. What is the goal of evolution? What should be formed by this process? That we are not told.

Science can only tell us what is, not what should be. For instance, scientists can manufacture the hydrogen bomb—a wonderful triumph of man over nature. But can science tell us when to use it—if we should use it—how we should use it? Science tells us what is, but not what should be. And so an education based upon this naturalistic and scientistic attitude can in fact set no ultimate goal before us except that of further and further dominating nature and aiding the evolution of the cosmos; but where evolution is to lead us we don't know. Science can't tell us what is the aim of evolution or what should be the aim of man's progress. In consequence now, education based upon this view lays the emphasis on means and on the technique of education. We get that now —it is the emphasis on means, on the technique.

These means and techniques are usually good in themselves, and even necessary. We can and we must use them in our Catholic schools. We have to keep in step with modern advances in science and with techniques in the means of education. But we cannot accept the view that education is entirely a matter of technique. Nor should we be unduly influenced by it. For instance, I don't think that in a Catholic college we should have the same reliance upon psychological testing as is common in secular colleges. Testing depends upon the standards used and the aim proposed. You are testing a boy for what? For his intelligence. Very good. What do you mean by intelligence? Do you mean his power to manipulate instruments? Or the power to reason correctly with regard to truth? Or to know God? The value or use of any method depends upon the end. We should always have it clearly before us. We've got to use these new techniques, these methods and the instrumental advances in education, but always in a Christian way, not making them ends in themselves.

Many views on education which are common today neglect, if they do not deny, the ontological aspects of man's nature. They regard as real that which is measurable or quantitative. For this trend of thought, what is real is what counts. *Is* means *equals*. The only real sciences, in this school of thought, are the physical sciences. This means, of course, that the real nature of man is either denied or ignored, and in practice this entails a suspicion of and an aversion for other ways of thinking. The scientist, if he doesn't despise, will at least not appreciate the way of thinking of the philosopher or the theologian, which he regards as all up in the air, and as not based upon facts. Everything which cannot be empirically verified is relegated to the lumber room of discarded and useless notions.

The spirit corresponding to this first school of thought requires that instead of sterile speculation we must have practical knowledge, knowledge which can be tested, and which in practice can lead to results that can be seen. This implies an aversion for absolute truth. The scientist is very wary of using a term such as absolute truth. For it he normally substitutes probability.

Now in practice, what can we conclude from this? First of all I would suggest, in the light of what we've been saying, that in the Catholic college there must be a thorough grounding in the positive sciences of nature: physics, chemistry, mathematical physics, at least to some degree; biology, botany, and so on. They should be taught with awareness of trends in recent research. We have to be up to date, both in our teaching and in our equipment.

Secondly, there must be great care in the selection of textbooks. John Julian Ryan in his *Beyond Humanism,* now unfortunately out of print, instances Catholic colleges where there was a physics laboratory manual introduced by a quotation by Huxley stating that only the measurable is true and worthy of investigation. A wonderful textbook to put before Catholic students! An introduction to poetry where there is no mention of the Bible! Psychology textbooks in which man is treated as merely an animal!

Thirdly, there must be a thorough grounding of the student in the art and science of logic. Now by logic I don't mean just formal logic. I mean logic as conceived now by the great Scholastics, including not only dialectic, not only the laws of reasoning, but the different ways of proof. The logic of probability, rhetorical techniques, the art of persuasion. These various aspects as adapted to the college level are well treated in Father Ashley's book *The Arts of Learning and Communication.* This of course should normally be done in the high school, before college education if possible. Make the student aware of the different ways of knowing, so that when he comes to specialize in his way, scientific or mathematical, he will not have that contempt for other ways which one sometimes finds as a result of specialization. An awareness of the various approaches of the mind to reality, of the different kinds of certainty, may give the student a broadmindedness that will make him able to appreciate, or at least prepare him not to condemn, other ways of knowing besides that which is going to become second nature to him by specialization later on.

Fourthly, I think we have to be aware of and to stress the

34

role of the senses, of experience. There is need to counteract that dulling and dimming of our senses caused by the incessant bombardment of our whole being by these various noisy, distracting influences that surround us on all sides in our modern life, perhaps dulling our senses to the perception of things as they really are. Because we live in a man-made world, we may not see the world that God made, the world of nature, wild animals, and so on.

One must be aware of the limitations of the senses, and bear in mind the possibility of empiricism, of students taking it for granted that that only is to be accepted which is made evident by the senses. The senses are to be stressed, but not over-stressed, for they are only ministerial to the intellect.

Fifthly, there will be on the higher level of education a necessary specialization, which means a fragmentation, a pulverization, of reality. Now that is a fact; we've got to face it. We can prepare the student to avoid the dangers inherent in this specialization by recourse to philosophy and theology as basic ways of knowing and of integrating human knowledge. Now that means, in practice, that our teachers of science should ideally have a training in philosophy, and be aware of the fact that there are other ways of knowing besides their particular scientific approach to reality. Some formal inter-faculty communication seems essential. There are many books written nowadays on this lack of inter-faculty communication, of any real unity between the various departments of a higher institute of learning. Let me refer you to another essay in the volume, *Theology in a Catholic College,* one by Father Wallace, himself an eminent scientist, who is engaged in this type of work. He has some very practical suggestions to make in his essay "Theology and the Natural Sciences," which I very strongly recommend.

Now finally, in our colleges we must also insist upon the philosophy of nature. Here I am on very disputed ground. There are two main approaches among Catholic philosophers. There is the Louvain approach, for which essentially the philosophy of nature is a part of metaphysics. I reject that completely and I regard it as useless in this connection. There is the traditional approach of St. Thomas and Aristotle in this matter, that there is a generalized science of nature on the same level of abstraction as the natural sciences, and which we call the Philosophy of Nature. This is ideally adapted to completing the natural sciences and integrating the knowledge afforded by them. You'll find a very good textbook in that spirit in Vincent Smith's *General Science of Nature*.

Let me leave you with these questions: Do we make clear to students the end of the whole process of education? Do we see the whole thing in its full perspective? Do we see means as means, and ends as ends? Do we see education as a total process, the cultivation of the whole man? And then, are the means of knowing adequately presented? The scientific approach in its various ways? The mathematical approach and the approach of the philosophy of nature? The approach of the metaphysician and the approach of the theologian? The approach of the poet? These are the major areas of questioning which I think are suggested by the considerations I have offered here.

The Matter of College Education

FR. AMBROSE J. McNICHOLL, O.P.

We often ask—what is the matter *with* college education? Well, now we have to ask—what is the matter *of* college education? And here I hope to touch on three important and hotly disputed questions, questions which I have no doubt will set you afterwards grappling with one another, and grasping for one another's throats. I hope they will. Only don't put on record any of the attempted strangulations.

The three points that I wish to touch on, however briefly, are, firstly, the general question of the habits at which we aim in this ideal college education: we aim at forming habits of thought. Secondly, we ask what kind of habits, intellectual or moral? And thirdly, and more in particular, what habits in detail do we aim at cultivating in the ideal Catholic college?

I should begin by reminding you that the aim of the teacher is not just to develop the strength and skill and accuracy of man's mental powers, as though it were indifferent what the subject is on which they were exercised. We do not aim at any and every exercise of our powers. To develop our powers and bring out what is best in them, we must exercise them on what is best, what is most true, of most value. Why? Because that which sets the mind free, really free, is not exercise but truth. So the matter on which the mind is to be exercised is not a matter of indifference at all. It's not sufficient to say that it doesn't matter—that oft-used word—what the subjects are. It matters very much.

A mind can be trained to be quick, clever and smart, even brilliant in repartée, and yet be very superficial. The classic example of such minds trained to be quick and smart and responsive on any subject whatsoever are the Sophists, and they like the poor, are with us at all times. That will give us training, but not education. And what we have in mind is education, not training.

It is far better to lead the mind to penetrate, to understand, to see reasons and causes at work, even if that implies being slower and more ponderous. Very often you who are teachers will have noticed that, in oral examinations for instance, it isn't the quick, glib answer that counts. That can be learned, trotted out, merely by memory. But the person who won't commit himself at once because he sees the various aspects, and tries to make up his mind before answering, might give a bad impression. He may hem and haw for a bit. He may be a far better thinker than the quick answerer.

Now what we aim at in the ideal college education is to form the student, not just to inform him; I'm speaking now of college education, not elementary grade-school or high school. We have to form habits there too, but now I'm speaking particularly of college education. And that means the growth in the student's mind of habits of thought, a growth that is from within. Learning is necessarily a vital, inward process, but under the loving and wise guidance of the teacher. It means teaching the student to think for himself rather than simply to receive from others and to repeat what he has heard, to think for himself, to understand, rather

38

than to memorize, to know rather than to know how or to know that. I use the verb "know" in the Aristotelian sense of being able to see the thing in the light of its causes and thus to have certain, evident, demonstrative knowledge of it. What makes the mind free is not so much facts as truth. It is on truth that the mind feeds, grows, and develops.

The inner strength and vitality of the mind are nurtured, its growth preserved, and further growth assured only through the patient building up of habits. By habits I do not mean mere mechanical routine, as we so often do nowadays. Routine reflects the passivity of matter. A habit is not a conditioned reflex. That is something that pertains to the material side of our being particularly. Habits are living, spiritual, permanent growths, leading our powers to the peak of their perfection: they are spiritual things that grow up within us. This is almost a contradiction, since growth is normally automatic. We have no control over it. We can't help ourselves getting fatter or taller sometimes. We can't prevent our getting old; but spiritual growth habits we can control. Growth by habits is not automatic. It is willed —deliberate, acquired, conscious. Habits are spiritual qualities which enable our powers to act with all their energy, swiftly, deftly, and pleasantly, with a kind of sureness and infallibility that lead the power to its object, its true object. Think of the mathematician at ease, delighting, deftly, swiftly going through his process of reasoning. Think of the student before he has got the habit: he stumbles, he gropes, he is blind, he doesn't see connections. A man with the habit delights to exercise this new facility which brings his powers to their perfection.

Habits are permanent extensions of our powers, deeply implanted within them, fused into them so as to become with them one living source of connatural action. The moral and intellectual habits have been called very felicitously by Aristotle, second nature. They are indeed a second nature which we add to ourselves consciously, and do bring about our spiritual growth.

We should aim, then, at forming the student in this manner, from without of course, always as an extrinsic agent, following the course indicated by nature, the natural development of his powers, aiding him to grow inwardly, spiritually, by the formation of these habits, by which the mind and its various powers can move at ease, with sureness in the particular realm which is covered by the habit.

Now the second point is the controversial question whether the formation of moral virtues pertains to the college curriculum or program. Is it the aim of the college, the ideal Catholic college, to form moral virtues in students?

You might all be inclined to answer immediately—yes, because we're dealing with Christian education. Let's make some precisions on this point. First of all, we're all agreed that the education of the Christian includes essentially the cultivation of moral virtue. There's no doubt at all about that. That is more than evident because it is of divine faith, and should be quite clear from what we've said about the aim of Christian education: To form Christ in the souls of men, to fashion the real Christian man, to lead him to the conquest of spiritual freedom, and so on.

But our problem is not concerned so much with education as with schooling, which is the task of the school or the college. Now some things are quite certain. First of all, that moral formation is primarily the duty of those who have the natural right to educate. That means the family, the Church, particularly in the supernatural order, but also in the natural, and to some extent the state. These are the primary agents responsible for the moral formation of the child and of the student. Remember that the school is the secondary and instrumental agent of education, not a natural agent. It wouldn't have been in the Garden of Eden.

Now the teacher or the college as designed to teach is primarily concerned with knowledge and intelligence. The primary aim of the college is to aid the student to possess truth. But let us remember that truth is both speculative and practical, and practical truth has to be taught as well as speculative truth. Now the college addresses itself directly to the intelligence rather than to the will. I say directly. The intellect, however, has both a speculative and a practical function. People who get hot under the collar on this question seem to be unconsciously influenced by Kant, who, when he speaks of practical reason, identifies it with the will. Now we don't. The practical function of the intellect is not the will. So that, for instance, the practical intellectual habits of art and prudence regard not the will directly, but the intellect.

In other words, direct action on the will, or the shaping of character, is not the aim of teaching. That belongs to the primary agents of education. The child who comes to your school, and particularly to your college, is presupposed to have acquired the virtues already through constant practice. Now the school should aid the student to continue this moral formation, but it does this principally through instruction, by teaching the "why" of virtue. The student usually knows what is wrong; he doesn't do what is wrong; he has the virtue. But now why should he not do what is wrong? To enlighten the mind about this is to provide instruction of the

41

practical intellect. It is not to give moral virtue, but to teach, to give the reason why. It is to teach him to direct himself.

Indirectly, through intellectual formation, through illumination, our teaching bears upon moral formation in the student through forming the virtue of prudence particularly. Through the intellect, therefore, we indirectly aim at the moral formation of the student.

You will find a different view defended by John Ryan in his book *Beyond Humanism,* but rather than engage in controversy I will simply remind you of his book and go on to add one precision to what I've already said. Namely, we have to make a distinction between school and the college. The school is where normally the student passes some hours every day for part of the year. The residential college is where the student passes all his days for eight or nine months of the year. Now both the school and the college are delegated by the parents and therefore share in the responsibility of the parents. They take the place of the parent. The college therefore is far more intimately entrusted by the parents with the education of the child, since it is where the child resides, where the student lives. His whole day and night are under the care of the college authorities who thus have a far more intimate sharing in the primal authority of the parents, and therefore share in the responsibility of the parents for the moral formation of the students.

The teacher is always a delegate of the parents, and the more he is delegated, the more power he has, and the more he is responsible for education. So the college authorities are not merely teachers; they are also educators in a larger sense. But even there I think the principle remains true that their primary duty as teachers is the intellectual formation of the students.

Thirdly, what particular intellectual habits should figure in the program of the ideal Catholic college? This brings up the question of the liberal arts, for the liberal arts college is the one that we are thinking about. Here again we come into the realm of controversy. One reason for this is that many people seem to confuse the liberal arts with what are called the humanities. For them a liberal education is one based on the classic Greek and Latin texts. Now that is a confusion, for the humanities, the classics of Greek and Latin literature, form only part of the subject of some of the liberal arts.

The liberal arts derive from a system of education that can be traced back to pre-Socratic Greece. They seem to owe much to Pythagoras, that religious, philosophical, and mathematical teacher who founded a school which was as much a school of religion as it was of philosophy. These arts represent a system of education that was practiced by the Greeks before Plato. It was refined by Aristotle and the Latins, and was adopted into the Christian schools. In the Dark Ages, when Christian schools all but disappeared on the Continent, the torch of learning was kept aflame in Ireland. When the invading nations had settled down in Europe, the Irish monks were active in reviving learning in Europe, and brought back with them this system, so that it was called in the seventh and eighth centuries the "via Hibernica." It was this structure on which the faculty of Arts in Paris and in Oxford was built. It was commented on by St. Thomas. You heard Dr. Ulanov tell us how Shakespeare was brought up under this system of education. It was gradually superseded through the rise of the new physical and physical-mathematical sciences, especially from the seventeenth century onwards. It has continued to influence our system of education, but nevertheless as a system, rather a detailed system, it was gradually abandoned and replaced by what we all know to be our modern systems.

This liberal arts system essentially comprised the Trivium and the Quadrivium. Now the very words signify that this system of education was a way—*trivia,* threefold way; *quadrivia,* fourfold way—to knowledge. They are preparatory disciplines to something else. This further goal for the ancients was wisdom or philosophy; for the Christian it was philosophy and theology. They are the royal ways, the royal roads, leading to wisdom: the trivium, grammar, rhetoric and logic; the quadrivium, arithmetic, geometry, music, and astronomy.

Now these were called arts in a loose sense, in so far as there is an analogy between these mental disciplines and the arts. The arts for medieval men were mechanical arts, the practical arts, the arts concerned with making boats, making shoes, making tables and chairs and pots and pans. These disciplines were called arts by a kind of analogy because in them there is also the making of a mental work. We make syllogisms, we make figures in geometry, we do sums in arithmetic, and so on. They were called arts in this loose sense and distinguished from what were called servile or mechanical arts. These deal with matter, and imply the activity of the body. We mold clay with our hands, we paint, we cut wood, using our body. The trivium and quadrivium engage primarily only our minds. They were called liberal because for the Ancients they were the activities to which free men in their leisure time could devote themselves in order to realize their potentialities, to become full men. They were ways leading to that leisure, that ease, in which they could devote themselves to wisdom, to contemplation. (I refer you again to Pieper's book, *Leisure, The Basis of Culture.*)

They were called free because they were then ordained or directed towards the type of activity in which free men could engage and also because they pertained to that part of man which is essentially free—his mind. They engage directly only his mind, and that is essentially free—*liberum*—whereas the body is not free. And finally they are free because they have something of the character of play about them. In other words, they are cultivated for their own sake.

St. Augustine was brought up under this system and gave it his characteristic twist by saying that these are liberal arts, not merely for the reasons we've mentioned but because they are the arts which befit the *liberi Dei,* the children of God, the really free people, because they fit man to understand the Scriptures, to attain divine wisdom, to attain the knowledge of God.

For St. Thomas these arts are regarded as free primarily in that they pave the way for the speculative sciences that are sought for their own sake—philosophy and theology. They are means, not sought for themselves alone, but for the sake of philosophy and theology which are the really free sciences, the sciences of the free children of God.

Now for St. Thomas, though they have something of the character of art, nevertheless, these liberal arts, as we call them, are essentially sciences, and form a program of education. Grammar and rhetoric are studied in the preparatory schools, and so we call them grammar schools. Logic and the quadrivium, which is essentially mathematics, remain for higher education. These are the two sciences which particularly pave the way for the study of philosophy and theology. In the faculty of Arts in the University of Paris when St. Thomas studied there, one studied logic, mathematics, and philosophy—logic and mathematics as leading to philosophy.

For St. Thomas the ideal sequence of studies corresponding to this liberal arts system is the following: Presupposing grammar as having been done in childhood, we have the following order: logic, the mathematical sciences, the sciences of nature, that is, the physical sciences, cosmology, and psychology, then moral science, ethics, and finally metaphysics. That is the general outline based upon this liberal arts system according to St. Thomas.

Before going any further we should note that when we include music in the quadrivium, we don't mean the instrumental science or art of music, of melody making and so on. Music in this context means the mathematical study of sound, the science of numbers as informing sound. That is the Pythagorean concept.

We should note further with regard to this quadrivium, that mathematics in this scheme of things has a twofold status. It is first learned in the quadrivium as an art, the art of numbering, the art of figuring and so on. It is intended to grow into a science, the science of number, of magnitude and so on.

It does this in higher education. In this connection I recommend an article from the *Thomist* (1959) by Fathers Conway and Ashley, which has been reprinted, as a brochure, *The Liberal Arts in St. Thomas Aquinas.* In one page they sum up the position of the system of education based upon St. Thomas's idea of the development of human nature.

Starting from the very beginning of things and following the order of nature there is first the care of the body in children, before the soul, although simultaneously in the supernatural order both soul and body must be reborn in Baptism. Subsequently, as the soul awakes, the moral virtues dealing with the sense appetites are fostered by training, while waiting to develop the intellectual virtues. This moral formation from early childhood is under the care of the family and of the Church. With regard to the intellectual virtues, supposing the foundation of good moral practice, one begins first with training the mind itself to the art of thinking, or logic, as a prelude to the mastery of all the other arts and sciences as ordained to one thing, that perfection of the man which is his happiness. Logic is the method common to all the sciences. Next comes initiation to natural science, which leads naturally to metaphysics, although all practical inventions are also derived from it. Along with the intellectual virtues, there is also that one which is specifically practical, namely prudence, obtained by the combination of the knowledge of moral science with a right will, as perfected by the moral virtues, and which equips a man now mature to direct intelligently his own life and also that of the community.

Finally this sequence is kept in its true direction by the reservation of the ultimate position to divine science or metaphysics, as subordinated only to sacred theology, the scientific knowledge of God based on divine revelation.

There is the structure of the liberal arts education as based upon the traditional system we find Christianized by St. Thomas.

Now to come down to practice, what results from all this? First of all, this system or structure is something elastic, capable of variety and growth. When I say that, for instance, we should base our college curriculum upon the liberal arts, do I mean that we've got to go back to the middle ages, and do exactly what St. Thomas and the Scholastics were doing, or the Faculty of Arts in Paris in 1250? By no means. What we have here is the outline of the development of knowledge that is proportionate to the development of man's faculties, a reasoned structure of growth in knowledge corresponding to the stages in the development of man's intellectual growth. Needless to say, this system of structure is based on a realistic and spiritualistic view of man as a person.

There are various ways in practice of adapting this system to the particular college in which you find yourselves. I don't think there's any one way that you can say is the ideal way for a Catholic college. Within the structure there are many varieties possible. One possible variety which I think you'd find very interesting is Chapter 3 of Jacques Maritain's *Education at the Crossroads*. I don't fully agree with it, but I am sure you will find it stimulating to read. He deals there with the curriculum of the Catholic college—what you should do in the first year, the second year, the third year, the fourth year. I shall not discuss his proposals in detail because I don't think one can offer any universal blueprint. Each college, accepting this general structure, has to work out its own particular form of education. Secondly, and I think we're all agreed upon this, the main danger at the college level of education to be guarded against at all costs is that of premature specialization. Ideally, college education should be open to all. If we wish to have a really human and cultured society, college education should be open to all, and only after it should we pass on to occupational training. That is the ideal. How far it can be implemented in practice is another question.

Otherwise we get a society of dehumanized, highly trained

specialists, who are fundamentally uneducated, yet looked up to as leaders. Before a man devotes himself to being a businessman, he must devote himself to being a man. In other words, a student, before he aims at becoming a professional, should aim at becoming a person. That is the ideal. College education then should not unduly specialize. In practice its aim is not to turn out a philosopher, or an artist, or a mathematician, or a business administrator. It is aimed at turning out a fully-rounded, well-balanced, complete human person. Let's keep in mind the aim with which we started this part of our course. The aim of the ideal Catholic college is not to turn out a great pianist, a great painter, a great geometrician, or a scientist, or philosopher. It may do so. Let's hope it will. But first of all, it should aim at providing a complete education, without undue specialization, for everyone. The scientist, for instance, should have been made familiar with those subjects which aim at rounding out man's personality. The liberal arts system gives us a type of education which is precisely aimed at turning out a rounded human being. The scientist should know what philosophy is. The painter should know what history is and what logic is. Now that's a high ideal.

In practice in the ideal Catholic college there should be a course in logic. A basic course is better done in the high school, but since logic is such a vast subject nowadays—think of symbolic logic, and the theory of scientific method—the college should build on the basis given by the formal logic of the high school.

Grammar. Grammar is presupposed to have been done from grade school on, but grammar here will surely include scientific linguistics and communication theory. These are all connected with grammar.

Rhetoric. The third of the trivium is the vital art of persuasive discourse, fitting man to take a part in the social life of the community. In ancient times this art of persuasive discourse, of taking part in the governing of one's own city, was associated with politics and law. Among the subjects properly pertaining to college education we may include politics, and some study of law if possible.

The arts of propaganda and communication, and also, for Aristotle, poetics, are included in the trivium along with grammar. Poetics includes literature, drama, poetry, languages. All these, of course, should be done from a much earlier stage of our education. Nevertheless they are continued on a higher level in college education.

Here let me put in a plea—with regard to languages—for Latin and Greek. They are essential if we are to understand the civilization into which the Church was born and which she to a great extent consecrated and sanctified; and they are necessary also to understand the Scriptures, the Fathers of the Church, and medieval science and philosophy.

And let me also make a plea for modern languages, which perhaps have been rather neglected in your country, in some places at any rate. These keys open the door to communication with other worlds, other ages, other cultures, and free the mind from the error of identifying truth and the mode of its expression, as we often do.

The influence of language upon our thought is incalculable. Read the Scriptures in a translation. Not in the language in which you're used to reading them. Read them in French for instance. You will see what different meanings you may get from reading in that unfamiliar language.

Moving on to the quadrivium, mathematics must figure in our program both as an art and a science, and in higher education, it will be mathematics as a science particularly: pure mathematics, applied mathematics, and so on. Here let me note that St. Thomas is insistent upon the role of mathematics in the intellectual formation of man. It enables him to pass from the sensible order to the intellectual order.

Astronomy figured in the quadrivium, and it's important today. This does not need to be emphasized today, when people are whirling around the earth, and satellites are circling the moon and Venus. Pope Pius XII in 1952 urged Catholics to use modern physical theory to confirm and illustrate, mind the words, to confirm and illustrate, the proofs of the existence of God. Dr. Ulanov mentioned a book during our debate the other day, *Space and Spirit* by Edmond Whittaker, and I said I'd written an article on that book. He maintained that we should use science in our philosophy. We should, but not to prove; it is used to confirm and to illustrate, as the Pope very prudently wrote.

These sciences lead on to philosophy, the first branch of which is for St. Thomas the philosophy of nature; and that includes what we now call the positive sciences of nature. I shall simply say that the natural sciences form an essential part of a liberal education according to St. Thomas.

Now what about painting and music? Two reservations we must make, or two clarifications, very briefly. Where do the fine arts fit in? It's interesting to note that Aristotle, in his outline of education in the *Politics,* says that the education of a free man includes music, not the mathematical study of sound, but music as played instrumentally. Why? Because it is a fitting relaxation from intellectual labor and a proper employment of leisure. I love to recall the pleasure I had when for the first time—studying Aristotle in the *Politics*— I came across this. He says, music is necessary because intellec-

51

tual labor is so hard. We have to have some relaxation. A proper employment of this leisure is listening to delightful music. Should a free man be able to play an instrument? He says, yes, he should be familiar with the instruments and he should be able to play them indifferently, not expertly. The expert playing of the instruments is for the slaves who make the music while the wise man is enjoying it. We have to change that I suppose nowadays, but that is Aristotle's thought about it, and being Aristotle's it is worthy of some thought. So when I tootle on the recorder, inexpertly, I think I'm being Aristotelian. I'm certainly not being expert.

Also drawing, he says, must have a place in the free man's education because it is necessary to appreciate the work of artists, painters, and sculptors. So these two have a place, drawing and painting. But again, not in any expert way. You see, we have to think about free men. We're not turning out artists. After this global education, the students can specialize and devote themselves entirely to one special field; but during their college education they must be grounded in the basic human studies.

And here let me say how impressed I've been, in my very short visit, with some of the colleges in America. Some colleges have wonderful facilities for the cultivation of the fine arts, and very serious work is being done there.

Finally, what about history? Well, St. Thomas and Aristotle include history in all these sciences we've mentioned; they regard the study of the history of the sciences as essential. General history is included particularly in ethics, because prudence requires knowledge of both the past and the present. For a prudent judgment is aware of certain things that were done in the past, and so on. And politics

52

includes a study of the laws, customs, and institutions of the past.

But for St. Thomas and Aristotle, history has a secondary and limited value. They do not consider it a primary constituent of the college curriculum, because it is not sought for its own sake. It is regarded by them as a means of preparing men to vote, to take part actively in a democracy to be good citizens. And for that history is essential. Aristotle has a famous remark that poetry is more universal than history. Why? Because poetry gives you the idea, the essential. History deals with the contingent. So let me conclude with this remark, that a scheme of education based on history as the central focus, as it is proposed nowadays by a number of people, will not, for St. Thomas and Aristotle, be ideal. It will not have the same value as the scheme based upon the liberal arts. It is interesting, in conclusion, to note that the demand nowadays in this country for education which is scientific and mathematical agrees very largely with the liberal arts program set down by St. Thomas and Aristotle.

The Teaching-Learning Relationship

Willis D. Nutting

I have asserted here the proposition that the form in which higher education is carried on is a very important thing, and that when the wrong form is used then the full purpose of the higher education isn't carried out, no matter how good the teachers are, no matter how good the students are.

In order that we may perhaps be working to some conception of what that right form would be, I'd like to discuss the teaching-learning relationship. Certainly this brief discussion won't be adequate; but perhaps I may lead you to appreciate the wideness and the variedness and the richness of this relationship, and it's only when we recognize that, that we can even begin to think of the proper form for carrying on this enterprise of higher education.

Note that I say "teaching-learning relationship"—not the "teacher-learner relationship"—because both the so-called teacher, and the so-called learner, are at the same time teachers and learners. The so-called teacher is learning all the time from the people who are officially learners; as a matter of fact he's probably learning more than the official learners are. And the so-called learners are not only teaching the teacher, but they're also teaching each other, and so there is a constant pedagogical energy being exchanged. We want to explore the breadth of that thing that is or at least can be going on. Everybody is a teacher; everybody is a learner.

In a college you have a particular situation with regard to the learners: they are in general people who have reached what you might call the "age of realization." We talk a lot about the age of reason, but seldom talk about a thing that is much more important, this age of realization. In the development of a youth the time comes when he begins to make ideas his own, rather than just taking them from somebody else and not really committing himself to or against them. He begins to take these ideas very seriously, becomes fiercely loyal to them or turns fiercely against them. He's very much interested in them; fascinated by some of them. You might say that a person who enters this age comes to a realization of what a human being is, as distinct from an animal, and to a realization of his own higher capacities. That's the kind of person we hope we're dealing with. One of the difficulties of our system—I suppose of any system—is that it is not easy to determine when a person has reached this stage. Some people appear never to reach it. Some people reach it very early, and we hope that we can get them then. In our teaching-learning relationship, we're especially interested in the learners who are in this age of realization. And now, granted that our students have reached this age, we want to consider the character of the student and the character of the teacher. It's very important to realize first that each one of them is a unique person. There are no two alike. The student comes to us already part way along in his education. (As a matter of fact we'd have to take him as soon as he's born to get him right at the beginning of it.) He also comes to us part way along in the development of his character. He also comes part way along in his ability to think, to use his reason, and no two of them are the same way along in any of these things. No two students have the same potentialities for learning. They're persons—they're unique. And what we have to do is to take each one of these persons—not just take students in a mass or the "average" student (obviously, you can't do that)—we have to take each one of these students and in the time at our disposal have to try to lead each one to become wise. That is not an easy thing. If we were a trade school, we would have to try to lead each one to be a good dentist or machinist, a good engineer or a good doctor. That would be easier. But more fundamental than being a good engineer, or a good doctor, or a good dentist, or a good scholar, is to be a wise person. That's our job in liberal higher education.

We must also remember that the teacher is a unique person. No two of them are alike. No two of them have the same kind of abilities, even if they are all teachers, and there are some in the profession who are not teachers at all. But even if they're all teachers, they're not alike, and their potentialities are quite different. The teacher is unique. Each one has a different attitude towards students. Each one has a different way in which he can appeal to different students. None of them can be 100% successful. I think that any of us who have done much teaching will realize that if a teacher manages really to reach 50% of his students he's doing very well. That, incidentally, is why there should be a plurality of teachers. Because if there's only one teacher, 50% of the students wouldn't get anywhere at all. This shouldn't be too discouraging. It's very encouraging if a teacher can reach one person. Every time he does, it's a triumph, a reason for raising a flag and blowing a trumpet.

And as you know, there's very great satisfaction to the teacher when that happens.

Different teachers, then, not only have different things to teach, but different teachers have different ways of teaching the same thing, and here we ought to mention one of the pedagogical principles which makes college catalogues completely off the point. The principle is: it's not what you teach that counts, it's what your students learn. And anyone who is a teacher knows that there's a vast difference between those two things. Anyone who teaches knows that you can't look in a college catalogue to see what's taught, and from that infer what is learned. So the teacher has to try in the way that's best fitted to himself to lead a student to learn something, to think, and finally to become wise.

You can see from this that the whole nature of the situation, both the situation of the student and the situation of the teacher, makes an absolutely uniform scheme impossible if students are going to learn anything. And that's one of the reasons why the form that we have used in organizing our higher education, the form that copies the industrial corporation, is so very disastrous. It prevents almost every student and almost every teacher, in almost every relationship they have with each other, from doing what is potentially possible. Let's take an example.

Suppose I have to teach History 21. I'm not particularly interested in it. I'm interested, say, in the History of the French Revolution. But I have to teach History 21, which is a survey of everything that happened to mankind from whenever history began until last night. I'm not fitted to teach that. The student—Student X—is a person who likes to read certain books intensively. He has read quite a few in history. He has to take History 21. He's not fitted for that. It may seem to him complete drivel, complete childishness. A lot of the facts he knows already. He has already got hold of a certain historical sense and this kind of brush-off and generalization, the only things that can be done in a course like that, just irritate him completely and he's completely bored most of the time.

Take another person, Mr. Y. He doesn't like history at all. Well, by taking that survey course, he will learn to dislike it more, because in it he will never get the real understanding, the real joy, the real fascination of finding out through investigation what actually happened, because he will have no chance for investigation at all.

And so you see here is a uniformity, a mold, into which teachers and students are brought in which neither group can function very well. The whole business of courses which you take—required, unrequired, a sufficient number of them, etc.—is a poor way for teachers and learners to be related, considering the uniqueness of each one of them, and considering that you want finally to make them wise. So there is the situation: the uniqueness of persons does not fit into an industrial form.

I'd just like to speak about the different kinds of teaching-learning situations that are possible. This is not exhaustive. You can think of any number more—as many as there are persons. But we can mention a lot of different ways in which a fruitful relationship between student and teacher are possible, ways in which a certain person may be very good as a teacher, and ways in which certain people come to appreciate him and learn from him. But in any one of these ways, there are some teachers and learners who don't function.

First there is the formal lecture. A great deal of fun has been made about the formal lecture, but it's a very highly valuable thing, if it's good. Of course it can be very poor. But in a formal lecture, a man is given a certain amount of time; in that time he can present a subject without interruption. There are some people who can do that very well, for whom interruption just blasts the whole thing. They are able to present a thing so clearly that a lot of people will understand it, and it's a great misfortune to have a pedagogical theory which won't allow that. And it's a wonderful thing for certain students to find a teacher who is able to give such a lecture. What you want to find out is what his idea is, and you'd like to find it out by giving him free rein for a certain amount of time without anybody interrupting him. I know, I myself liked that method of learning very much. I disagreed with most of my teachers all the time, but I found that if I interrupted them, I didn't even know what I disagreed with. In my undergraduate days I very seldom asked any questions because I didn't want to interrupt, and I was irritated at people who did ask questions. But there are some students who simply don't get anything out of that kind of thing. They're bored with it. They hate it. They go to sleep. And you can say that that kind of student should not be compelled to enter that kind of relationship with a teacher. You can say that some teachers should not be required to give that kind of presentation of a subject because they don't like it and they're not fitted for it. The formal lecture is just one very valuable form of personal relationship.

Then, there's a relationship which is practiced very generally: the disciplined course of study. The student is required to do many things—required to read this, required to write that, as the teacher keeps a check on him. That is a thing which everybody admits is valuable for many people. But there are some that rebel against it. Some students, if a thing is put as a requirement, automatically hate it. There are some teachers who are not capable of doing that kind of thing at all. I'm one of them. I can't be strict. I often wish I could terrify a student by a glance. When I try, they just laugh. I'm absolutely incapable of a strict form of discipline of my students, or my children, or my dog. I have learned not to try, and everything goes along very well. Now strictness with students is a very valuable thing. There should be people around doing that, and there are some people who like it. I'm very glad to have as my colleagues people who are strict. But that doesn't mean I should be. Very definitely I'm a fish out of water when I try it. And although the University requires teachers to be strict, I very definitely refuse to obey the regulations that make that requirement, because it isn't the way I function.

There is a way of learning that a person has to acquire sooner or later, and that's the way of self-discipline. That is, setting himself a course of study that he will carry out rigorously. You ask how a person is going to learn this. Some people learn it by having external discipline imposed first, and some people are prevented from learning it by having that external discipline imposed. However self-discipline may be learned, there is a good motto that any person can adopt with profit. I suppose maybe it's the only valuable thing that General Ulysses S. Grant ever said, the only thing that should become eternal. I'm sure you remember that he wrote back to Lincoln in the campaign in Virginia in the summer of 1864, "I propose *to fight it out on this line* if it takes all summer." That is the kind of discipline that we hope that a student will acquire. A person who wants to learn is not to shy away from difficulties, but to keep fighting until they are overcome. When he learns this, then he really has got something. But how you get them to learn this, I don't know. As I say, sometimes enforced discipline leads to it, sometimes it doesn't.

Sometimes inspiration leads to it. That is, you see a teacher or a student who has this "self-startingness," and you're inspired to copy him. The teaching-learning relationship has a great deal of the poetic or charismatic in it, in the sense that things are learned that are not taught. There are plenty of things, of course, that are taught and not learned, but also things are learned that are not taught. By something a teacher says or does, the student may get an inspiration toward something that is not what the teacher is now intentionally saying or doing. He may get an inspiration that may last him all his life. That is one of the beautiful things that comes with the age of realization, and it's one of the joys of a teacher—to find that there's something that he has said quite casually, or something that he hadn't intended at all, something that perhaps he had forgotten that he had said, that has struck a spark in the mind of a student and that the student has carried that out into a blazing sequence of ideas. Sometimes self-discipline comes in a way like that.

Then you have another way, another kind of teaching-learning situation, the one that comes with directed discussion or dialogue. That's a thing that has very high value at the present time. Certainly many people write and talk in favor of this thing as against the formal lecture. It certainly can be good—good for some people and for some teachers. But other teachers find themselves incapable of doing it; and when they're forced into the mold of doing it, they have all sorts of difficulty. Quite often the effectiveness of this kind of thing depends not only on the teacher but on the students who make up the discussion-group. Some groups go very well and some don't, even with the same teacher.

Then you have what you might call a roving discussion. That is, the discussion just goes along wherever it wants to go. Undisciplined, yes, but it can be a very fruitful thing. You can get enlightenments from such a haphazard discussion that you may not have gotten anywhere else. Henry Adams in his very discouraging book on his education (in which he finally concludes he wasn't educated) speaks about the accidental education that he values most highly. And to be autobiographical, I think that is the kind of teaching-learning relationship that has personally helped me the most. Insights come as out of a clear sky, insights I wasn't looking for. Here is just another bit of autobiography. When I came into the Church a lot of my friends took the matter very seriously; they'd say, "Did you find what you were looking for?" And I would answer, "I wasn't looking for anything." Very often in informal roving discussion you find *what you're not looking for,* which may turn out to be the most valuable thing that you ever found.

Then of course there comes reading. And a library. And paperbacks, because now libraries are becoming obsolete because it's so easy to buy books for yourself and such very good ones. I don't mean the kind you see in the drugstore, but I mean the kind you see in a store that really goes in for paperbacks. There can be *assigned* reading, and I think all of us who have studied have blessed people who have made us read certain things. Well, again I don't want to make a blanket statement. Perhaps some people never read what they are assigned. There's that reading, and then there's *private voluntary* reading. There is the opportunity of setting yourself a task of reading which nobody has assigned to you. When I was in college, I discovered the Christian religion. It wasn't what anybody was officially teaching me. I'm quite sure that the University of Iowa would go out of business if they found that they officially taught me that. But being a faculty child, I could go anywhere I wanted. I went deep into the stacks in the Library and just stayed there for, oh, half days, just reading about Christianity. Some of the books I read were pretty queer. But that private reading of one book after another as you see them on the shelves can give you a thorough grounding in a subject you have chosen for yourself. Following an inspiration, or following somebody's suggestions, with no examination in the offing and no credit involved—here is joyful learning for the pure love of coming to know. There are a lot of people who are educated in just this way and in no other way at all. I am sure that the personal relation with the teacher is also part of the complete learning process, and that a man who has learned simply from books has missed something. But you can learn a great lot from books as teachers and this is one of the very definitely valuable teaching-learning situations.

Then there's a thing that I suppose you'd call a use of solitude. You'd call it meditation or contemplation. You know the story of the man sitting on his front porch with the chair tilted back against the wall. He just sat there and sat there and sat there, and somebody said one time, "What do you do when you sit there?" "Well," he answered, "sometimes I sit and think and sometimes I just sit." And I'm not sure but what the just sitting is the most valuable of all. Contemplation, I think it is. Not trying to find out anything, but just letting something happen to you intellectually. Things clicking together perhaps that will not click together as long as you're furiously trying to fit them together. Enlightenments that have meanings that come from something that has been said or has been read, meanings that come to you without your seeking for them at all. It's not without cause or relevance that the really great universities of the world always have long vacations. This idea of having twelve months' school is horrible. Not only from the point of view of a lazy man like me, but from the point of view of learning at all. That is, there must be periods of quiet when nobody is trying to get you to do anything, and when you're not fiercely trying to get yourself to do something. I think you might say that if a person has never, either by someone's help or by his own experience, learned to make use of solitude, he's in a pretty bad way. Periods of solitude could become a kind of a keystone, you might say, of the educational arch. This is where things become your own, and this is where you pass from Newman's notional assent to real assent in some very essential matters.

These are just some examples of what the teacher-learner relationship is, and you see it's a very complex thing. You could think of plenty more relationships that I haven't mentioned. Now, *all these are valuable, and in any formal organization of the enterprise of higher education—all these must count and must count equally.* No matter how you order your institutions of higher education, if you're going to conform at all to the human situation that exists, you're going to have to make it possible for all these different ways of teaching and learning to count *so that a person, no matter how he learns, will have what he has learned recognized, officially.* In the course and credit system that can't be done. And that is really my biggest objection against it. The thing that you have learned that's not in the course doesn't count. It may be the most valuable part of what you're learning, but still it doesn't count. If you're going to evaluate people at all, some way has to be found so that you don't evaluate merely one kind of thing they do; because some very good people may not be able to do that one kind of thing very well. You have to make your evaluation so elastic that you can evaluate their excellence—their knowing and their ability to use their intellect—no matter how the knowledge is acquired, no matter in what way their intellect is exercised. Everything must count and that's got to be the central organizational idea in the form of an institution of higher education.

Now I'd like to mention one other thing which is very important, and that is an educational process which our Western tradition has produced, and which as far as I know is unique to it. There are many civilizations that have handed down the things that they regard as most worth knowing from generation to generation simply by a kind of tradition in which the elders speak to the younger, and the younger listen with reverence. The attitude of the elder is one of authority; the attitude of the younger is one of docility. The younger then, when they have received the tradition from the elder, certainly use their intellects, but they use their intellects to be sure they've got their elders right. That is, you can talk, you can discuss, like this: I wonder, did he really say this? Is this what he meant? And so the highest intellectual work you do is commentating, or commenting. You make commentation. You make commentaries. Our Western tradition has had that, but it's had something else besides, and that's the *dialogue*. The teaching-learning process has been one of *argument*. There has been something besides the teacher and the learner involved, and that's truth. And truth has been regarded not as something that's completely possessed by the elders, but something that is to be gained by everybody, to be striven for by everybody because the elders may miss it. So when you take up a matter, you take it up by discussion, and you give arguments pro and con. The young man questions what the elder says. He may doubt it. He may hustle around to find arguments for proving the elder wrong. And this has been a central element in our intellectual tradition, in our educational systems. You don't have this absolutely unrestrained reverence for the people who came before you. You doubt the old boys. There is perhaps a kind of irreverence in it. You read a Socratic dialogue, and you find that young men here are very eager to show up the ignorance of the people who are supposed to be wise. They like to prick balloons. It's fun and it can be carried on much too energetically, but it has become a part of our tradition so that there has been a tension in that tradition. Never a "yes-sir" to the elder, but a "let's see," an "I wonder," a "Let's think about that for a minute." And so there has been this tension, this argumentation, almost an unease in our tradition. You find plenty of people who are at ease with what they have discovered. They think they have discovered a truth. But somebody else says, "No. I don't agree with him." So there is this unease, and it's been a very fruitful unease. For instance, it's led to great discovery. You want to prove your own point, or disprove somebody else's point, so you go out for evidence. This questioning attitude has led to a dynamic character in our tradition which you don't find elsewhere. And as the discussion moves from one thing to another, people are anxious to find new arguments; they are anxious to find new facts, and they bring all these things back to the discussion through this dialogue. The dialogue is something like an eternal poker game. That is, some people sit in for a while, and then they retire and take away their winnings and other people sit in. The thing has been going on for about 2,500 years. It has grown. Its interests have shifted somewhat from time to time, but it has continued to go on.

Now there is a particular kind of unity that exists in this dialogue. It's not the unity of agreement. It is rather a unity of mutual understanding and communication. You don't agree with your opponent necessarily, but you know what he means. You can talk to him. As a matter of fact you have. You've talked to him a lot. You've argued with him. So there can be communication. In this Western tradition, there have been very few points which have been agreed on. Some fundamental ones, perhaps, but comparatively few. But where the dialogue remains intact, there has been a real understanding of what the other person believes. That's the only way you can honestly criticize anybody—when you know what he's talking about, when you know what he means. Thus there has been that kind of unity, a unity of dialogue.

Historically, our process of higher education has been to draw young people into a rather intensified form of the dialogue for a while, so they become familiar with it. You have the Socratic schools in which people just walk back and forth and talk. You see no property and no equipment. It's a wonderful kind of a school. If it rains you just go where there's a roof. If it doesn't rain, you're out in the sun. No football teams, no stadium. Sometimes it's been a more formal situation in which you have a place, a definite time for enrollment and finishing. Sometimes, as in a medieval university, you become a member of the Teaching-Learning Guild and stay in it for a while. There have been all sorts of ways, of forms, in which people have been drawn into the dialogue and have been then, I wouldn't say dismissed, but have been given the stamp of approval as the process goes on and on.

One of the disasters of modern thinking came when the great dialogue was broken up, and in place of it there arose nice intensive little dialogues, each with its own participants. Very nice little intensive dialogues on literature, and nice little intensive dialogues on metaphysics, on physics, etc. But the people in the physics dialogue never got into the metaphysics dialogue, and the people in the literature dialogue never got into either of them, so we have instead a separation, and the modern intellectual world lacks the unity that came from the great dialogue. The fragmentation of the great dialogue did not come simply because there was so much knowledge. No man can master all of it, of course. That's quite true today, but I rather think it always was true. But the break-up came because people in their specialties ceased anymore to be interested in other kinds of thinking. C. P. Snow, the scientist-novelist, has called attention to the disastrous division in the modern world between scientific culture and humanistic culture; he said the literary man and the physicist don't understand each other at all. Well, I think Mr. Snow is very optimistic, because there are more likely *three* cultural worlds rather than two. There is the world of the sciences, there is the world of the humanist, and there's another world that people like to put in the humanistic world, but as far as humanists are concerned, it isn't there, the world of metaphysics, of ethics, of theology. And the literary man finds himself just as alien to a knowledge of metaphysics as a physicist is. And so we have at least three dialogues and a lot of little dialogues in each of the three, and there is no great dialogue any longer.

But now if wisdom is to be the thing that we are finally seeking—that is, if we are trying to put a student at least on the road to it or the beginning of it—there has to be, within the form of our educational enterprise, a provision for the dialogue to go on. And the complete dialogue, not just a lot of little dialogues. There has to be at the center of the process some way in which people who are interested in studying different things are brought into communication with people who are interested in studying other things. So that they can communicate back and forth, so that each person can know what the other person means when he says something. And there has to be a provision for both teachers and learners (because, remember, everybody is a teacher and a learner) in the institution to take part in that dialogue. Some may take much more part in it than others, but the dialogue has to be there, as a going concern.

And so we come to the necessities, the things that must be provided for in the *form* of organization of our educational institution: 1. the students and teachers must live together in a dialogue in some form or other, and 2., all the manifold teaching-learning relationships must be allowed to flourish and, 3., both teachers and learners must be allowed to make use of the kinds of relationship that will suit the particular persons involved. If you don't establish something like that, you haven't got an institution of higher learning. And I would say, then, that in this country we haven't got institutions of higher learning, because I don't know any place that really provides these necessities.

Educational Challenges of the Space Age

WILLIAM A. WALLACE, O.P.

Space age, electronic age, atomic age, nuclear age, age of automation—call it what you will—there is little doubt that we live today in an age of science. And in this age of science, the educator is challenged on all sides. How is he to synthesize and transmit the vast accumulation of knowledge that is characteristic of our age? How is he to teach science effectively? How is he to integrate science into the college curriculum in a way that does not destroy the intellectual heritage of the ages? How is he to utilize twentieth-century technology in education? These are some of the challenges that the educator must face. For example, we have all seen the recent growth of the communications industry. We are very much impressed by telestar, the communications satellite. What will telestar permit? Perhaps some of you have been reading reports telling us that, a few decades from now, we may have person-to-person communication everywhere in the world, over the entire sphere of earth. The art of all nations, their languages and their cultures will be at our fingertips. Libraries will no longer be remote from the general public. Merely push a button, and information will flow from library to home. Everyone will have at his disposal the masterpieces, the rarities, the source materials that were formerly given only to privileged scholars. There will be almost instantaneous retrieval and dissemination of information. Language laboratories are already receiving extensive use in education. Teaching machines and other electronic techniques may revolutionize our ways of drilling young students.

All these might be referred to as educational challenges of the space age. But since I am speaking to a group of Catholic educators, it is not my intention to dwell on such specific technical applications. I should like to go somewhat deeper, and point out a challenge that has been brought forcibly to my attention during the past few years at MIT. Undoubtedly we are now witnessing a science explosion. We are living in momentous times, and it is quite possible that we will soon be faced with one of the most challenging intellectual crises in the history of mankind. I am going to take an extreme view at the outset, and say that the adventure we are facing as educators will be an adventure born of conflict. I see in the offing a conflict of the type that occurs when an irresistible force meets an immovable object. To put it briefly, it will be a conflict where secularist and scientific knowledge, which is now gathering terrific momentum, will crash head-on with the established Christian synthesis of traditional knowledge. Finding a resolution to that conflict is the special challenge that the Catholic educator will be called upon to face in the years to come.

Now, this is a peculiar challenge, but it is not a challenge that is completely unique. There has been such a conflict before in the history of mankind, and it took place seven hundred years ago. It was an intellectual conflict, centered at the intellectual capital of the medieval world, the University

72

of Paris. The conflict arose from an influx of pagan, of secularist, yes, of scientific knowledge into a world that was dominated by a stable Christian tradition. There was the influx, the conflict, and finally the resolution, which came about largely through the efforts of two men whose names I am sure are not completely unfamiliar to you—Albert the Great and Thomas Aquinas. The source of this conflict was the physical science, or the secularist knowledge, if you will, of the Greeks, which was revivified by the Arabs, and which made its way into Western Europe through newly arriving translations from Spain, Italy, and Greece. When Albert and Thomas arrived at the University of Paris in the early part of the thirteenth century, the University was already in a state of turmoil. Two streams of thought were then prevalent at Paris, and both of them have significance for us.

The first I would refer to as an anti-scientific movement; it was a movement that spurned pagan and secularist knowledge in the name of Christian philosophy and theology. It looked to St. Augustine as its patron. And it worked hard to exclude from the University the incoming translations of Aristotle and of the Arabs. An attitude of mind that was hostile to scientific knowledge was thus rampant at the University. Against great odds, and almost in the face of an accusation of heresy, Albert and Thomas took up battle against this radical Augustinianism. The battle was hard fought, but with Albert's ready knowledge of the science of his day and Thomas's tremendous integrating intellect, the issue was quickly decided. Writing in our own day, the great Louvain scholar Canon van Steenberghen pays tribute to the victory that was forged by Albert and later by Thomas. He observes that for the first time since the origin of the Christian Church, these men distinctly established and clearly defined the status of science in Christianity. By that fact, he goes on, they furnished the principles that enabled the crisis provoked by the introduction of Aristotelianism in the Christian world to be resolved, and thus contributed in a decisive manner to the integral development of a Christian intellectual life.

A second stream of thought that was likewise newly arriving at Paris and that was also concerned with science is that known as Oxford Platonism. This movement received its stimulus from Robert Grosseteste, Bishop of Lincoln in England. It was brought to Paris presumably by Roger Bacon, who was later to become a Franciscan friar. The Oxford scholars—such men as Grosseteste, Bacon, and Peckham—early had an acquaintance with Arab thought, even before the professors at Paris, and they too had great interest in the natural sciences. But they were soon overcome by the attraction of mathematics and by a Neoplatonic metaphysics of light that rapidly came to dominate their view of science and of knowledge. The Oxford school went rapidly in the direction of idealism—and ultimately into a form of mathematicism—which tried to reduce all knowledge of the physical world to mathematics. As a consequence, beginnings were made even in the thirteenth century for a type of scientism or mathematicism that diverted science from a search for physical causes and over-emphasized the mathematical. This development marked the beginnings of the British empiricism that was later to come from William of Ockham, Francis Bacon, John Locke, and David Hume in a consistent line of development. This was science within the Church, but science that had begun to degenerate into a type of scientism.

Albert and Thomas, even in the middle of the thirteenth

century, perceived in the teachings of this Oxford school the beginnings of a rupture between science and philosophy. Again they took up the challenge, just as they had taken up the battle against Augustinianism. They began a battle that has not yet been resolved, but that I think we will have to resolve in our lifetime. While granting to science its independence from the data of divine faith, and thus assuring complete absence of conflict between science and theology, they would not grant the autonomy of science from philosophy. They would not allow that one can have a scientific type of knowledge that is purely mathematical, or purely empirical, and that thus is divorced from philosophical knowledge. Rather, Albert and Thomas saw all of science as completing in specific detail the integral view of the physical world attained by the natural philosopher. Science might fall outside the pale of revealed truth, but for Albert and Thomas it could never be divorced from philosophy without doing violence to its very nature.

Let us jump in one tremendous leap over seven centuries and come right to the present day, to the crisis that is being provoked by the rise of scientific knowledge. Science was a thirteenth-century infant when Albert and Thomas tried to protect it from the attacks of philosophers and theologians at the University of Paris. In our day, in the twentieth-century, it has become a giant that threatens to crush beneath it both philosophy and theology—its persecutors of old.

J. Robert Oppenheimer, writing recently in the *Bulletin of the Atomic Scientists,* points to "an alienation between the world of science and the world of public discourse which has emasculated, impoverished, and intimidated the older disciplines and given them a kind of arbitrary, unrooted, unfounded, quality." The slight crack that originated seven hundred years ago in the teachings of the Oxford school has widened and widened into a huge gulf. The gap between scientific knowledge and philosophical knowledge is so great now that the cleavage between the two is no longer even discernible. Historians have difficulty recognizing where the cleavage even originated. To all outward appearances we have two diverse departments of knowledge so far apart that people do not even recognize that there is a gap between them. Yet, paradoxically enough, philosophy has not disappeared completely from the contemporary scene. There are still wise men—if you care to use the nominal definition of philosopher as "a wise man." There are still intellectuals, thinkers to whom we go for direction and guidance. Who are they? I am not going to attempt an enumeration; I would merely suggest that day by day their ranks are being swelled from the physical sciences. In the generation past we turned to Albert Einstein, and Bertrand Russell, and Alfred North Whitehead; today we turn to Julian Huxley, and Edward Teller, and Robert Oppenheimer, and Werner von Braun. These are the men from whom we seek answers about the nature of the universe, the origins of life, the destiny of mankind. Science has grown and grown; it is now pushing its frontiers into fundamental questions and problems that have always been the domain of the philosopher. Without going into great detail, I will indicate two areas where science and philosophy are merging, where they have within themselves the seeds of conflict, and thereby present the great intellectual challenge of our time.

The first area deals with the origin and the ultimate nature of things, i.e., of the material universe. The past century has seen a tremendous growth in knowledge of the fundamental structure of matter. The stuff of which all things are made is being plumbed to its depths by the discovery of subatomic entities. Already we know of electrons and positrons, of protons and neutrons, of mesons and neutrinos and anti-neutrinos. More important, we have unleashed the tremendous potential in matter for its own transformation. Now we can decompose and synthesize the elements, we can produce artificially things that were never known to have existed before—new types of chemical compounds, synthetic materials, etc. Daily we learn more about the extent and the structure of the universe. And our knowledge of all these things tempts our minds to reconstruct the history of their origins: how the universe itself was formed, how the stars and the planet Earth, how the wide proliferation of types that are found on its surface. Is science interested now in the abstract questions that were treated for centuries in the dusty tomes of philosophers: What is life? Can living come from nonliving? I would say yes, these are the questions that are spurring on researchers in our laboratories. At MIT, for example, a vast team is trying to produce life from non-living matter. And, always in the background, is the big question—is everything really only matter in motion? This question keeps suggesting itself to the modern mind. And the tremendous simplification that would result from an affirmative answer, tempts many to say yes, all there is, is matter in motion, and this even at the price of excluding from the world God, the soul, and anything else that cannot come within the compass of scientific instruments.

The second big area is that of technology and the tremendous feedback that it has on the culture that produces it. This is a development that threatens to modify a species—the species in which we are most interested, *homo sapiens*—

and, not only modify it, but possibly wipe it completely from the face of the Earth. Atom smashers have startled men's minds with the tremendous detail that they have shown in the structure of matter. They have also put fear and dread in men's hearts when they produced the atom bomb. The threat of destruction from nuclear weapons or, possibly even worse, mass mutilation from radiation, is so instant that it is before our minds all the time. I am therefore not going to dwell on that here. Rather I would pass to a related threat, one that is not so widely feared but that could, in the long run, have even more disastrous consequences for mankind. At the moment this passes under the familiar name of automation or electronic control—without which, for example, orbital flights would be impossible. Automation may be described as a type of automatic control that produces the supermachine, capable eventually of displacing the human agent in the tedious work of production. I think all of us know how the pattern of men's lives was changed by the first industrial revolution. There machines replaced man's muscles and eventually did work man himself had not the strength to do. Now planners tell us that a second industrial revolution is in the offing which will have socio-economic consequences that none of us can imagine. Science has shown how man can be most efficiently coupled to a machine—not only with his body, with his muscles, as in the first industrial revolution—but also with his nervous system and, ultimately, with his mind. Engineers are now working on the impedance matches by which a few highly trained technicians, coupled to their information machines—which are in turn coupled electronically to their regulators, which are in turn coupled to heavy machinery—will soon displace the laborers, the workers, the craftsmen, now necessary to

78

supply the needs of a complex society. The trend has already started. We already have automated factories in many branches of industry. What are the advantages? Vastly greater productivity, a more uniform product, a better product, a cheaper product. Soon we will notice the change in labor force. First, the depletion of menial workers, those whose labor is really beneath the dignity of man anyway, but who unfortunately know nothing else to do. Then, a gradual cutting into the white collar force, where secretarial work, for example, can be done more efficiently by machine. Slowly a premium will be placed on the technical mind: the mathematicians, the physicists, the engineers will come into their own. They will assume the leadership in our society. They are the bright young men of tomorrow. Possibly we, as educators, are pushing more and more people into these very lucrative fields. Now when this happens, and it surely seems that it will, what about those who do not have a scientific mind? What about other mentalities—the imaginative people, the artists, the literateurs? What about the average or the low I.Q.'s, those who constitute the majority in our society? Isn't there the danger that they will be adversely affected by this second industrial revolution? After all, the argument will go, production is for their material well-being too. So, at the least, they will be conditioned to have the proper needs, to want the products of an enlightened technology. Not many years ago, very few people had television sets. Then, thanks to production techniques, soon everyone could have them. (This was effected largely by automation, without which one could not produce television tubes in all their intricacy.) Then, that peculiar socio-economic feedback—the phenomenon we have seen in our own lifetime— soon everyone *must* have television! The vast majority of

Americans simply cannot live without it. Now, does this product of automatic control radiate back on its users? Does it condition its viewers and make them creatures of desire, of want, of need? I would say that already our society is undergoing a peculiar reflex phenomenon where a significant percentage of its activity is directed toward satisfying artificial needs that create other artificial needs in their very satisfaction. (Perhaps here is the place to inveigh against TV commercials: the inducements given to the masses to buy products to amuse or indulge themselves, and the vicious cycle that this creates; also, the problems TV creates for the educators trying to teach young people to read.)

There is no need to point out what such artificiality, what repeated conditioning of this type, can do to the average or low-mentality human being. Already there are enough neurotics in our society to point out one possible consequence everyone can see for himself. And I would maintain, as all of you would maintain, that we cannot rely on science alone, or on its methods, to deal with the psychical disturbances that are produced by this impact of technology on the human being. I suppose most of you have seen this morning's papers. Marilyn Monroe was found dead, apparently a victim of suicide—A poor unfortunate creature, who, in a sense, is a victim of a technological development, viz, the movie industry. Make no mistake: science is already preparing to meet the challenge presented by neurosis. Drugs are being produced (and evidently Marilyn Monroe died from an overdose of some drug) that are expensive now, but will become cheaper later—as mass production techniques come to be employed. These are drugs that seemingly quiet tensions and anxiety; they induce a feeling of well-being, almost as good as going to church. Aldous Huxley was lecturing at MIT while I was there and much of his concern was with the development of a drug that could induce a religious, mystical experience. This would supplement the diet of ordinary people. Instead of having to get out of bed on Sunday morning, they could get their rest and their religion too, simply by taking a pill. And, having gone so far, there is no reason to stop there. Too much frustration from not having enough to do in a completely automated society? Insuperable problem? Too many people? Population explosion? Control production. Control production of people. A simple pill, an oral contraceptive—science will do it.

Here may be the place to call attention to a book written a number of years ago by the same Aldous Huxley, *Brave New World.* Some of this is a bit jarring to religious, but some of its insights—idle speculation, mere fantasy, when first written—are now more plausible in the light of new developments, e.g., eugenics, drugs, automatic control. For those who prefer a more temperate (and certainly a more Christian) view I would recommend C. S. Lewis's *Out of the Silent Planet.* This is a thin book that exploits some of the effects of original sin, as known on Earth, when compared to what might be the case on other planets. Another good book has been written by Walter M. Miller, Jr., *A Canticle for Leibowitz.* All these are science fiction, but they address problems that must be faced by succeeding generations who would salvage the human race from an uncontrolled development of science. Every one of these writers attempts to show that the great problem confronting man today is the effect of science on the society that produces it. You know that Karl Marx's thesis can be summed up in the words, "What man makes, makes man." And, the scientist with the materialistic orientation will maintain that this is true. Many present-day scientists think in this direction. Many scientists hold views of the Marxist type. They regard Marx's thesis as true. In fact, they explain it very well. Their view is this: man evolves. It all starts with matter in motion—that's the primary reality. The motions within matter cause it to evolve . . . into the plant, into the animal. Then, the peculiarly communist note, the particular motion called labor makes the animal evolve . . . into man. So man is essentially a tool-using animal, a producing animal. Labor and production give birth to man. They also give birth to society. But society evolves, too. Capitalism gave the world that marvelous invention, technology. Technology tends to the mass-produced, uniform product, which has such feedback on the humans that produce it that ultimately it demands social control, a completely controlled society. Complete socialism is one step removed from materialistic communism. Surely you see the direction in which we can go. Hydrogen bomb or automatic control, take your choice! Nikita Khrushchev is right: "The future is ours, comrades."

The point I am making, I think, should be clear. The idea men of today are forming the world of tomorrow. A tremendous tide is swelling. Ideas are being multiplied, but, in the intellectual circles most influential in the United States—I am talking now about the Boston-Cambridge area, with which I am most familiar from my experience at MIT and Harvard—there is little consideration of the Christian tradition or of what we teach in the Catholic college. In fact, there is often an outright rejection of our ideals—and much of this in the name of science. In the field of knowledge: a refusal to be committed to anything that is not detectable by scientific instruments; a declaration that man's knowledge cannot surpass the sensible, the material level. (We run

82

into this even in our students in Catholic high schools and Catholic colleges.) From this, a secularist indifference to, and an outright denial of, the spiritual in man. Another rejection in the field of absolutes: no absolute truth. If you want to get into a fight on a secular campus all you have to do is to hold for anything and say it *has* to be so. Anything. Right away you are a target, someone who is benighted, still living in the Middle Ages! No absolute truth, no unchanging goal for man's life, nothing for man to aim at above the flow of matter; and, certainly, no life after death! In the field of motivation: a desperate effort to deny freedom of the will, to emphasize biological drives, sub-conscious influences, animal parallels for human behavior. If man's origin is from matter, if his knowledge is limited to the sensible order, if his soul is not spiritual and immortal, there is no point in talking about freedom of the will. And since there is no freedom, there is no moral responsibility. Morality shifts with social custom whose violation is a matter of taste rather than of tragedy (and this thinking afflicts our young people in the secular university and unfortunately sometimes moves across social borders into the Catholic college). In the field of creative thought a long list of scientific triumphs bolster the confidence of our youth. The millennium seems just around the corner. The possibilities for progress are infinite. In the exciting maze of progress there is no time to ask fundamental questions. These students, and I am talking now about our Catholic students at places such as Harvard and MIT, although I see vestiges of it even in the Catholic colleges, are young, vigorous, sure of themselves, riding a wave of triumph that is extending forever forward. For the non-Catholic God is not a problem; He is not something that is speculatively interesting; He is merely an encumbrance—

something to be worried about and then dismissed from the mind because He gets in the way of what one would like to do. To a great many the idea of a Creator is a religious luxury and a scientific absurdity. The world seems to be self-sufficient, self-explanatory. A wholesome grasp of the notion of man and of God has been so wholly lost on this "brave new world"—this proud, young, self-sufficient world—that it feels it can do without God and base its pride on a caricature of man.

It seems to me that this is the way in which secular education is going in the present day. It seems the way in which our scientific culture, gravitating toward the materialistic culture, is influencing our development of industry, of technology, of educational techniques. And, if we do not watch out, this imminent surge of secularist knowledge threatens to sweep the Christian ideas of God, of man, and of society from the minds of men.

Without going further into the problem, I would like to mention one insight that may be helpful. I think that this whole development of scientific thought has shown the tremendous intellectual vision of Albert the Great and Thomas Aquinas and that it has vindicated their concern over the separation, or divorce, between science and philosophy. Let me enumerate some signs of the times that seem to bear out the truth of their conviction. It is true that the methods of science are different from those of traditional philosophy. But what is most important and what must be conceded is that both science and philosophy are studying the same basic questions and, ultimately, getting answers to them. Already the testimony of our society shows that the philosopher who knows no science forfeits his title of philosopher. He is no longer the supreme, wise man. And, conversely, our generation has seen that the scientist, whether he is conscious of it or not, will ultimately be a philosopher. He will have a philosophy. No matter how narrowly he may have been trained, no matter how specialized his area of competence, he will have adopted certain basic options and explanations that color his thinking about the universe as a whole. And his philosophical commitments are all the more influential, and, should I say, all the more dangerous for never having been reflected upon, explicitly stated or, for that matter, compared with the intellectual heritage of the Western World.

There are many scientists, and many Catholic scientists, who do not know the difference between the thought of Augustine and Thomas Aquinas—who could not tell you the difference between one philosophy and another. Many scientists are out and out positivists. Many are materialists. Some are Communists. Most scientists are by implication Cartesians, some are Kantians, a few are idealists. In America there are skeptics all over the place, pragmatists, relativists, and there are realists too. There has also been a surge in realist philosophy—something that provides grounds for encouragement. But among Catholic scientists it is surprising how many are intellectual schizoids—professing one truth with their faith, implicitly embracing its very opposite in their so-called scientific thinking. And, will I scandalize you if I tell you that some are on the faculties of our Catholic colleges wearing the habits of Sisters, Brothers, and Priests.

To me this is the great intellectual challenge of the space age—and it is a great educational challenge.

How to close—not the missile gap, not the space gap, not the nuclear energy gap or the automation gap—but how to close the gap between our science and our philosophy so that science and technology will develop in a free society to the benefit of that society without destroying the values that we all hold most dear—I propose that that is your job, whether you be a science teacher, a philosophy teacher, a literature teacher, a religion teacher. Unless we can bridge this gap in our own educational system, we are not doing anything to foster the ideals of Catholic education. In fact, we may well be introducing within our system the very forces that will lead to its ultimate disintegration.

Education in a Pluralist Society

Rev. Francis Canavan, s.j.

I want to talk in this lecture about education in a pluralist society. What I mean to present here is not a plan or structure of education, but a way of thinking about it. I will therefore start with a text which reads:

> Our public school, if not a product of Protestantism, at least is more consistent with it than with the Catholic culture and scheme of values. It is a relatively recent development dating from about 1840. *It is organized on the premise that secular education can be isolated from all religious teaching so that the school can inculcate all needed temporal knowledge and also maintain a strict and lofty neutrality as to religion. The assumption is that after the individual has been instructed in wordly wisdom, he will be better fitted to choose his religion.* Whether such a disjunction is possible and if possible, whether it is wise, are questions I need not try to answer.

Those words were written by the late Justice Robert H. Jackson of the U.S. Supreme Court in a dissenting opinion in the case of *Everson v. Board of Education* in 1947. As a dissenting opinion, they have no particular authority. But the part of the passage that is in italics was quoted by Justice

Tom C. Clark in the 1963 School Prayer and Bible Reading decision.

Although the lines quoted by Justice Clark appear in a majority opinion, they do not thereby become the constitutional law of the United States. The constitutional law is what was actually decided. What leads up to it, as in the definition of a dogma by the Church, is argumentation and does not enjoy the same status as the decision itself. But I think it is a pretty good expression of the philosophy of education that the Court has understood as underlying the public school system. That is to say, formal education can be split off from those ultimate beliefs and values that we call religion. It will be remembered that, to the Supreme Court today, all ultimate beliefs and values qualify as religion in the constitutional sense.

A second point to be noted here is the idea of education as being the inculcation of all needed temporal knowledge. I think that means the sort of thing that Professor Paul van K. Thomson has described as "useful knowledge." Because of "cultural lag," we tend to think of present-day realities in terms of out-of-date situations. Much of our thinking about public education is still dominated by the myth of the Little Red Schoolhouse on the frontier, where they taught children the 3 R's: reading, 'riting and 'rithmetic.

These, you will notice, are all technical subjects. They are skills. They have in themselves no content. One reads, but what? The first thing is to teach the child to read. Whether he reads Jack and Jill, or Dick and Jane, or whatever it is that children are reading in primers these days, does not particularly matter. What is important is that he learn to read. Then to write. Then to do elementary mathematics in the form of arithmetic.

Now, to the extent that one conceives of education as being technical and useful in this sense, it is obviously easy to split it off from anything in the realm of belief and value. The higher we go up on the scale of education, of course, the more impossible this becomes. But the Supreme Court was not thinking about universities. It was talking about the elementary school.

Justice Jackson said that the public school conception of education, as he expounded it, is more compatible with Protestantism than with Catholicism. It is particularly compatible with Protestant individualism. The sentence, "The assumption is that after the individual has been instructed in worldly wisdom, he will be better fitted to choose his religion," makes sense in an individualistic Protestant culture. To a Catholic, or to a member of one of the Eastern Orthodox churches, or to an Orthodox Jew, it does not make any sense. Believers in these faiths do not educate people in order to fit them to choose their religion. To think that this is an aim of education is to read into the theory of education the assumptions of an individualistic philosophy or theology. Yet this conception of education underlies a great deal of what the Supreme Court has had to say about the relation between religion and education in public schools.

The principle, however, which I think even more fundamentally determines what the Court has decided is the proposition that the state offers all children a common education. This proposition really has nothing to do with the establishment of religion clause in the Constitution. One could arrive at the same conclusions without the establishment clause. The court has taken the clause as the peg on which to hang its decisions. I think it is a bad peg; there are other clauses in the Constitution that would have been better ones. But, be that as it may, the true premise of the Court's decisions is that in the public school the state offers to all children a common education.

If the secular, religiously neutral, uncommitted state undertakes to educate all children alike, it will inevitably wind up giving them a secular education. What else can it give them? It cannot impose on some of the children the religious beliefs held by the parents of other children. Therefore, when the state gets into the business of educating, it tends necessarily toward giving a purely secular education; and this is the real significance of the School Prayer and Bible Reading cases.

Certain questions can be raised about the court's decisions in these cases and should be raised repeatedly. The first question that should be raised is this: Is the public school nothing but the state functioning as a teacher? I think the general assumption of the American people is opposite: the public school is the people's school, the community's school. But the Supreme Court, in every case that it has decided in this area, has begun with the premise that the public school is the state in action. The conclusion at which it has arrived is that what the state cannot do, the public school cannot do. Since the state is secular and has no official religion to teach, it cannot teach religion in the public schools. Furthermore, as the court decided in 1948 in the *McCollum* case, it cannot allow religion to be taught in the public school, even if the public school itself is not doing the teaching.

On the other hand, if we look upon the public school as being an agency of the community, rather than of the state, we can take account of the fact that the community is religious, although divided in religion. The community's members and the groups that make up the community hold ultimate beliefs of some sort, including secularist ones. I would suggest that, if the public school represents the community rather than the state, there should be some way of incorporating the community's beliefs into its teaching. That would mean that for certain periods of instruction, the school ceases to give a common education, and divides children into separate groups for religious instruction.

This is what was done in Champaign, Illinois, in the 1940's. A released-time religious instruction program was operating in the public school, for an hour or two a week. The Council for Religious Education, a private inter-denominational body, supplied the teachers during the time allotted for this teaching. The children split up and went to classrooms according to the choice of their parents. The parent had to apply in writing to have his child go to these religious instruction classes. In fact, every child in the school did go except little Terry McCollum, whose mother was an atheist. She went to court and claimed that this program going on in the public school was an establishment of religion. When the case eventually came before the U.S. Supreme Court, it accepted her argument and declared the whole program unconstitutional.

It is true that three years later the court stepped back a bit and, in a New York City case, said that released time was permissible if the religious instruction classes were conducted outside the school building. I cannot see why it makes an essential difference whether the classes are carried on in the school building or elsewhere. Nor am I saying that released-time religious instruction within a public school is a particularly satisfactory substitute for a religious education. But if we accept the existence of public schools as permanent, and I certainly do, some accommodation with the wishes of those parents who want their children to get religious instruction as a part of their education is necessary. It could be made if the court would drop the premise that the public school is nothing but the state, and that the education it gives has to be given to all children in common. On the other hand, the education that the public school does give to all children in common will have to be non-religious. To that extent the school prayer decisions will stand.

A further question is whether the state is competent to educate. The Supreme Court assumes that the state can educate but, on the other hand, the state has to be neutral in the realm of belief and values. This looks to me like a dilemma. Can an institution educate with this limitation placed upon it? If one defines education as consisting only of those things that the state can teach, then, of course, the state can educate. But such a conception of education, whether true or false, is only one philosophy of education among several that are held by Americans. There is nothing in the Constitution that makes it the official, orthodox philosophy of education. It is simply a conclusion that happens to flow out of the premise that in public schools the state offers all children a common education. The premise itself is not found in the Constitution because the Constitution says nothing about education.

I do not mean to question, nor did Pius XI in his encyclical *On the Christian Education of Youth,* that the state has an interest in education and a role in education. In modern conditions it has a very large role to play. There is only one institution in modern society that can get everybody educated and that is the state, if only because the state is the only institution that can tax. It does not follow that the state itself has to do the educating or that it is particularly well qualified to educate.

That raises the third question. Is the state, in the performance of its proper function in regard to education, limited to supporting only secular public schools? If the function of the state is not so much to educate as to see that people get educated. One could argue that the state can stimulate the foundation of schools, coordinate them in a general system of education and support them; but it does not have to own and operate all of them. One could also argue that the state could and should support general education, reflecting any religious point of view, provided that it meets the public standards of what an education is.

Fourthly, in the schools that the state does operate—and I assume that the state will always have to operate a good number of schools, because if it did not there would be many young citizens who would not get educated—are these schools limited to that kind of teaching which the state can impart? Or can it allow agencies to take part in the teaching process whose competence goes beyond the competence of the state? In other words, could the state accept some way of incorporating religious instruction into a scheme of public education? It would not be the state that was teaching religion but some other agency or teachers coming in from outside. This would not mean that the state was going beyond its competence. It would only be a recognition by the state that its competence is a limited one, that education has dimensions beyond what the state itself can do, and therefore that the state should cooperate with those who can do what the state itself cannot.

So much for the role of the state. In order to understand this problem of education in a pluralist society, it is necessary to say something about the role of the Church. The Church is different from the state in that it has a mission to teach. The Church is a teaching body, as the state is not. Nonetheless, the mission of the Church to teach is a limited one. The Church's mission is to teach the Christian revelation and those natural truths that are necessarily connected with it, and nothing else. All the rest of the range of human knowledge that must be included in a complete education, falls outside the peculiar competence of the Church.

It seems to follow that a Catholic school is not merely an agency of the Church to do her work. The Catholic school teaches a great deal that goes beyond the competence of the Church. The Catholic school, therefore, need not be an ecclesiastical institution under clerical control. I am not advocating that the Jesuits, or the Dominicans, or other religious communities should get out of the business of running schools. I am only saying that a Catholic school is not by definition an ecclesiastical institution under clerical control. Rather, it is a school run by and for Catholics. It represents the Catholic community rather than the hierarchical Church or the official magisterium of the Church.

The Catholic community is certainly subject to the hierarchical Church in matters of faith and morals, and therefore in matters of education in so far as they involve faith and morals. But the Catholic community can organize and operate schools which are outside of the hierarchical structure of the Church, and in fact this is done in some places. In the Province of Ontario, for example, and in two or three other provinces in Canada, the Catholic schools are called "separate" schools. The taxpayer is taxed for the support of public schools. But if he chooses to do so, he may pay his taxes to the separate schools. If he chooses to do this, he has the right to vote in the election of the school board that administers these separate schools. (In Ontario they are all Catholic schools.) On these schoolboards, it is usual for a priest to be among the members, but he has to stand for election like all the other members. For this is a lay schoolboard, which may or may not have a priest as a member. The school is usually taught by nuns if the schoolboard can get them. But the school's administrative body is a legally elected board, representing the Catholic community.

In the Netherlands, the state supports equally three school systems, neutral, Protestant and Catholic, out of general taxation. A school is established by a parents' association which has to show the state that there are enough families in the district with enough children to justify the existence of the school. The state then builds the school and pays the operating costs, the salaries of the teachers and the other expenses. But the parents' association administers the school.

The Dutch Catholic schools are run by Catholics, for Catholics; they give a Catholic education. But they are not ecclesiastical institutions. I do not suggest that we should switch over to the Ontario or the Dutch system in this country; in fact, I do not see the slightest practical possibility of doing so. But with regard to the Federal aid to education question, certainly one of the things that we have got to get across to the public is that, if aid is given to Catholic schools, it is not done to subsidize the Catholic Church, but to subsidize education. That means that in our own thinking we have to conceive of the Catholic school as not being merely an agency of the Church.

Finally, we must consider the role of the parents in education. We have put a very heavy stress on the primacy of the right of parents to choose the education of their children. It does not follow, however, that a school is simply an extension of the family, or that the teacher is simply a substitute for the parents. Obviously, the family is an educational institution and gives a child the most important part of his education. But the family is not an educational institution in the sense that a school is. Especially in a highly developed society like ours there is much that cannot be taught by the family and has to be taught by institutions, dedicated to "formal" education, which we call schools. The school is not the family writ large.

It performs a service to the family, of course, as it performs a service to the Church (if it is a Catholic school) and to the state and the community at large. But the school is not simply an agency of the state, or of the Church, or of the parents. It is an institution of formal education and its character is determined by that function. It is responsible to the state, to the Church, to the parents, but without wholly belonging to any one of them. Therefore, it ought to enjoy a certain autonomy from all of them. Not a total autonomy, of course, because the school is not a supreme society that operates completely under its own rule: it is a subordinate institution within society.

A Catholic concept of society, as opposed to all totalitarian concepts or all radically individualist concepts, is in this sense organic. Organic is perhaps a poor word to use because it has connotations, not all of which we want to accept. But in the Catholic tradition we do not look upon human society as being the state, and under it the individuals. For us, society is an "organic" structure of institutions which serve human needs. Because they are parts of society, these institutions have to be directed toward the ultimate goal of society, and therefore must be subject to regulation by higher authority. But on the other hand, if they are to do their work properly, they can not be mere subordinates and instruments of higher authority. They have to have a certain freedom, and therefore a certain autonomy to do their work and to determine their policies. That is what I advocate for the school. I propose therefore that we should recognize that to pose the problem of religion in education as a problem in Church-State relations is to falsify it. It is really leaving the school out of the question. It means asking: does the school belong to the state or to the Church? My answer is: to neither. It belongs to itself. And, if we have to think of it as being an agency of some society, it would be better to consider it as an agency of the community.

In our divided society, that would mean a judgment on two levels. The school first of all belongs to the whole community, to American society. It educates American children; it is supported, or should be supported, by the whole of society through taxation; it trains children to take part in society. Society as a whole therefore has an interest, even in a Catholic school. Children who are being educated there are not only Catholics. They are also members of society, being trained to take their part in society.

But since society is religiously divided, certain schools represent certain groups within the community, groups which have ultimate commitments in the light of which they want to form and educate children. It is no offense to society as a whole that Jews should educate their children Jewishly, and Catholics should educate their children Catholicly, and

Protestants should educate their children Protestantly, or, for that matter, that secularists should educate their children according to the tenets of Ethical Culture. The school thus is an agency, on one level, of society as a whole, and on another level, of some group within society and acts for this group in a particular way. So Catholic schools act for the Catholics, or the Catholic community.

This way of thinking about the school, I submit, would first of all heal the split between factual knowledge and the realm of belief and value that is produced in education by the Supreme Court's philosophy of education. Secondly, it would enable a pluralist society to have an educational system that educates everyone but still respects the pluralist character of the society. And, finally, it would free education from undue subordination to societies that are not fully competent to educate: the state, the Church, the family.

I have spoken so far about elementary schools. Let me close with some suggestions about the future development of higher education. In Canada, which is blessed with having no established Church and no First Amendment, and therefore is much more free to adopt flexible arrangements, there has been a wide range of experimentation with the incorporation of church colleges into general universities, some of them private, some of them Provincial. (A Canadian Provincial university is equivalent to an American State university.) The Canadians follow no single pattern. In one Province they do it one way; in another Province another way. But in most, if not all provinces, church-affiliated colleges in one way or another can become constituent colleges of Provincial or private universities. I should like to see their example initiated in the United States.

First of all, without involving public institutions, there could and should be much more cooperation among Catholic schools. There could also be cooperation with non-Catholic colleges and universities. If a private university were being put up new, different groups might join together and set up a single university, whose constituent colleges would belong to the different groups, whether religious or secular. It would mean a considerable saving in cost; it would also mean that students would have the benefit of contact with people of other points of view within the same university without being thrown back entirely on their own resources or on those of a Newman Club for the religious aspects of their education.

Finally, may the day come when State universities will accept Catholic and other religious colleges as constituent colleges on their campus. There might be a Catholic college, for example, that would not attempt to give a complete university education. It would be a college in which the student would matriculate, and in which he would get those courses that its faculty was particularly interested in giving, but he would get the rest of his courses from the State university.

This sort of thing would require the breaking down of many fixed ways of thinking about the structure of education. It would be naively optimistic to promise anything like immediate success in setting up a college of this kind. The immediate reaction of people would be: "This just isn't the American way of doing it." But there are some signs of a greater openness of mind, of a willingness to think differently about the structure of education. Today, when the question is asked: "What are we going to do for parochial schools?", the great Protestant cry is: "Shared time." What I propose is shared time on the university level. It is an idea that may have a future.

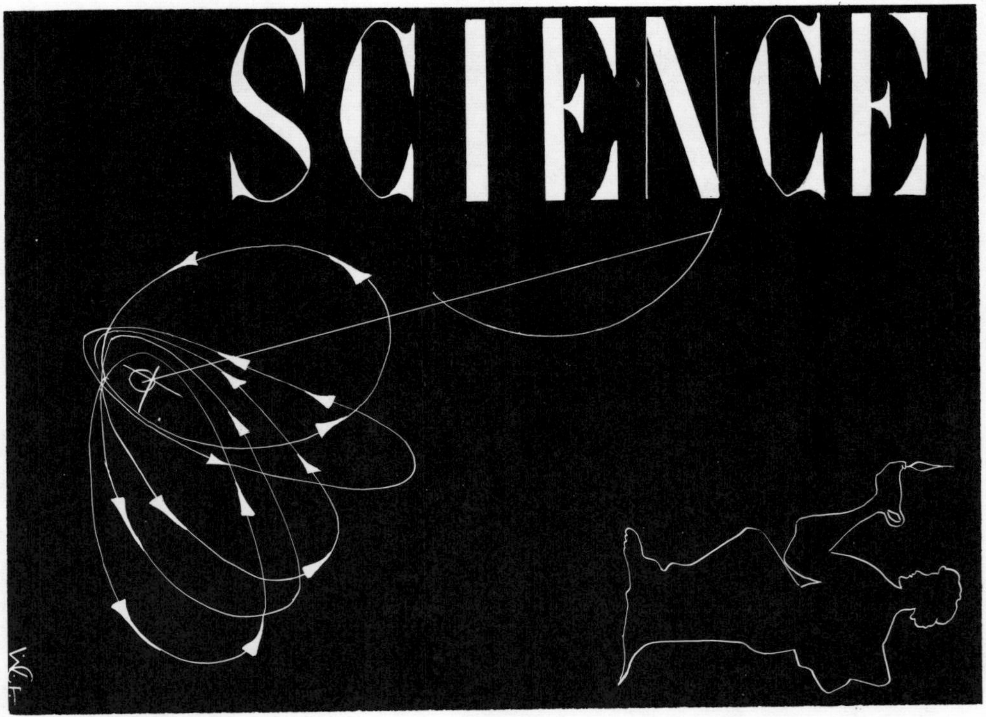
SCIENCE

Science and the Humanities

CHARLES DE KONINCK

I

Our subject is to be Science and the Humanities, and I am
proposing that we consider these first of all from an historical point of view. May I recall to you a book which itself
has made history in this great discussion, *The Two Cultures,*
by Sir Charles Percy Snow. In this celebrated work, Sir
Charles maintains that we have reached something like a
final and irrevocable divorce between science and the
humanities, the last stage of a divergence that began in the
Renaissance, and of a divergence which, in my opinion, was
somewhat natural. Indeed, it was perhaps inevitable. Sir
Charles, you will remember, describes the opposition between the group of mathematicians and so-called pure scientists on the one hand, and the men of letters on the other.
These two parties stood sneering at each other, so to speak,
with utter contempt for what their adversaries were doing.
The men of letters knew no mathematics; the mathematicians
had no Greek. Hence the divergence, which could of course
grow into something quite serious, for it is important to observe that here we have not a mere division by reason of
specialization, but a division which will ultimately affect

even the average reader of a newspaper. That one scholar or scientist should find himself isolated from another by reason of concentration on a real field of study, is unavoidable and not necessarily harmful. But the condition of things which we are examining, and which began in the Renaissance, though it may have been unavoidable in the beginning, did not carry the learned people of those early times as far as it must carry learned people now, and it has become indeed serious.

It has been suggested that what is wanted to bring together the humanist and the scientist is a third man. This third man's duty would be to explain the mathematician, mathematical physicist, biologist, and their comrades, to the gentlemen who make a name for themselves in the fields of literature, history and the arts. Well, Sir Charles does not propose this solution. No, the suggestion which he advances, though somewhat vague, approximates to that which I will make myself, namely, that the third man should be simply the first and the second. In other words, each of these two fellows who are supposed to be in opposition should function as his own go-between. The first and the greatest of their needs, then, is to possess something in common which would make it possible for them, on their own, to discuss their respective problems. They must be capable of a certain kind of thinking, leading to certain results, which will enable them to talk directly to each other instead of calling in that third man and interpreter, whom they themselves could not hope to understand unless they already possessed something in common with him—the very thing which would make the interpreter unnecessary if each of them could lay hold of it.

The only way out, as it seems to me, is that each should

be his own mediator, and this will be possible only if we return to the Ancient Greek idea of *paideia.* What is this *paideia?* It is simply good instruction in basic matters: music, which should begin with childhood, indeed with infancy; grammar; then a great deal of poetry. When I say a great deal of poetry, what I mean is not talk about poetry but the reading of poetry itself. The reading should be supported by interpretation from someone competent to draw attention to that which matters in the art: how this is said; how well it is said; and perhaps why it is well said; why this should strike us so deeply, and so on. After poetry should come rhetoric, a more advanced form because containing much more explicit reasoning. For in rhetoric we find arguments by *exempla* and enthymemes. The enthymeme may not be an entirely sound kind of syllogism, since it is composed of only two propositions. But still it is a reasoning process. One proposition is left tacit and for this very reason in certain matters the argument is more forceful. If the concealed proposition were brought out into the open the total effect would be too weak. Finally, part of a man's basic training should be logic in the true and scientific sense of the word. By this I mean logic studied with a view to the acquiring of science by application of logic in this or that field of investigation.

Now a man would be ready. He would have a general formation. For instance, he would know something that very few people do know, namely, the difference between what he knows and what he does not know. And this is perhaps the most precious fruit of *paideia,* of good elementary education: that a man come to possess judgment even in matters in which he is not a specialist. For example, upon listening to some lecture, he would at once be aware that

105

this fellow was not talking mathematics—that he was making rhetoric for the cause of the intuitionist, or something of the sort. Because in mathematics there is no place for persuasion, but only for strict, detached argument. Many people do not know even this. Indeed many people cannot tell the difference between poetry and rhetoric, nor even between poetry and science or poetry and theology. Yet, the differences in these cases are radical. Now, in order to possess judgment in these matters one must have benefited by *paideia*. Thanks to good early discipline, one's mind has become well-shaped. And the discipline should be tough and thorough like that demanded by grammar.

As remarked in the beginning, the cleavage between scientists and humanists began in the Renaissance, and in the very early Renaissance, but as yet there was no overt opposition on either side. The third man, later to become so badly needed, was still on the scene. As a matter of fact, until only a few years ago, there still existed a few excellent writers in English on scientific subjects; and men like Sir Arthur Eddington, who was a fine writer, could find scholars like themselves in Germany, thinkers like Max Planck, and eminent physicists who also wrote splendidly, and even Heisenberg, although he did not possess the skill in expression of the two others. At any rate, all these men still enjoyed the support of a classical education. But with the final divorce between science and the humanities, the classical education was abandoned, at least in the country of my birth.

Now, here is how I think the separation came about. After St. Thomas, who represents the highest point of intellectual achievement in the Middle Ages, and who was a late contemporary of St. Albert, philosophy and theology became extremely, and sometimes absurdly, technical. This is true

106

both of the work of his commentators and of the work of his attackers. (We must not fall into the illusion of thinking that St. Thomas was well received in his generation. Not at all. Nor was he readily accepted by the next generation—as a matter of fact, he has never been well received. Not at least until the time of Leo XIII. Of course there were earlier popes who had also welcomed his work, but Leo XIII resurrected him at a time when he was unkown. In fact, only a few hardy Dominicans were studying him. And St. Thomas, even today, is not well received. But, of course, there is no cause for surprise in all this. After all, *bonum ex integra causa, malum ex quocumque defectu.* And the *bonum ex integra causa,* that is, the *integra causa,* is extremely difficult to achieve. I mean that it is easy to miss a target, as the Pythagoreans realized. It was they who pointed out to mankind that it is easy to hit the side of a barn but difficult to hit the bull's-eye. They may not have used these terms, but what they thought amounts to this.)

So philosophy and theology degenerated by becoming more and more technical. The decline can be seen in the breakdown of philosophical and theological vocabulary, which departed farther and farther from familiar meanings. An urge was felt to make distinctions before any reason could be found for making them. No attention was paid to that concerning which the distinction should be made. I can offer a very simple example. Take the expression "distinguished according to reason," which in Latin is translated *distinctum ratione.* Very good. Something is distinguished from something else by a distinction according to reason. But in St. Thomas this phrase has seven or eight different meanings, whereas for the later authors it is fixed and rigid. Ask them "What do you mean by distinguished according to reason?"

But what is happening to our philosophical vocabulary? Take the distinction between matter and privation. Are these distinguished only according to reason? Of course, but what of the distinction between essence and existence? Is this the same sort of distinction? Hardly. And are there not things concerning which one can make one distinction which has no foundation whatsoever in that which is being distinguished? Then if you call upon these decadent Scholastics (and the non-decadent are few, mind you, in all schools of philosophy) for a distinction, they refuse, protesting that they cannot understand you, by reason of the single meaning which is the only one they will allow. And this impossible complication has come about by the multiplication of univocal meanings. True thinking is now confined in a straight jacket of terminology.

I am afraid that I am losing myself in something of a digression. But it is a profitable digression because we are learning one of the ways in which philosophy can be killed. It is by destroying the philosophical vocabulary. The typical Late Scholastic would walk into a class-room in order to give a lesson on causes, and would begin by declaring that there were four causes. Furthermore he would most likely present them in some reverse order, e.g., formal, material, efficient, and final. But what do you mean by a cause to begin with? This kind of philosopher does not dare stoop to such simple inquiries because, if he faced this question, and was indeed able to answer it, he would find himself stating that the word cause, in both Greek and Latin, originally meant responsible, or a person responsible for something. When it first became a technical term, its meaning was legal. This fellow called before the Court, as responsible for an accident, stood there as its cause. But my point is that we are often reluctant to go back to things that everybody knows. We seem to feel obliged to take a great deal for granted, to start halfway. Yet why try to impress people with a vocabulary? So there are four causes. Good, let us distinguish them. As a matter of fact, we could distinguish about forty-nine different kinds of causes. Will it not be wiser to find something upon which all of us can and do agree. Of course this agreement will make itself known only when we start talking. Yet even though, in our talking, we contradict one another, such contradiction cannot go on without some basic notions and basic truths accepted by all. And it is this familiar error that we are inclined to. Wisdom, we seem to think, will be achieved by abandoning all of this and rebuilding it from the ground up.

If we hold to our example of the causes, such a procedure will eventually yield causes existing only in text-books. Such causes are destroyed when you throw the text-book into the fire. If all you had in mind were the words that you use in making your distinctions, then when the text-book goes up in flames, so do your distinctions. But this was not true for Aristotle, the great Greek Commentators, and the Scholastics who were loyal to him, among them St. Thomas. For example, they would never employ the phrase "final cause", without reference to the basic significance, "that for the sake of which." One builds a house for the sake of shelter, shelter being the final cause. But the typical professor of Late Scholastic philosophy, will be thoroughly confused. "That for the sake of which?" Such a phrase will have little meaning for him. Yet it is the only expression Aristotle ever employed. "Final cause" is a phrase made in Latin by the Scholastics, not objectionable itself, but which in English might lead us to think that final indicates the very end. As when we make a decision and declare that it is final. So the term final applied to cause is not entirely helpful. But we still say that a man acts for the sake of something, for a purpose. We still declare that we did something purposely, and everyone knows what is meant.

So the wrong mode of procedure, in our example, one that takes ready-made terms which are half-comprehended as its starting point, will surely lead us farther and farther away from primary and familiar knowledge. The whole point is that the obvious is being concealed, or disregarded as trivial. Now, in all probability the obvious is what everybody knows, and if it is concealed, the less known will then be employed to explain the more known. In his commentary on the *Physics,* St. Thomas makes reference to this wrong-headed type of argumentation. At some length, in defence of Aristotle, he points out that there is no way of demonstrating the existence of nature. Because everyone knows that nature is. We all use the word. As when we say: "Is not nature wonderful in making such trees, or in making an elephant, or a lion, or a porcupine?" These things we attribute to nature. Of course, such knowledge of nature remains quite vague. To be sure, we desire knowledge that is distinct, but distinct knowledge is not necessarily arrived at by demonstration. It can also be achieved by what might be called determination or decomposition, that is, dividing in view of a definition. This is one way of acquiring distinct knowledge, and it is supported and furthered by more investigation. But there was one thinker—I am thinking of Avicenna— and although a very great philosopher he was indeed the victim of impatience, who did not respect the human mode of knowing which moves from the vague, and the general, towards the more distinct and more particular. He was resolved

110

to squeeze distinct knowledge immediately out of vague knowledge. (And to do this by way of demonstration, to boot.) But it cannot be done. It cannot be done, St. Thomas warns us, because it will mean expressing what is better known in terms of what is less known: that is, making something clear by means of something obscure. There could be no more glaring instance of putting the cart before the horse; that is to say the horse is forgotten. Alas, from the very origins of philosophy, there have been thinkers ready to attempt it. And they are still with us. For instance, only recently, at the Annual Meeting of the Canadian Philosophical Association, I had to deal with some logical positivists and analytical philosophers. Now just as soon as one mentioned something really basic, upon which all could agree,— and most of Aristotle's strictly philosophical work is of this sort—they would protest that this was trivial. Trivial it might be, but there are such things as tremendous trivialities. Nothing is to be dismissed because it appears trivial. The trivial should be weighed and considered. For example, what do we mean by rational when we say rational animal? What do we mean by animal? What does this word signify? Of what sort of thing do you say animal? This must be searched out. Similarly, what does one mean by a circle? The question may be trivial, but everything can depend on it. What is meant by a point on a line, by a curve, and so on?

St. Thomas, then, in the passage already referred to, lesson 1 of his commentary on the *Physics,* Book II, repeats after Aristotle that the existence of nature needs no proving. Although everyone might well agree; this would not mean that we all possess a distinct knowledge of nature. Here is where science gets to work. Because we want more and more distinct knowledge of the world about us. But such research cannot dispense with that vague knowledge with which all thinking has to begin. St. Thomas goes on to explain the extraordinary remark made there by Aristotle that to speak of things without reference to the common basic knowledge preliminary to all right thinking, is to behave like a man born blind who is determined to discuss colours. A physicist of course will assure you that even the blind man can discuss colours provided they are described in terms of angles of refraction. But if colours stand for what we see with our eyes, proper sensibles, the blind man can talk about them, to be sure, but never with any knowledge of what he is talking about. He will only be using words, something all too easy to do. The blind man is able to utter the sound "red." This much he can do. And it is astonishing how often philosophers are doing no more than this. Because such occupations usually characterize what is called a school of thought. The members erect a kind of vocabulary that any of their colleagues can manipulate in the approved fashion, without knowing to what the terms actually refer. In other words, our man born blind talks of things he does not know as if he did, whereas whoever wants to demonstrate the existence—already self-evident to all men—of something like nature, talks of things he and everyone know, as if he did not; the muddle is the same: both men lack the most elementary *paideia* of the mind and both stand in what Socrates (and Plato, in the *Sophist*) had so rightly judged the most crass and unfortunate ignorance of all: that of being quite unable to tell knowledge, even the humblest, from ignorance. This is my understanding of the criticism made there by St. Thomas. And the same condemnation is found in his commentary on the *Ethics*.

112

Those of us who are at all familiar with the vocabulary of the kind of Scholasticism which arose after the thirteenth century will know what I am talking about. Most men of this period showed little desire to recover the primitive meanings of words. Whereas, in Aristotle, this concern is always dominant. Book V of the *Metaphysics* is a good example. It is entirely devoted to the basic words which we use, not merely in philosophy, but in common speech. We are asked to consider what is meant by a beginning? by a cause? by an element? by a part, a whole, a power, and so on? And our author forever leads us back to the word in common usage. St. Thomas is only repeating Aristotle when he formulates the general principle that *nominibus utendum est ut plures utuntur*—we must use words as they are used by the general public.

It is also interesting to observe how little concerned were most Scholastic philosophers after St. Albert and St. Thomas with the question of what a word is. And this notwithstanding the nominalists. Indeed, nominalism only became possible because of all sorts of tacit assumptions which were made concerning the nature of words, the nature of concepts, and the relations between these. Nominalism is never concerned with what a name is. The nature of the name itself is a most embarrassing problem for your run-of-the-mill nominalist.

There are many reasons why the mind should be formed by contact with poetry, before proceeding to training in rhetoric, or in scientific logic, that is, in the logic which leads to scientific knowledge as the instrument of such knowledge. The psychology of youth yields one of those reasons. But the reason to which I would draw your attention here has nothing to do with the psychology of youth. It is that both poet and philosophy use words whose first meanings are commonly known. Remember your Shakespeare: "Now is the winter of our discontent turned glorious summer by this son of York." Winter is winter, and discontent is discontent. But the winter of our discontent, that is known too, as soon as the poet has said it. There is an initiative that words and meanings do not take of themselves. The poet is a maker and a midwife. He can put the familiar world ablaze, sometimes quite noiselessly, and make us understand what we had never seen before, or never seen that way.

Words first signify things as we first know them. They first belong to ordinary language. Then the poet becomes aware of the inner wealth of what our words stand for—that these cover so much more than they do in ordinary usage. He can talk to us because the materials he constructs with are already known, yet by arrangements (e.g. the metaphor), he throws new light on what we already know.

It has been said that the poet is a person in love with words. This is materially true, for he does love words for what they are: sounds proclaiming our concepts which in turn signify the things that provoked us into giving meaning to the vocal sounds in the first place. And he wants further to make them living voices, to render them incantatory.

But what we are concerned with right now is that the poet cannot afford to abandon ordinary meanings and become so allusive that every line he speaks calls for a tome of commentaries without which the line has no meaning, without which the line itself remains mute. This is just another way of saying that the poet must abide with the well-springs that remain hidden in ordinary speech, and that when he poeticizes he must remain direct.

114

The philosopher too must use ordinary language, up to a point; but when he goes beyond this point, when he has made distinctions and imposed new meanings upon a word, these new meanings must never be divorced from some well-known, earlier, meaning. If they become so divorced—as is almost invariably the case with words such as "matter", "form", "act and potency", "essence and existence", "genus and species"—they will lose their soul, their animation. This is, I implied, what happened to Late Scholasticism, which had nothing in common with what the Ancient Greeks, nor later the Neo-Platonists, nor the splendid tradition which you see at work in the Berlin corpus of the *Commentaria in Aristotelem Graeca,* nor Boethius, nor Albert, nor Aquinas, had ever meant by philosophy.

Do we begin to see, perhaps, why St. Thomas insisted that poetry be taught before philosophy. The mind must acquire a kind of refined determination before stepping into the field of strict science. This is indispensable. For otherwise the field of science itself will soon become empty. Not that science is based upon poetry, but a mind that is not shaped by poetry cannot use words with wisdom. Please be careful not to misunderstand me. I do not mean that the scientist or philosopher must use words as the poet does, nor somehow learn from the poet how to use them. No, what I am talking about is the quality of mind acquired by a man who is sensitive to poetry. Not all people have to become poets. Indeed the poetic gift is found in only a few. But all have to know poetry, which is something different. And the shape of the mind, its power of using words which are tools of the mind, will depend upon the formation acquired by an intelligent reading of poetry, under the guidance of a competent teacher.

115

Charles DeKoninck

II

In our previous lecture, we insisted that poetry, and even before poetry, grammar, is the most basic of all disciplines. Perhaps I did not put sufficient emphasis on the indispensable character of grammar. Training in grammar is something which no mind can do without. Let us not fail to notice, of course, that there is something irrational about grammar. And, among irrational grammars, that of the English language easily carries the palm. I myself never had an opportunity to learn or study English grammar. Indeed, when I asked for it, the reply which I received—and this from English scholars—was simply: "Well, we have none." Apparently, it is just something one picks up as one goes on. A French grammar does exist, at least in some measure. But really to lay one's hands on grammar, one must return to the classical languages. There are a certain number of philologists and linguists among my acquaintances, and to a man they insist that if it is grammar we want to learn, we must study Latin, Greek, or both. With these as our point of departure, we may then move into our own language.

Allow me a remark or two on the irrationality of grammar. It is good to realize that in this life things are not completely rational. Grammar, heaven knows, is one of the earliest instances of the irrational which we encounter: all those exceptions, idioms, declensions, conjugations, and so on. None of them is ever completely rational. If to you they appear rational, it is because you are seeing intelligibility where none exists. And it is good that our first encounters in the long slow process of learning should be with matters that are not completely intelligible. If mental formation began with something as simple and lucid as counting, by which I mean here the operations within the power of a computer, the effect might be to communicate a quite false outlook on life for the future. Will you not agree that this is the case with many mathematicians, who sometimes, when it is a question of dealing with reality, reveal themselves to be the most irrational creatures on earth? It is not my intention to make light of mathematicians, nor of their science. But it is remarkable how proficient a man can be, especially in the art of calculation, while in all other respects his mind is quite formless. I should explain again that by the art of calculation I do not mean mathematical science in the true sense, that is, as Euclid for example understood it. I am speaking rather of that computation which proceeds through algebra, calculus, and so on. A man may be thoroughly effective in this field and worthless in every other. I am sure some of you have met the kind of men that I have in mind.

In our earlier lecture we insisted on the immense wealth latent in ordinary language. And we remarked that here is why no poet needs an eccentric or technical vocabulary. We suggested that the good philosopher will also use ordinary language. At least up to a point. But it will be his duty, as he observes how words are used in different meanings, to bring out these shades of meaning explicitly. When he speaks to us, he should be careful to indicate what the word which he will employ is going to mean. As a favorite contemporary example let us take the word "being." The philosopher employing such a term ought to warn us from the start that whether it be taken as a noun or as a verb, this word carries about fifty different meanings. Here is a fact most distasteful to the existentialists, who assume that it has only one meaning. But, whether we like it or not, it bears a multitude of significances. So that one must try to fix the particular value with which one is concerned. For instance, it means one thing in the phrase: "Socrates is a husband," or "Socrates is a relative of such and such a person by blood," "Socrates is five and a half feet tall," or "Socrates weighs 200 pounds," and so on and so on. In all this, "is" is involved, but the "is" means something different in each instance. If it be asserted that the equilateral triangle exists, there we have one meaning of existence. But when it is stated that Socrates exists, a quite different meaning is implied. And if the statement be made that "nothing is nothing," there we have still another meaning. Of all these different significances we must be keenly aware. But I am reserving some classical examples for later mention. The example of being which I have just offered to you stands, I think, as a relevant one, for the reason that so many people nowadays assume that the term "existence" has a privileged meaning. Of course "existence" may well be of a privileged kind, if you mean that existence which is identical with the nature of the thing that exists, and this is the privilege of divine being. Do not trouble yourself if this sounds a bit confusing. These matters can be taken up later, and with perhaps clearer result.

Now it is the duty of the philosopher to be explicitly aware of these matters. He must be conscious that words, some words at least, and these the key words of his science, each bear many meanings. It is the relatedness of these different significations that he must try to detect. And I say relatedness because the meanings are not utterly different, as they are in the word "seal", for example, which may mean an animal, or the seal placed upon a document. The two meanings of a term like this one have been acquired entirely by chance. But the words which I have spoken of as carrying more than one meaning, vary in their significance by design, and by design not necessarily established through public convention. No, somehow, as a language develops, a word grows in meanings. And there is always reason why these subsequent meanings are new with respect to previous ones, and yet related to them. All significance somehow grows from a primitive significance. And the philosopher must try, not merely to detect the diverse meanings, but to identify the fashion in which they are related and discover how the original word grew and proliferated in various directions. For example, let us take the Greek word "logos": it carries many meanings—indeed so many as to make it one of the most difficult of all words to translate. Now the primordial meaning was just that of the spoken word, the basic part of speech. But then, very naturally, the word *logos* came to mean that which we express by means of words. Already, then, our term bears two distinct significances, though these are not unrelated. I utter a word. You hear it. That is, you hear a vocal sound, and a significant one. Now that which the sound signifies, its meaning by convention, is also called a word. Now it is the mental word to which reference is made. And so the process goes on. Finally, *logos* can mean the definition of something, that is, the clear exposition of what I say. I may utter the term *circle,* for instance; then I define what I mean by a circle. The definition will also be called *logos.* And here we are with a third meaning. Now whenever we use a word, we ought to make clear at least by the context in which we employ our word, just in what sense we intend it.

Now why is ordinary language so important? All the words which I have suggested to you so far are part of ordinary language, like the word "word," and the word "definition." Well, to explain why, let us take a word which is a Scholastic term. I choose a Scholastic word because these are the terms so much abused in the period immediately preceding the Renaissance, and which went on being abused throughout the Renaissance. It is important that we see how disastrous it can be to ignore the meanings, and the interrelation of the meanings, of any crucial term. So let us direct our attention to the word "matter". What does this word mean? Last year at Notre Dame University, an entire symposium, the results of which made a stack of pages, was devoted to what matter is, or what the word means. Those pages I have not examined, but from the dictionary I know what the word "matter" meant first in Latin, and what the word *hulê* meant first in Greek. Now, if you talk to a scholastic and let fall the word "matter," then of course he will take it to mean prime matter. But this is not at all its primary meaning. He is accepting a very late imposition of the word. In Greek, matter first of all meant wood under its most familiar form. Not just wood, but wood cut down and useable either for burning or for building. It meant timber, and lumber. Now here, surely, we derive a much more concrete grasp of what the word stands for. Lumber is so much more intelligible than wood, because lumber means wood considered with respect to building, and building we understand, and the need for building materials we understand. Our practical conceptions are always much closer to us. Why is this? Because actually they come out of our own heads. Wood, as found in nature, must inevitably remain something rather mysterious. Those trees out in our park are not exactly intelligible even to a botanist. Should a botanist tell you that he does understand a tree, don't believe him. Ask another

120

botanist. And you will soon learn that what we know about trees is not quite so thorough as this. But lumber is a thing we can comprehend. To be sure it is wood, but above all it is a human convenience. The stuff we need for building. So finally, the Greeks call any sort of building material *hulê,* and in Latin *materia,* which led to our word matter. Then, at a still later stage, matter became whatever anything at all was made of. Thus even a syllogism has its matter, for the terms of the syllogism are the stuff, so to speak, of which it is made. But please do not fail to notice how this word is changing its meanings all the time. And when and where does the meaning of prime matter appear? Only at the very end, and at the very end because this meaning can be attained only with great difficulty. The primary matter is something most obscure and hard to come at. We cannot possibly know such a thing directly. All we can do is to speak of it through examples. In the example of a wooden block, it is easy enough to see the proportion between the shape of the wooden block and the wood of this object. Then, we are able to make a kind of parallel and to detect the proportion by which anything at all is the kind of thing that it is, and that of which it is made. Thus even man must be made of something, and, besides the something of which he is made, there must be something else about him by virtue of which he is a man. And so we attain the notion of an ultimate material and of a form which makes this material to be a thing of a certain kind. Of course, what I have been telling you would require long discourse to make plain. Aristotle, indeed, devoted a whole book to this question. Only at the close of the first book of the *Physics,* does he finally attain, among other things, to this ultimate material, this first matter. But you see how very far it is from being what matter first meant.

Now the vital point is this, that the original meaning must never be lost sight of. If you forget the significance with which you began, you will wind up with a vocabulary that hangs in mid-air, so to speak, and hence with a primary matter that exists only as a printed phrase in textbooks. And it will be hardly even that, because it will be a word which is no true word at all. It will possess only the look of a word. Because words ought to have meaning, and that which has only the look of one bears no meaning.

Still another example is, of course, that of *eidos* or "form." Now what does form mean to the typical scholastic of today, that is, to the kind of man who has entirely lost his hold upon nature and who lives in a maze of terminology, much as do many modern philosophers of our time. It is these latter gentlemen who are the true successors of the decadent scholastics. But now for our other word, "form." Well, what does this mean first of all? It means simply the shape or figure of a sensible thing, the outline of a horse, let us say. But the shape of things is very often that by reason of which one comes to know, somewhat extrinsically, what the thing is. If we make a difference, at distance, between horses and cows, we do so primarily from their shapes, not by reason of distinctive colours. Now, since the shape of a creature is so good an indication of what sort of creature it is, it will be natural to extend the word shape to indicate, let us say, the interior shape of the object. That is, whatever inside it makes it to have the peculiar outside shape that it does have. The outside shape is what St. Thomas calls a proximate sign of the nature of a thing. It is not the nature but is a sign of it. Then, what this external shape is a sign of, the interior shape so to speak, is also called *eidos* or "form". Again, a new imposition, though not entirely without dependence on the earlier one.

In your libraries you can find, I am sure, Liddell and Scott's Greek Lexicon, or you might turn to any good Latin dictionary; such works will reveal to you all those meanings. These are really not technical at all. Every word Aristotle used, every term to which he gave a special significance, is usually to be found in Liddell and Scott.

As another instance of the principle which we are explaining, let us take the word "order": in Greek *kosmos,* in Latin *ordo.* What is its meaning? In present English usage the meaning is somewhat vague. But in the beginning this word carried a markedly concrete significance. For it was a term used of weaving, where the cloth bore a definite pattern. You see how at the outset the term was essentially a practical one. May I recommend another dictionary, the *Dictionnaire étymologique de la langue latine,* by Ernout and Meillet, which is something like a chronological dictionary of the Latin language. All such words are revealed by this work as possessing meanings which originally were quite concrete. Let me have you notice once more that Aristotle and St. Thomas, more than all other philosophers, were greatly concerned with the origin of a word, with its earlier impositions. Plato too, at least in his *Cratylus,* shows himself to be very concerned with "etymologies," his primary intention being, quite rightly for a philosopher, to make the meaning of certain words clearer, rather than to lay bare their historical past and various vicissitudes. Now, in St. Thomas, the etymologies proposed are often quite false. This is because he takes them from Isidore of Seville, or other uncertain scholars, who will tell us, for example, that the word *lapis* is derived from the two words *laedere* and *pedem* meaning to hurt the foot. This etymology is absurd, historically. Yet it is a very interesting one because at least it brings us back to something concrete. A man stumbles over a stone and injures his foot. The important principle is the need for achieving that early imposition which is related to sensation. Historical truth is in no way so important.

We may come to the matter of truth a little later, and I will then show that sometimes a false example is better than a true one. Many of the examples offered by St. Thomas, and by Aristotle, are quite deliberately false. Why such choices were made we shall learn in a moment.

I shall now propose two more words which are common enough, heaven knows, but which are supreme examples of vagueness and multiple meanings. These are "whole" and "part." Nothing is more amusing than to watch certain modern philosophers of mathematics manipulating these words, while remaining totally unaware of their many different significances. As when they say, for instance, that there are parts which are equal to the whole. One example would be the series of whole numbers. This series contains within itself the series of even numbers and the series of odd numbers. It would appear beyond question that the series of even numbers is part of the series of whole numbers. Yet each of these series is infinite since we can establish a one to one correspondence between the items in each: for there are as many even numbers as there are of whole numbers. Therefore the part, which is only half of this whole, is equal to the whole. Now this is amusing, a kind of parlour game, but designed for children rather than for serious people. Obviously, if you subtract your even numbers from the first series, you will be left one series of odd and another of even. So this yields you two equal series. If you play your game fairly then you must grant that the whole numbers form a series twice as big as the even. But if you concern yourself only with what you can put down severally and call one series whole numbers, and another even numbers, then of course you can allow yourself as many as you like. You can enjoy an infinity; indeed there is nothing to prevent you from having an infinite series of a single number: the number two, for instance, repeated to infinity. For I can take the number two, then take it again, and take it again, and so rejoice in the possession of as many twos as I wish. Is this the true state of things? Then I shall be able to say that the number two, a single item in the series of whole numbers, is equal to the entire series. And if we chose to take the time, we could discover still more silly paradoxes than this.

When you talk of "part," you see, you should be aware that it has diverse meanings. Is the meaning that of part universally taken, or of part taken particularly? Is it, say, a physical part? A logical part? If a logical part, then it must be part of a logical whole, and you should remember that the logical universal, that is, say, "animal", is a whole that is wholly found in each of its parts. For when I say that man is an animal, this universal, "animal," is said of all men, and of each man. As a matter of fact, you can say animal of me. I am an animal. Now, animal signifies as a whole. But the parts then are subjective parts: that of which this whole is said. So here we have something one, "animal", that can be identified with many "men, dogs, horses and so on". So "whole" is a thoroughly equivocal term. The same is true of part, and again of *genus* and *species*. This word *genus* no longer exists, that is, it is hardly used anymore in treatises on natural history—though a good exception is George Gaylord Simpson's work entitled *Horses,* where I recommend the first chapter, called *What is a horse?* But the term was much employed for a long time. And, though found still in Scholastic textbooks, it is precisely one of these terms that might safely be burnt. Why has it become so useless? Because we now ignore where it comes from. *Genus,* unfortunately another word which English had to borrow from Latin, actually means a race. The human race, a certain race of cows, these are examples of the *genus.* So first of all it has a natural meaning, then much later an imposition which speaks of some kind of universality. Something now becomes predicable as a *genus.* Figure is thus predicable of triangle and circle: so that figure stands as their *genus.* Equilateral triangle is predicable only of individuals, so that equilateral stands for a *species.* But what about the term *species?* Where did it originate? For unless we lead this term also back to some original meaning we shall not be able to make a verification. The term *species* is a fair translation of either *eidos* or *idéa.* It means something narrower than the race: a certain type within the race differing within that same race from certain other types. But earlier still, it meant something recognizable, the *eidos,* or "extrinsic shape".

Now, already in ordinary language, several levels of meanings are established by the people unthinkingly. And to this popular language the great philosophers are generally faithful. Even the names which Aristotle gave to fish and to beast, he preferred to take from the fishermen or countrymen.

Let me not be understood as objecting against the coining of, let us say, chemical names half a mile long. There is no harm in this, but we should not forget that these are not really names. They are "technical." Philosophy should as a rule try to avoid such practices.

The levels of meaning, the new impositions, which are

precious in the development of human knowledge should, as I say, arise spontaneously. They should seldom be the product of special investigation. They should just come about as the human mind makes its natural advance into greater understanding. Let us consider the various meanings of the word "nature."

Nature in Aristotle has about thirteen different meanings. I will now record seven of them and then an eighth taken from a much later author, namely, Boethius, but which is generally accepted. The very first meaning of all is almost sure to be unfamiliar to the average Aristotelian scholars. In order to discover it we need the help of a good etymologist or a good philologist, a man expert in the Greek language. He will show you that *phusis* first meant the generation of animals as a process, their coming to birth. The meaning is primary in animals and, by extension, is also attributed to plants. So here is our first imposition, which stands for the process of being born, the acorn growing out of the oak tree, then falling to the ground to yield still another oak tree. It is this sort of process that is called *phusis*. So in its first meaning the word stands not for something fixed, not for a principle, but for a living process.

Then, by a process equally natural, the word came to stand for that from which the birth process took its rise: the living parent being the principle of a process. So nature now means a principle, something intrinsic to a thing, and from which there comes forth something by way of process, not the being born, but the birth.

The third meaning now becomes that of an intrinsic principle of any change which occurs in nature, a principle found essentially within the thing itself. Let me beg you to look at this piece of chalk as it falls. I am not pushing it down, as

127

you see. All by itself it moves in that direction. This change of place we attribute to something intrinsic in the object, whatever it may be. The force concerned is not extrinsic, as when I break the chalk. In order to make clear the differences between an intrinsic and an extrinsic principle may I suggest the example of a natural organ. My eyes grow from within. Hence it is to nature that I attribute my eyes. I did not make my organs of vision. But now, what of my spectacles? Their principle lies outside me, it is extrinsic. Our spectacles are made by men, deliberately fashioned. They grow, not from nature, but from our own heads, and by planning. Hence the difference between artificial and natural things. The natural comes from within. But how is this? What does it mean? I do not know. But I do not need to know in order to make this supreme distinction: that which holds between those things which are by virtue of something intrinsic in them from which springs whatever they do, or whatever their behavior may be; and those things which are as they are by virtue of a principle outside them.

A fourth meaning of nature now arises and again by natural extension of the preceding ones. For that out of which things are made, their natural material, now comes to be called nature. And this can be done because the material of a thing is often responsible for its motion.

Finally we have nature coming to mean form. By form now we indicate that by reason of which a thing is of a certain kind, and by reason of which when propagating itself, it will produce a second thing of the same kind. That in an oak tree which causes it to produce another oak, that in a horse which causes it to produce another horse, are the forms of these objects and may truly be called their natures in this last sense. Now if by nature you mean the source or principle of the characteristic motions or behavior of natural things, then their form, though this means nature by a later imposition, will be nature most of all.

But I beg you to observe that we have a kind of reverse order here. If you compare the first meaning of nature (the process of coming to birth) with the last meaning of nature just mentioned you are forced to admit that the last is far more nature than that meaning which is the root of all the rest. Because matter would not be a principle of characteristic motion without form, and no object could be nature in any sense without both matter and form. In other words the third meaning of nature is: an intrinsic principle of motion or rest that is within a thing essentially and not incidentally. But to explain all this now is out of the question. What I mean to insist on is merely the multiplicity of meanings, how one comes from another, how they follow a determinable order, and how the last is the most determinate meaning of all. St. Thomas's way of putting this is as follows: "It is the order of naming which reflects the order of our knowing, where we first know this and later know that, and where what is most knowable itself is least known to us, whereas what is least knowable itself is most known to us, because of the inverse order between our process of knowing [where we depend first on our senses] and the order of things in themselves." Hence, if we could at once arrive at the order which things possess in themselves, we could at once put our finger on that which most of all deserves to be termed nature. But if we follow, as we must, the order of our knowing, then that which for us is nature first of all, is something quite different. In more technical language the primary analogate in the order of naming is not the primary analogate in the order of being. But we have not finished with our meanings of nature. There remain two more which again are related to those already given. There is nature not just in the sense of material, but in the sense of raw material, like iron ore with reference to all objects made of iron and steel. The French speak of such a matter as primary, *matière première,* namely, the raw materials of a given industry. And then there is form, in a new meaning, which leads to a very different significance for the word "nature"—a significance different from all those already given. For instance, we speak of the nature of a circle. We speak of the nature of the English language. We even will allow ourselves an expression like the nature of time. But neither the circle nor a language nor time is a nature in any of the senses already set down. All the meanings which are studied above have this in common that they refer back in some fashion or order to that primordial sense of a coming forth, or of coming to birth. But is it not true that in our examples of circle, language, and time, we seem to have contact with this primordial meaning?

What we mean by nature, when speaking of the nature of a circle, is that which is expressed in a definition. Let me suggest an example of this employment of our word. In the definition of "person" given by Boethius, he offers us the following formula: *Rationalis naturae individua substantia* —the individual substance of a rational nature. How is the word "nature" used here? Does it mean nature in any of the senses employed already? It would seem not, and we might have advised Boethius to avoid the word "nature" and substitute something like *essentia.* Why does he not make the choice which we would prefer? St. Thomas explains that a person is a special kind of essence. Now, essence is a very common term, indeed too common for the purpose of Boethius. You see, essence stands for that which is the content of a definition. But what is there which we cannot at least attempt to define. We can define circle, time, language, and indeed almost anything which you might care to name. Hence if essence and nature are used interchangeably, the implication is that anything which can be defined possesses, or is, a nature. But the thing which Boethius is attempting to define is a very particular kind of essence indeed, namely, that unique essence which is rational. Hence St. Thomas tells us, Boethius chose the word "nature" because it has a narrower meaning and is more appropriate for an essence so peculiar. But I beg you to notice above all how here you witness such very great minds going to so much trouble in order to learn how an author came to use his term as he did, and searching back into its original meanings. Why all this bother? It is because they do not want to drift from their moorings, from the things we know first, and most commonly.

The dreadful mistake, then, is to start halfway. Show me any textbook that you like on this subject. Do you know where the man will begin telling us what nature is? He will begin with one of the late, and derived meanings. But this will never do. It is too abstract. Take the definition of person which I just offered you. It can be established and verified only by a lengthy argumentation which is not demonstrative. And notice that St. Thomas when he explains the meaning of the word nature, in its third significance, which corresponds to the use made of it in Aristotle's *Physics,* insists that he derives his definition from the way in which we talk about nature in everyday conversation. And this is of the highest importance. Because then we are expressing what? We are expressing what we know of the thing. Stick to this law and nobody will ever be able to say that you do not know what you are talking about.

But the textbook will not protect me from this disaster. The textbook will pounce on the most important meaning of the word nature, but will never lead me back to its primitive meanings. The result will be that I will never know clearly what I am talking about.

Of course these primitive, familiar, and basic meanings are always vague. But this vagueness is something we must respect. Should we despise our vague knowledge, as if whatever was only known vaguely could never be relevant, then we might as well do away with all knowledge and sleep out the rest of our days. No, we must grasp a meaning which is basic, basic as to us, and upon which later meanings depend for their comprehension. The man who fails to do this can never be talking sense. The dead-end of scholasticism, to which reference was made in a previous lecture, became inevitable when later meanings of words used in philosophy were divorced from meanings known by the men in the street. If you want modern examples of this kind of collapse an example might be found in the word class. I mean the term as used by modern mathematical philosophers. They speak to us of classes which boast only one member, of parts severally greater than their whole, of relations without terms, not to speak of words that do not signify. And expressions like these are in current use by certain people today. Now, I know what a null class is, but if I had anything to do with the naming of such a concept I would call it something else. Never a null class, because for me the term class signifies multiplicity. If all I have is one of them, I am not going to call it a class. There are of course reasons for invoking the notion of class here, yet the two things concerned should be

132

kept apart. To do otherwise is to foster confusion: to encourage the rise of a kind of secret society, and in philosophy there is no place for a secret society. Of course far back in the beginning, philosophy did contain a secret society. It was that of Pythagoras, and it existed for a mysterious reason, mainly because of irrational numbers.

Science, Education, and the Christian Person

SISTER ADRIAN MARIE, O.P.

Those willing to think deeply about the problems of our times, to face the reality of the burdens of fear, of impoverishment, of racial prejudice, of ignorance, of miseries of one kind or another, with which modern man is afflicted, must admit that modern science and technocracy are not unmixed blessings. Mauriac said he believed in twentieth-century science, in the progress which it promised, until one day he saw a carload of German Jewish children headed for one of the concentration camps and for slaughter.[1] This he knew was not progress. It has even been claimed that it is science that has brought us to the plight we are in. Written a century before the advent of jet planes and 50-megaton bombs, the words of Thomas Peacock sound prophetic. According to him the results of modern science consist almost totally in elements of mischief:

See the complications and refinements of modes of destruction . . . See collisions and wrecks and every mode of disaster by land and by sea, resulting chiefly from the insanity for speed, in those who for the most part have nothing to do at the end of the race, which they run as if they were so many Mercuries speeding with messages from Jupiter. Look at our scientific drainage, which turns refuse into poison . . . Look at our scientific machinery, which has destroyed domestic manufacture, which has substituted rottenness for strength in the thing made, and physical degradation in crowded towns for healthy and comfortable country life . . . The day would fail, if I should attempt to enumerate the evils which science has inflicted on mankind. I almost think it is the ultimate destiny of science to exterminate the human race.[2]

Short of the actuality of man's destroying himself with the aid of the instruments provided him through his modern scientific venture, there are other horrors which man has contemplated and is in danger of bringing to fruition. " 'The anti-Utopias,' the 'Brave New Worlds,' the 'Nineteen Eighty-fours' project into the future a vision of society more dark than the deepest pessimism the ancient world ever conjured up,' " warns Barbara Ward.[3] These books arouse in us a much greater concern for what modern science and technology have done to man, than for the way they have changed his surroundings. Many men are now doomed to spend their lives in industrial slums and factories, cut off from contact with the soil, with the sweet smelling honeysuckle, with the beauty of the brilliant red and yellow autumn leaves, with the playful scampering to and fro of the chipmunks, with the early dawn choruses of mockingbirds, catbirds and jays, with the silence of forest life at mid-day away from the frantic hum and buzz of our modern cities.

There are some people even more deprived than those involuntarily cut off from nature. These, Father Gerald Vann writes, are the "people who do live in contact with Nature, who are free to walk in field and forest, to listen to the voice of river or sea, but who in fact are blind and deaf to these things: having eyes they see not, and having ears they hear not, because psychologically speaking they are dead, and they are dead because, as we shall see, they have lost the faculty of wonder." [4] "Many generations of scientific discovery seem to have dulled the primeval appetite for wonder," [5] for in "the triumphal march of the practical sciences," the magic of life been crowded out. [6] The world does not lack for wonders, but man is seriously sick for lack of wonder. Modern science explains a man, a flea and a nasturtium each as a different arrangement of the desoxyribonucleic acid molecule, DNA. The DNA-defined man in turn renounces the child-like attitude of reverent wonderment which prompted Blake to write:

> To see a world in a grain of sand,
> And heaven in a wild flower,
> Hold infinity in the palm of the hand
> And eternity in a hour. [7]

As modern science strips the mystery from the grain of sand and takes heaven out of the wild flower, man blindly turns his dull dispirited thoughts on himself and his neighbor. J.B.S. Haldane was thus blinded when he wrote: "I am far more interested in the problems of biochemistry than in the question of what, if anything, will happen to me when I am dead . . . When I am dead, I propose to be dissected." [8] How different from Hamlet's epithets on man: "What a piece of work is man! How noble in reason! How infinite in faculty! in form and moving, how express and admirable! In action, how like an angel! in apprehension, how like a god! the beauty of the world! the paragon of animals!" [9] Is man an animal, an angel, a god, or is he merely a biochemical? The answer he gives to the question "What is Man?"

will greatly determine what man will make of himself in the brief span of time given to him on this earth. His outlook on the world largely determines his viewpoint of himself and his fellow man.

Why is he deaf and blind to his own nature? To the mysteries of a leaf or of a star? How has man come to his present state? Where did he get the drab picture of our twentieth-century world as a meaningless conglomeration of random, moving atoms? It is conjured up as the modern scientist sits watching index needles, revolving drums and sensitive plates. Withdrawn from the nature he attempts to explain, he looks only at that aspect of nature which is heavily controlled by and geared to the artificial environment of his own design. From the pointer readings, "the little shivers and wiggles" [10] of his apparatus, from these symbolic manifestations of the world he wants to know, he sketches the world as it appears to him. The results are strange, to say the least. Here is Bertrand Russell's account. "Academic philosophers . . . believed that the world is a unity . . . The most fundamental of my intellectual beliefs is that this is rubbish. I think the universe is all spots and jumps, without unity, without continuity, without coherence or orderliness . . . Indeed, there is little but prejudice and habit to be said for the view that there is a world at all." [11] If scientists accepted Russell's conclusion, actually there would be no point in any scientific investigation or explanation. A non-existent world is scarcely a suitable object of study. The modern scientist seems to be in Alice's dilemma as she asked the Cheshire Puss:

"Would you tell me, please, which way I ought to walk from here?"

"That depends a good deal on where you want to get to," said the Cat.

"I don't much care where—" said Alice.

"Then it doesn't matter which way you walk," said the Cat.

"—so long as I get *somewhere*," Alice added as an explanation.

"Oh, you're sure to do that," said the Cat, "if you only walk long enough." [12]

It is of the very nature of the human mind to want to move toward some goal, some end or purpose, even though the person involved, like Alice, denies that he has any particular one in mind. William Beck's fable [13] may be a little overdrawn, but it illustrates the point that every man, including the scientist, must at least implicitly have a goal. The main character in this fable is Sigmund, a fairly typical modern scientist, except for the fact that Sigmund has an unusually strong faith in his ability to reach certitude through experimental science. He knows that all experiments, up to his time, have failed in certitude because of some uncontrolled element in the experiment. If sufficient care were taken, if every possible eventuality were foreseen, surely an experimental animal could yield the kind of certitude he so devotedly seeks. He proposes to perform a perfect experiment in which every element of uncertainty would be ruled out. The frustrations he encounters with his experimental animal, the amoeba, are carefully recounted. Finally all is in readiness for Sigmund to achieve experimentally the kind of certitude he has so long sought. Months of anxious work had brought on a stomach ulcer, colitis, and he knew that he was near a nervous breakdown; but he must push on, as he is close to his goal. The author's description of Sigmund at this stage of the story seems to me significant of what may happen to any man who loses himself in the finite. "Sitting there at his desk, Sigmund looked rather like a plant that had been grown in a cave." [14] The dramatic conclusion of Sigmund's experiment comes as two inadequately insulated wires on badly overloaded electric circuits cause a flash of fire to ignite vapor seeping out of a poorly constructed solvent locker. Sigmund and the entire science building are burned to a crisp. Sigmund has given his life in his search for certitude, which according to Beck was actually a search for the Infinite. The fact that Sigmund failed is related to the fact that his knowledge of science was as unsound as his knowledge of himself. Beck says of him: "Had it not been for ill fortune, he might have achieved his mission and immortality —or so it would seem. As it turned out, however, Sigmund's sublime moment turned him into a cinder instead of a saint." [15]

The likeness of the scientist to the saint is not completely untrue. Isn't there a resemblance, call it a caricature if you like, between the dedication of the scientist and that of the saint? Both are looking for the Certitude which alone can satisfy the human heart. The scientist willingly gives up his time, his dreams, his hopes, in a word, himself, in pursuit of his goal. Is it any wonder that the world bestows on him the role of "wise man, the Magi of our day," provides him with money and time to retire to his monastic laboratory to contemplate the mysteries of nature, and then accepts him as the seer and the diviner of reality? [16]

Is it not the scientist who today bears witness to the following words of St. John of the Cross?

> To win to the knowledge of all,
> Wish not to know anything.

To win to the tasting of all,
Wish not to taste anything.
To come to the possession of all,
Wish not to possess anything.
To win to the being of all,
Wish not to be anything.

The scientist is willing to give up the knowledge of all except his one tiny specialty; he is willing to forego the taste of pleasure and social life; he is not ambitious for wealth; he will even give up health of mind and body—for what? In order to arrive at Certitude in the one area in which he thinks it is to be found. And It is there. God is everywhere. But the scientist is doomed to failure because he has stripped nature to the dimensions of his own thoughts about the world; he denies that there is any more to her than what he has unearthed and can control. His sense of wonder gone, the modern man next denies that there is any mystery in the natural order and finally repudiates the supernatural, thereby cutting himself off from God. "Where there is no God, there is no man," Berdyaev wrote.

If the modern scientist does believe in God, he is pitifully silent as his colleague Julian Huxley ascends the pulpit: "With the substitution of knowledge for ignorance . . . and the growth of control . . . God is simply fading away, as the Devil has faded before him, and the pantheons of the ancient world, and the nymphs and the local spirits . . . A faint trace of God, half metaphysical and half magic, still broods over our world, like the smile of a cosmic Cheshire Cat. But the growth of psychological knowledge will rub even that from the universe." [17] We hear in Huxley's words the modern scientist's testimony that he has cut himself off from God. Let us now bring modern science to the witness

141

stand to see what retribution has been demanded of man in return. Man radically removes God from His creation, but only to be uprooted himself in the process. According to the data of ten years ago:

In the United States during 1956, close to one million persons were hospitalized for mental disease, more than ten million were thought to be in need of psychiatric treatment, and there was reason to believe that a good percentage of the total population would spend at least part of their lives in a mental institution. In 1955, 16,760 persons were known to have committed suicide and not a few of those who had died a violent death had directly or indirectly been victims of abnormal or antisocial behavior. On the other hand, it was considered a great medical advance that tranquilizer drugs had become available to all. Three out of ten prescriptions were for these drugs in 1956, and more than a billion tablets of meprobamate alone were sold in a year! [18]

Would we not declare a national emergency if any other disease reached such proportions? Chesterton once observed that it was strange that men should see sublime inspiration in the ruins of an old cathedral and see none in the ruins of man. While our skyscrapers go higher and higher, it is time that we look at what our toil and trouble is doing to the launcher of this bigger and better world. Man reduces nature to the mechanical models and mathematical equations of the laboratory and classrooms and ends up disintegrated himself because his fellowman measures him by the same yardstick. D. H. Lawrence has well expressed our dilemma: "We are perishing for lack of fulfilment of our greater needs, we are cut off from the great sources of our inward nourishment and re-newal, sources which flow eternally in the universe. Vitally, the human race is dying. It is like a great uprooted tree, with its roots in the air. We must plant ourselves again in the universe." [19]

What can education do in the face of such a dilemma? As educators can we help man to relocate himself in nature, to reclaim his sanity and his health? Can we fulfill our own function, to bring man along the road of the arts and sciences toward that Wisdom which will set him free? One hundred years ago Longfellow wrote:

> Were half the power that fills the world with terror,
>> Were half the wealth bestowed on camps and courts,
> Given to redeem the human mind from error,
>> There were no need of arsenals or forts. [20]

Where shall we begin? If man is to reclaim the job of thinking from the machine, if man is to be restored to health and sanity, if man is to be free to search for that Truth which makes him free, among the imperatives must be the creation of a different atmosphere in our schools. "The frenzied tempo, the confusion, the activism of modern life, its hatred or fear of silence and stillness" is like a death house for the life of the mind. Father Vann says that

> Education could set itself to combat this state of affairs; but in fact it is itself too often determined by the prevailing atmosphere; and becomes itself a frenzied rush, a scramble for examination marks, for degrees and diplomas; it becomes itself so activist that there is no time to think and live; it becomes itself so utilitarian that it defeats its own essential ends; it may provide a great deal of information, it can hardly hope to be a royal road to a deep and vivid culture. [21]

143

A school that provides a homey atmosphere for students away from home, that concerns itself with human problems, that is interested in man's need for creativeness, that helps him to find his roots in nature, is preparing to .meet the challenge of the times. If we can lead our students back into the fields to lie again in the rich soft carpet of green grasses that provide so many benefits to man, or take them to the sea shore to see the feeding of the fiddler crab and the stealthy movements of the ant lion, and teach them to rejoice again in the song of the bird, we may bring them to realize that their problem is far less that of fighting nature than of fighting for nature. Krutch, in his provocative book *The Great Chain of Life,* claims that in this age of mass education and conformism, man may even have to relearn the basic lessons of his own dignity and individuality from the animals.

If we are ever to regain a respect for ourselves it may be that we shall regain it by the discovery that the animals themselves exhibit, in rudimentary form, some of the very characteristics and capacities whose existence in ourselves we had come to doubt because we had convinced ourselves that they did not exist in the creatures we assumed to be our ancestors. Even if man is no more than an animal, the animal may be more than we once thought him.[22]

Life out-of-doors is healthful for the body and tranquilizing for the spirit. In a recent public lecture Werner von Braun said that if American youth are to be educated, we must create an atmosphere of study in our schools. Televisions and cars must be removed from the campus. Without TV as a constant distractor, students might seek the out-of-doors for purposes other than the attainment of that much desired and eagerly sought status symbol, sun-tan. They

144

might return from the out-of-doors with a tranquil spirit that makes study and meditation a possibility again, without tranquilizers.

Contact with nature could also restore to man a sense of cosmic affiliation which would offset some of his anxieties and tensions. Man needs to feel at home in his world, in God's world. He needs to know that this is his home—one prepared for him by a loving and tender Father. Jean Daniélou says that before the time of Abraham, God had already made promises to His people. Through the regularity of the seasons, the promise of rain, through the soil and the fruits thereof, through a kind of cosmic liturgy, God had already made a covenant with his people. Man could re-discover these truths, if he would approach nature humbly and be attentive to her message. As Wordsworth put it:

> And hark how blithe the throstle sings!
> He too is no mean preacher.
> Come forth into the light of things,
> Let Nature be your teacher.[23]

Chesterton is a good example of a man in close contact with the reality of nature.

. . . When Chesterton shook himself out of his reveries and gazed on reality, then miracles happened. Romance is always something brought to a thing, and Chesterton invested the whole world with the great goodness of his heart. Chesterton in contact with a thing, be it a lamppost or an umbrella, was like the fuse that ignites a Roman candle. Anything at all set his intelligence off on a brilliant fireworks of paradoxes that penetrated into the heart of reality. He was a symbolist, and the inner meaning of creatures was never hidden from his concentration.

This world diaphanously let through the glories of another order, and Chesterton could see God in a gable. If his world looks like a pasteboard toy theatre created by a father for the sheer joy of his children, Chesterton could demonstrate that the analogy was strictly true. If the toy was out of order and deranged, the contrast fingered more sharply than ever the primeval origin of the world in goodness.[24]

How are the schools to develop men of such wisdom and vision who can help man to relocate himself in the world? How can individual teachers contribute to this enterprise? Teachers in the elementary schools might take their children out into the fields to discover the burrows of moles, the quick nervous movement of the towhee, the noiseless gliding of the water beetles over the surface of the water. Or better still, students can be asked to write about their own adventures into the out-of-doors, to tell of the antics of the birds and bees that they have observed. The horned toad and the preying mantis brought into the classroom may well serve as invitations to the students to observe other animals in their natural habitats where they will reveal themselves more fully.

In high school boys' and girls' interests turn more toward themselves. They want to understand the changes in their own bodies and minds. These are closely related to the rhythms in nature. These changes in the adolescent are not so frightening to one who has seen and has understood the natural rhythmic cycles in the lives of animals and of plants from season to season and from year to year. As a result of a deeper appreciation of the natural world, these students will see man less in the image of the machine, and more as the highest manifestation of organic life. First-hand experience with animals and plants in the pond and on the plain will offset some of the effects of mechanization on young people and prepare them to accept themselves and others as creatures fashioned in the image and likeness of God, with some of His freedom and daring to create.

At the college level, students who are re-rooted in the world of nature will again be prepared for the kind of scientific study which the genius of Aristotle and of St. Thomas left them as their heritage. If their lives have been enriched through an understanding of the likenesses and differences in natural things, by having a natural basis for an appreciation of the dignity of man and of the natural laws which provide for and protect him, students will be ready to undertake a Thomistic and truly scientific approach to nature. This approach does not strip away wonder, but admits of more wonder and mystery as all the causes of natural things are carefully investigated. Man will never succeed in exhausting the riches of the blade of grass, or of the petal of the flower, but he can gain much through an orderly approach to their study. Aristotle's and St. Thomas's conception of the universe, as a hierarchical one, as a plenum, is in accord with a common sense view of the natural world. It is less sophisticated, but not necessarily less true, than the highly technical and mechanical explanation of the world in terms of aggregates of atoms in blind and meaningless motion. There is an even greater challenge for college teachers to help students to recapture some of the wonder of childhood, to capitalize on their native curiosity in developing their imaginations, emotions and intellects, ultimately to awaken in them the vision of a Chesterton, a Pasteur, or a Teilhard.

No violence need be done to a student's courses in modern experimental science while teachers supply for the deficiencies in contemporary man's view of the world. Eminent contemporary biologists are trying to reinstate the organism as the focal point to a necessarily multi-level scientific approach to the world of living things. This could be accomplished more easily if graduate students had learned to know and appreciate the world of oak trees and lizards at an early age. Outstanding scientists in all fields are now beginning to realize the necessity of teaching each discipline within an historical and a philosophical perspective. Such a perspective is only acceptable to students who have understood the possibility of more than one view of a man and of a flea.

Ultimately an education in tune with nature and with the best traditions in the western world, will more fully nourish the Christian person who is in danger of becoming only a cog in a wheel of a massive impersonal society, of being regimented in schools, factories, armies and even in suburbia. The Christian person can thus keep alive his faculty of wonder which makes him a contemplative first of the world of nature. For the contemplator of nature, the windows of life will open on to infinite horizons in an atmosphere of mystery. If we bring our students to behold such a world, then the words of Daniel (12:3) will be applicable to us: "But the wise shall shine brightly like the splendor of the firmament, and those who lead the many to justice shall be like the stars forever."

References

1. In the foreword of *Night* by Elie Wiesel (New York: Hill and Wang, 1958), p. 7.
2. Quoted in *Great Essays in Science* ed. by Martin Gardner (New York, Pocket Books, 1957), p. 262.
3. Barbara Ward, *Faith and Freedom* (New York: Image, 1958), p. 14.

148

4. Gerald Vann, O.P. *The Water and the Fire* (New York: Sheed and Ward, 1954), p. 13.
5. Rene Dubos, *Mirage of Health* (New York: Harper, 1959), p. 27.
6. Walter Grompius, "The Curse of Conformity" in *Adventures of the Mind* ed. by Richard Thruelsen and John Kobler (New York: Knopf, 1959), p. 265.
7. "Auguries of Innocence," 11. 1-4.
8. J.B.S. Haldane, *Possible Worlds and Other Papers,* (New York: Harper, 1928), pp. 221, 214.
9. *Hamlet,* II, 2, 315-320.
10. Susanne K. Langer, *Philosophy in a New Key* (New York, Mentor, 1942), p. 16.
11. From *God is Not a Mathematician* quoted in C. Stanley Ogilvy, *Through the Mathescope* (New York: Oxford, 1958), p. 8.
12. Lewis Carroll, *Alice in Wonderland and Through the Looking Glass* (Kingsport, Tennessee, Kingsport Press, 1946), pp. 66-67.
13. *Modern Science and the Nature of Life* (New York: Harcourt, Brace, 1957), pp. 71-78.
14. *Ibid.,* p. 76.
15. *Ibid.,* p. 77.
16. Barbara Ward, *op. cit.,* p. 281.
17. Julian Huxley, *Man in the Modern World* (New York: Mentor, 1944), p. 133.
18. Rene Dubos, *op. cit.,* pp. 172-3.
19. *Apropos of Lady Chatterley's Lover,* p. 83.
20. "The Arsenal at Springfield," 11. 32-36.
21. Gerald Vann, O.P., *op. cit.,* p. 44.
22. Joseph Wood Krutch, *The Great Chain of Life* (Boston: Houghton Mifflin, 1956), p. 143.
23. "The Tables Turned," v. 2.
24. Frederick Wilhelmsen, *Hilaire Belloc: No Alienated Man,* (New York: Sheed and Ward, 1953), p. 22.

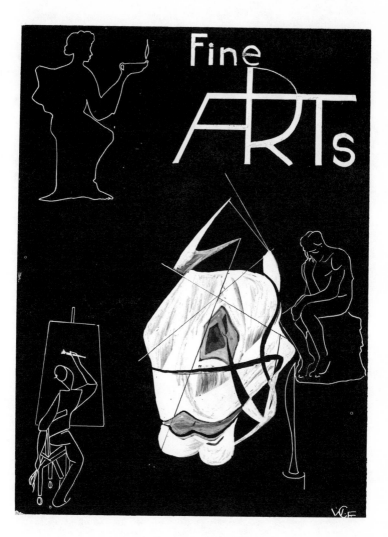

Literature and Personal Values

Dr. Paul van K. Thomson

The term "literature" as I understand it in this context refers to prose or verse designed to give pleasure to the reader. The expression "personal values" signifies the ethical and theological dimensions of experience.

As teachers of literature and indeed as persons concerned with Catholic education in general, we find ourselves confronting today what Pius XII described as the "depressing contradiction" between the technical skill which marks so much of modern intellectual life and man's fearful anxiety, his physical misery, and the profound preoccupation of many writers with the theme of anguish.

The Christian teacher of literature finds himself at a point where he might say truly that the history of the intellectual life of Western man, from the Renaissance to the moment at least, lies between a passage from Christopher Marlowe and one from T. S. Eliot. The Marlowe passage is from *Tamberlaine*. It seems to me to express the spirit of an ebullient humanism devoid of the levels of ethical and theological values. It is, in other words, something of the forebearer of what might be called natural humanism.

> Nature that framed us of four elements,
> warring within our breasts for regiment,

Doth teach us all to have aspiring minds;
Our souls, whose faculties can comprehend
The wondrous architecture of the world,
And measure every wand'ring planet's course,
Still climbing after knowledge infinite,
And always moving as the restless spheres,
Wills us to wear ourselves and never rest,
Until we reach the ripest fruit of all,
That perfect bliss and sole felicity,
The sweet fruition of an earthly crown.
(Part I, Act II, Sc. vii, 18-29)

Having experienced the impact of what is represented in those lines, many men and women in our time have come to the state described by T. S. Eliot in Choruses from "The Rock":

"Oh, weariness, of men who turn from God
To the grandeur of your mind and the glory of your
    action,
To arts and inventions and daring enterprises,
To schemes of human greatness thoroughly discredited,
Binding the earth and water to your service,
Exploiting the seas and developing the mountains,
Dividing the stars into common and preferred,
Engaged in devising the perfect refrigerator,
Engaged in working out a rational morality,
Engaged in printing as many books as possible,
Plotting of happiness and flinging empty bottles,
Turning from your vacancy to fevered enthusiasm
For nation or race or what you call humanity."

We who are involved in Catholic education, we who are therefore, involved with personal values, find that there are

154

many voices raised to suggest either a relationship or a separation between the ethical and theological dimensions of life and the dimension of aesthetic experience. We hear of those who speak of the absolute autonomy of literature or of those who speak of art as the servant of ethics and theology. And we also know of some who see modern literature in particular as a threat to faith and morals—the devil's wine.

Yet, there are others who see literature as a possible replacement for traditional Christianity in a post-Christian age. I attended a round table conference at Harvard, some years ago, which concerned itself with the topic "What is the responsibility of the modern university toward the transmission of the Judeo-Christian tradition?" A professor of physics rose to inform us that if anybody in the university had responsibility for the transmission of such a tradition, it must be the department of English literature.

This, of course, was much the position taken by Matthew Arnold in his essay "Literature and Science," in which he says that in the modern university, man's need for a guide to action and for the experience of beauty, which was satisfied for him by theology in the middle ages, must now be satisfied by the world of literature.

Another position is that there is a complex working relationship between literature and personal values in which proper distinctions can be discerned and mutual interactions grasped. This is the position which I would hold.

Yet we Christians might well ask if literature can be, as Wordsworth said in his well known Preface to the *Lyrical Ballads*—"a rock of defense for human nature" in our world, a world where traditional personal values appear to be losing ground. As Karl Stern points out in his very valuable little book *The Third Revolution,* there is everywhere to be seen the effect of the notion of a determinism based on the social sciences, behavioristic psychology, and the views of some physicists and some biologists. And once determinism takes over, personal values begin to decline.

I would suggest, however, that works of literature point to the inescapable question asked in the world's shortest verse: "I, Why?" The question of I, Why?—even when there seems to be no real "I," and the pursuit of "Why?" may be abandoned as hopeless—remains deep in the heart of man.

This is manifested in the work of Hemingway, where sheer animal courage, stoic dignity in the face of what seems to be inevitable disaster, for one who stands, a tiny animal, on a rolling ball of mud, hurtling into nothingness, is none-theless put forward to capture the responsive imagination of readers. Or again, as Marcus Aurelius writes in that dreadful confrontation which was his from day to day, as he stood holding back the pressure of barbarism upon the Roman Empire, "I say to myself, 'Get out of your bed. Stand up on your feet and do the work of a man.'" So do many of Hemingway's heroes.

Or again, one sees that the theory of individual involvement, which is so important to Sartre in a play like *The Flies,* is offered to the reader as an oblique approach to the question of existence. For poetry, like Christianity, is concerned with what is personal.

There is an interplay of concerns here, for the notion of men as persons is a Christian notion. In fact it arises in the world, not first as a result of a discussion about man, but rather as a result of the Trinitarian controversy—a discussion of God. And the concept of person, which is a very strong and important Christian contribution to human thought, has

156

so greatly affected the whole stream of our culture, that of course our literature is inescapably involved with it. And that is one reason why we find, even in our time, that the search for identity theme is so characteristic of much of our modern writing. As R. W. B. Lewis' book *The Picaresque Saint* shows, there is so often the Christ-figure in much of modern literature, for the Christ whom many men may think they have abandoned continues to haunt their dreams.

The whole subject of exactly what the relationships between religion and literature might be, needs a good deal of exploration, and some of the kind of exploration which it may be given is to be found in a volume called *The New Orpheus,* in which one finds a very searching analysis of the pretentions of the autonomous imagination.

As several of the contributors to this book suggest, this is a time when we ought to explore the possibility of a truly Christian theory of literature. And many of them are doing just that. The contribution of Allen Tate, for instance, suggests that for us the doctrines of creation and incarnation show the world as a glass of vision, and an arena sufficiently significant to be the theater for the drama of man's redemption.

Those of us who are teachers of literature may find some practical help in the formation of our own working critical judgment by applying categories suggested by the Christian, if not Catholic, philosopher, T. H. Greene, who suggests that when one studies a work of literature, perhaps the first thing one owes to it is the effort to get a sympathetic and personal impression of what this work indeed is. A great practitioner of that kind of thing was, of course, Walter Pater, whose description of the Mona Lisa is one of the magnificent passages in English criticism. And it is one of the reasons why

Oscar Wilde, in his perverse way, could say that the critic oftentimes is more creative than the creator. The mind which is open to examine, to receive, to respond, to have at least an awareness and a desire to have a sensitive impression performs an important critical service, although I would not argue for a theory of criticism which says, with Anatole France, that criticism is the adventures of a sensitive soul among masterpieces.

As Greene points out, we are also bound as intelligent readers to consider the historical moment in which a word appeared. Admittedly this has been overdone, and some of our scholarly journals are absurd in this regard. But there is a value in gaining a proper understanding of the historical problems which may be associated with a work of literature. When Milton says, "Admire not that riches grow in hell," it is well to know what the word "admire" meant in the seventeenth century.

There is a third area any critic must enter into—the area of judicial discriminations, which involves both aesthetic analysis and value judgment.

When we, as educators and administrators, ask ourselves how we are to evaluate modern writers like J. D. Salinger in relation to Christian personal values, I would suggest that what we owe to these serious writers of our own age is a respect and a charity for honest seekers and craftsmen. Faulkner, Hemingway, and Dylan Thomas were such men. Salinger, too, is such a man.

Moreover, we must have a concern for the relationships that can be found to exist between new knowledge, when it is real knowledge, and revealed truth. And we must display an absolute intellectual honesty. Those of us who are Christians are not limited by our Christianity in our teaching.

158

We are given the perspective which enables us to do, if we will do it, what Matthew Arnold said the great poets of classical antiquity had done: to see life and to see it whole. For us this means seeing life in terms of the Incarnation.

The view of the Christian humanist is a view that faces physical reality and the imaginative treatment of it with absolute equanimity. To fear so to face man's response to this aspect of his being is to lead to the heresy of docetism on the one side, or of Jansenism on the other. The Christian critic may rightly declare that Christian dogma will aid an artist, not by giving him a privileged and special subject matter, but rather by defining for him a perspective from which full light can be had on any subject matter.

Aristotle long ago understood that poetry incarnates universals, and that the artist, in his human and limited way, is carrying out again and again through the works of the imagination an incarnation of sensitive response to human experience. The Christian accepts the whole of life and ought to be able to see with sufficient insight to understand that the enduring works of literature ultimately are personally significant. This is not only true of the works of Sophocles or the works of Shakespeare; it is also true of the works of the serious writers of our time.

Excellence on the Catholic Campus

DR. PAUL VAN K. THOMSON

I would like to begin by telling you what in the middle ages would have been called a beast fable, because near the end of my remarks I may be saying something that might sound overly critical of some of the work in which we are all engaged. The beast fable is this, and I hope that it will exhibit to you something of the spirit in which my closing remarks are made.

There once was a rooster who lived, as roosters will, among many hens. One day he escaped through a hole in the fence and wandered across the road to a nearby farm where the farmer was raising ostriches. In the middle of a field the rooster suddenly beheld an enormous ostrich egg. Thinking of himself always as something of an expert in the matter of eggs, he was appalled by this object that reached dimensions far beyond his wildest imagination. He hurried home, ran into the barnyard and crowed. All of his group of hens came out. The rooster said, "Girls, follow me." They went across the road, and drew up in a respectful and somewhat awed circle around this enormous egg. The rooster looking around said quietly, "Girls, I brought you here not because I want to criticize your work. I just want to suggest what can be done."

Now, my subject is Excellence on the Catholic Campus, and in the spirit of Christian humanism I thought it might be appropriate to begin with a quotation from Hesiod: "Before the might of excellence the high gods have set exertion. Long is the road thereto and steep and rough at the first, but when the height is achieved then there is ease, though grievously hard in the winning."

Many years ago, with the optimistic slogans of World War I still fresh, G. K. Chesterton wrote: "The world will never be safe for democracy. It is a dangerous trade." No one who lives in these days and takes his American citizenship seriously would be disposed to doubt the truth of that remark. The fact of the cold war, which promises to be with us for some time, is a sufficient reminder of the dangers surrounding those who would live as free men and women. So also are the conflicts taking place within some of the so-called new nations undergoing the transition from a colonial state, which perfectly illustrate what DeTocqueville meant when he said, "There is nothing which is more difficult than the apprenticeship of liberty."

True democracy surely is not a cult of mediocrity. On the contrary. It concerns itself with the extraordinarily difficult enterprise of affording to each of its members the opportunity to develop his fullest personal talents. In fact, the very life of freedom requires that each person should regard the job he has to do as so important to the common good that it must be performed with the highest degree of competency of which he as an individual is capable. The men who made the American Revolution were generally convinced that the common man is in reality most uncommon. They had respect for the dignity of personal differences. Thomas Jefferson did not set up the lowest common denominator as his standard when he wrote the Declaration of Independence. Democratic societies flourish on the very paradoxical notion that men are in some sense unequal equals. Their peculiar greatness rests upon their striving after equal civil rights, and opportunity for all. At the same time they seek to provide each person not only the chance but the civic responsibility to develop those talents which are distinctly his own.

Now I think you would agree that we in the United States have never hesitated to encourage and reward talent in business, sports, and the entertainment arts. No one among us, I suppose, would venture to suggest that hard work in a business enterprise should not receive some kind of recognition. As for sports, we do not consider it undemocratic to idolize our favorites and to pay large salaries to professionals who perform in an outstanding fashion. Many American institutions of higher learning have developed remarkable techniques for discovering and recruiting talented athletes. It might even be said that some of our colleges and universities seem to regard their proficiency in this form of public entertainment as being one of their primary responsibilities. And their alumni associations would not appear to disagree.

In recent years however, many thoughtful Americans have noted that we have not always looked with equal favor upon encouraging and rewarding intellectual attainments. But we are now becoming aware of the fact that scientific leadership and technical leadership are among the primary tests of national power in the contemporary world. Yet it is still true that we have not done more than to begin to meet the educational issue with which the demands of our age confront us. The National Manpower Council, for example, has estimated that nearly 41% of those students in our secondary schools who rate in the top 1% for tested scholastic ability either do not enter higher education or do not remain to graduate.

The production figures regarding the number of scientists and engineering professionals in the Soviet Union are frequently cited to indicate where and how there are serious gaps in our development. Recognizing education as a vital source of power in the struggle for the world, the Soviets are reported to be spending almost 5% of the Gross National Product on education, as compared to about 3.6% in the United States. Moreover, like all traditional European systems of education, that of the Soviet Union is highly selective. Only those of better than average ability are permitted by the authority of the state to enter education at the secondary and higher levels.

This is disturbing. But even more disturbing is the notion which one sometimes encounters among those who suggest that we in America ought to follow the Soviet model. One consequence of such a course of action would be ultimately the virtual elimination of the American liberal arts college. A free modern society of course needs scientists, and engineers, not only for its defense but also to meet the needs of an expanding industrial economy. But it also needs the talents of those who can lead it in the cultivation of the basic human and personal values. It needs philosophers, writers, artists, theologians, linguists, historians. It needs leaders in public life who have learned how to bring their free intelligence to bear upon its complex issues. It requires humanists who are acquainted with the goals and concepts of science, and scientists who have not neglected the development of their humanity.

Some years ago the distinguished mathematician and philosopher, Alfred North Whitehead said, "In the condi-

164

tions of modern life, the rule is absolute. The race which does not value trained intelligence is doomed." Happily the signs are abundant that Americans are becoming more aware of this truth.

The National Defense Education Act, the growth of ability grouping techniques, the increased numbers of honors programs and programs of independent study, the work of private foundations to aid the gifted, the national scope of the activities of the Inter-University Committee on the Superior Student—all these developments are encouraging. Our secondary schools in many areas have already made such progress in promoting programs for gifted students that they may be said to be far ahead of most of our colleges in this regard.

It is, of course, not only the talented who will benefit from the extension of higher standards of quality and performance; experience has shown that procedures designed primarily for the more able students generally serve to raise the whole tone of the school where they have been adopted. The evil—and it is an evil—of intellectual élitism need not necessarily plague us where wise administrators see to it that a proper balance is kept between ability grouping and general participation in the classes and school activities.

We who are Catholics must, however, view this issue of academic excellence from another dimension, for we cannot be satisfied with a humanist and liberal view that makes man the measure of his own perfection. Nor can we, on the other hand, take refuge in pietism or attempt to regard man as a disembodied intellect. We cannot, of course, go with the tide of that kind of materialism that stresses physical skills and transient activity. Nor do I think we can stand with the modern existentialist concept that each man in the end creates his own nature from day to day.

Thomas DeQuincey, writing in the *North British Review* for August 1848, made what has become a very well known distinction between what he called the literature of knowledge and the literature of power. There is, he pointed out, a vast body of reading material which appeals to the discursive understanding and imparts information, as in the case of a work like Newton's *Principia*. There is also a great body of reading matter which, while it may appeal to the reason, does so through the affections of pleasure or sympathy, as in the case of the *Iliad* of Homer. What we owe to the literature of knowledge is the information we gain from it. I quote the somewhat aureate prose of DeQuincey: "A million separate items, still but a million of advancing steps on the same earthly level." What we owe to the literature of power is, again to use DeQuincey's words—and they do have about them something of the ring of his romantic imagination— "exercise and expansion to our own latent capacity of sympathy with the infinite. Every pulse and each separate influx is a step upward, a step ascending as on a Jacob's ladder from earth to mysterious altitudes above the earth." In short, then, one might say that the literature of power breeds in us a deep sympathy for the grandeur and the immutability of truth.

But it has been left to our century to demonstrate that there is a kind of pseudo-knowledge, which is actually deadly in its effect upon our power to have that profound sympathy for truth which is of the essence of academic excellence. It is the dubious distinction of our times that our civilization has produced an intellectual life which dries the blood and enervates the will to seek ultimate truth. This dreary fact

166

is effectively expressed in the question asked by T. S. Eliot, "Where is the wisdom we have lost in knowledge?"

That such is the plague of much of our modern academic life I think is undeniable. And students in Catholic colleges do not altogether escape it simply because they are exposed to courses in religion. Like students in secular colleges, and I was brought up that way myself, their motives for appearing on the campus are far too often dominated by the false notion that the purpose of higher education is primarily to prepare them for some occupation which will give them an upper middle class status and a secure income. And far too many products of Catholic colleges are most eager to fit neatly into a society which extols the doughnut and commends the mediocrity of the common man: A creature who satisfies his employers, buys the newspapers, reacts in a normal way to advertisements, purchases adequate insurance, takes full advantage of the installment plan, holds the proper current opinions, has the right number of children for his generation, and possesses a house, a car, a frigidaire and a television set.

That power which is a profound sympathy for truth does not live and grow in the mind which supposes that the aim of education is to prepare students for occupations. It grows only in the mind which understands that education is greatly concerned with arming students against the dominance of their future occupations, so that they will become the masters and not the slaves of the work they do. It is not only because, as Robert Hutchins pointed out a number of years ago, "utilitarian motives in higher education produce futilitarian results" that we find so many students lacking in sympathy for truth. More profoundly, it is also because of the widespread triumph of certain superstitions regarding natural science—a triumph which dominates the world of the half-educated.

Ideas which were popularized by the Victorian scientific materialism of such men as Thomas Henry Huxley, one hundred years ago, and which are not held by the great majority of self-respecting scientists today, in any part of the world where science is free from Marxist control, have taken hold of the popular mind in our times. As a result of this, which we might describe as a cultural lag, many students come to our American colleges, and too many depart as graduates, suffering from four great illusions, which make such knowledge as they possess the enemy of that powerful sympathy for ultimate truth which marks the whole man and which has always been peculiarly characteristic of the truly Catholic mind. Holding first place among these illusions is the idea that there is no real knowledge other than that arrived at by the process of inductive reasoning, by which the mind proceeds from many individual instances . . . to a generalization, which is at best highly probable but never really certain.

Following from this is the illusion that the admittedly incomplete and tentative picture which the natural sciences give of man and nature is the only really reliable picture there is. For after all, it is based upon the purity of empiricism.

Coupled with these two fundamental illusions are the deceptive hope that the methods of the natural sciences can be used to solve our social problems, and the equally illusory notion that the world will become a more pleasant place simply as the result of increased technical progress toward plastic palaces, synthetic steaks and free vacations on the moon.

Now it is of course to be hoped that the graduates of Catholic colleges will become possessed by that power of sympathy for truth which gives life to knowledge and leads on to real wisdom. And so they will be if, like St. Athanasius, the leaders of Catholic education are able to stand *contramundum*, to stand against the pressure to conform to the world's pattern of the moment.

In a world which insists that its colleges like its cars must become streamlined in order to make the educational process both fast and comfortable, we must uphold the painful and often expensive truth that the way to real knowledge and intellectual power is both long and hard. In a world in which many would gear education to the demands of the race for arms supremacy and dominance, we must provide a bulwark against the threat of a society controlled by technically proficient illiterates. In an age of "religious" agnosticism which often masks its doubts of God's very Being by the use of conventional religious language in a highly equivocal fashion, we Catholics, above all others, must stand firm in our grasp of the basic issues of life and death. Ours is the solemn obligation to hold fast to the sober clarity of the truly Catholic mind.

The sober clarity of the truly Catholic mind is an essentialist clarity. Far from being a stereotype, this Catholic mind has expressed itself in such diverse personalities as St. Augustine and Cardinal Manning, John Henry Newman and Evelyn Waugh. Far from attaining its intellectual goals by suppressing nature and denying the world's cultural goods, the Catholic mind devotes both knowledge and power to the service of God while at the same time it enriches and ennobles every legitimate earthly activity.

I would propose a thesis that there is no area of human attainment, either in the arts or in the sciences, which cannot be shown to have built its finest attainments and most enduring works upon those principles of reason, those traditions of creative beauty, those appreciative evaluations of the multiplicity of goods, for which the Catholic Church has ever been the guardian, patron and expositor. It is not western civilization that has produced the Catholic mind. But rather it has been the Catholic mind which has produced much of whatever is civilized about western society.

The Catholic mind is a theological mind, and no Catholic college can hope to be worthy of so great a title that does not give the scientific study of theology a central place in its curriculum. This is not to say that a Catholic college should become a seminary for the laity, or what would be worse, far worse, a place of indoctrination or exhortation, a besieged citadel of faith in a world whose knowledge and power it fears. What is meant by saying that the scientific study of theology, even more than philosophy, deserves a central place in the curriculum is that through theology we gain the supreme integrating force between what we have called the literature of knowledge, or information, and the literature of power, by which we have signified those studies that develop our love and sympathy for truth. Those in whom the habit of thinking theologically has been developed, will see not only the extent of knowledge, and thereby perhaps gain in humility, but they will also see its unity.

To give a central place to the scientific study of theology is to do more than integrate the literature of knowledge and the literature of power around knowledge of God. It means also putting all things in their true proportion, contrary to the tendency of the modern expert to see his own specialty as having a dominating significance.

Ideally, at any rate, the study of theology would seem to offer the surest way for the Catholic college to assure the student of that kind of excellence which only the Catholic college can provide. Yet, the late middle ages built its intellectual life around the scientific study of theology and still failed to apply theology's integrating power to the new discoveries and interests which finally issued in the Renaissance, the Protestant revolt, and the rise of secularism. The late middle ages had the *Summa Theologica,* but it did not have St. Thomas, who was wise and good enough to say that all which he had written seemed to him to be so much straw when compared with all that there is to know of God. The late middle ages had the scientific study of theology, but it also had many teachers and students who were bored by it because they had become satisfied with a sterile and uncritical presentation. The truth is that the mere communication by a teacher of so many pages of theology, however scientifically arranged, has little or no bearing upon putting knowledge and intellectual power together to build a man excellent in the service of God or himself.

St. Thomas, let it be recalled, began with questions rather than pat answers. Furthermore, he was quick to draw upon the thought of his time in answering the objections to his own position. Nor did he hesitate to introduce new problems or new objections. In short, the scientific study of theology, if it is to be fruitful, requires the fullest amount of intellectual curiosity, rather than a simple docility.

More than these things however, it is the one science which must be studied at a prayer desk, for unlike philosophy, theology must be studied in the light of faith and under the magisterium of the Church. The mere study of theology, at which he appears to have been quite adept, did not, it will be remembered, save the humanism of King Henry VIII who, with some assistance from St. Thomas More, prepared a theological reply against the errors of Martin Luther and won the title Defender of the Faith, one of the most ironic titles ever conferred on anyone. To possess knowledge of the truth is one thing, but to be possessed by the truth is a higher, a greater, and supremely more difficult thing.

Christ tells us that we must be like little children if we are to attain to true wisdom. Not in the sense of having an undeveloped intelligence, but as those who recognize God as their Father. What is most perfect belongs to God, Who is always able to teach us more than we know. The role of the child belongs to us, all of us who are teachers, for we must always be learning. The children of the Church are, in the words of Clement of Alexandria, "new spirits." They are forever young because they have heard new, good things. In a passage which every scholar might read with profit at least once a year, Clement says, "The fertile time of life is this unaging youth of ours in which we are ever at the prime of intelligence, ever young, ever childlike, ever new, for those who have partaken of the new word must themselves be new. For whatever partakes of eternity assumes the qualities of the incorruptible. Therefore the name childhood is for us a lifetime of spring, because the truth abiding in us is ageless."

To the modern children of the Church who are engaged in intellectual work, a great opportunity for excellence is open. A new synthesis is needed to give the Christian world what Cardinal Suhard once called "a humanly effective action based upon a completely Catholic doctrine." The first apostolate is therefore in the realm of the mind, for as the

Cardinal of Paris concluded, "The greatest error of the Christians of the twentieth century and the one its children would not forgive them would be to let the world take shape and unite without them, without God, or against Him, to be satisfied with recipes and tactics."

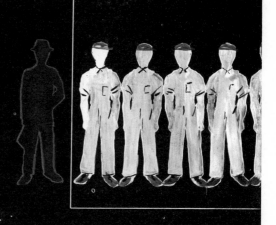

SOCIOLOGY

The Social Encyclicals

ANNE FREMANTLE

"The Church, which is the universal society of the faithful of all languages and all peoples, has its own social doctrine, profoundly elaborated from the First Century to modern times, and studied in its progressive development under all its approaches and aspects." So wrote the late Pope Pius XII in his allocution of February 22, 1944. Already St. Paul had much to say on social efforts, especially in the letters to Timothy. But possibly the greatest of all Christian social principles was enunciated by St. Augustine when he said that "Charity is not a substitute for justice withheld." Yet it was not until the latter half of the nineteenth century, when materialist and atheist assumptions challenged the Church's position on social questions, that the expression of a social doctrine became an integral part of theology, rather than of ethics. Then only was a theology of justice explicitly and separately stated. Only when a particular theological proof has been challenged or threatened, has the Church countered by defining it. Thus every one of the great Trinitarian definitions and the great Christological definitions was made only in response to challenge; the Church has never initiated a statement. So too, when issues of social import and social existence itself became obscured by false solutions, the full authority of the Church was summoned to enunciate its social doctrine in clear and contemporary terms. In every instance, not until the menace was distinctly present was the definition made.

Nor is this social doctrine, as spelled out in the twelve encyclicals of Pope Leo XIII that have become to be called the Leonine Corpus, and repeated by Leo's successors in their various encyclicals, which culminated in *Mater et Magistra* on 15th May 1961, a sociology. For sociology is a science based on the classification of social data, from which facts are deduced to permit the adaptation of empirical laws, which laws in their turn form the subject of social philosophy. The social doctrine of the Church, on the contrary, as outlined in the so-called social encyclicals, is more properly to be called a morality of society and also of sociology. It is based on and rooted in the Gospels, defined in the epistles, and expanded upon by many of the fathers (St. Basil, for instance, has a very comprehensive social doctrine), and discussed by St. Thomas Aquinas in the context of the virtue of justice.

Pope Leo XIII, from the moment of his accession on February 7, 1878, found himself confronted by the violence of social upheaval. He had to cope with vehemently anti-clerical France, with Bismarck's Kulturkampf in Germany, and with Italian revolutionaries who almost succeeded in chasing the Papacy out of Rome. He also had to contend on the one hand with an unprincipled laissez-faire capitalism, complacently accepting the horrors of the English factories and the London slums, and on the other with Marxist philosophy, militantly atheist and materialistic. All of his 86 encyclicals, produced during a Papal tenure of twenty-five years, originated from his awareness, as he put it, of the greatest tragedy of the nineteenth century, which was the loss to the Church of the working classes.

"The cause of civilization lacks a solid foundation," he wrote, "if it does not rest on the eternal principles of truth, and on the unchangeable laws of right and justice." This was in his first encyclical, *Inscrutabile Dei* (April 21, 1878). Two years later, in *Arcanum,* (February 10, 1880), he discussed Christian marriage, and insisted among other things on the equality of the rights of husbands and wives in marriage, quoting St. John's statement: "That which is unlawful for women is unlawful for men also, and the same restraint is imposed on equal conditions." He also refused to concede that any part of a Christian marriage—can be handed over to the State, since the contract is inseparable from the Sacrament: Not only is marriage a sacrament, but the contract itself is sacred.

In *Quod Apostolici Muneris* (December 28, 1878), his second encyclical, the Pope declared that the basis of authority, whether that of husband over wife, parents over children, or master over servant, originates in God and from Him is derived its nature and character. In *Aeterni Patris* (August 4, 1879), the first of the round dozen of encyclicals that make up the Leonine Corpus, the Pope observed that the best way to restore social order was by restoring the teaching of Christian philosophy in Christian schools. This was followed by a reiteration of that philosophical position and a definition of the terms in which the Church would state her arguments—all authority, even in a democracy, comes only and directly from God. It is not conferred by the electors on the elected, any more than it is inherited by birth in a monarchy, or inherent in some divine right of kings. The electors in a democracy merely determine who will be the next President, just as in the case of royalty, the birth of a young prince or princess establishes who will be the successor to the throne. Neither birth nor election confers power. They merely indicate who will administer it.

In *Diuturnum illud* (June 29, 1881), Pope Leo discussed the basis of sound political government, and in *Humanum Genus* (April 20, 1884) he denounced naturalism, and those who set nature and human reason above the supernatural order. The natural order and its laws are seen as part of the divine order, and subject to the supernatural order of grace. In *Immortale Dei* (November 1, 1884) on the subject of the Christian constitution of states the Pope clarified Church-State relations. The state holds its authority from God, he declared, and this divine origin of the temporal power is the most powerful guarantee the State can claim. From this it follows that states should regard the Church the stablest of their allies and recognize their indebtedness by making public profession of religion. (He would have had no use for the present situation here in the United States in which the State is constantly disavowing any relationship to religion.) Then he reaffirmed the traditional doctrine of the two powers: each is in its own sphere supreme; each has fixed limits within which it is contained, for the powers that be are ordained of God. *In Plurimis,* addressed to the Brazilian bishops (May 5, 1888), emphasized that error and moral evil are the true roots of social injustice. The Church never approves of the latter, but she does not believe that violence is the proper way of curing the disorders of nature. The Church, the Pope said, always disapproved of slavery, which was never a natural condition, but a consequence of sin; yet she has never urged slaves to rebel. However slavery finally

178

disappeared as a legally recognized institution because the Church steadily over the centuries disapproved of it.

In his next encyclical, the Pope defined human liberty and articulated its limit. In *Libertas* (June 20, 1888) the Pope clearly distinguished between natural and moral liberty. Natural liberty is the power of free choice and belongs as his birthright to every man who has the use of reason. "As the Catholic Church has declared over and over again in the strongest terms the simplicity, spirituality and immortality of the soul, so with unequaled constancy and publicity, she ever also has asserted its freedom." But liberty belongs only to those who have the gift of reason, said the Holy Father, and he went on to affirm that freedom of choice is identical with the will. Moral freedom—as distinguished from natural freedom—is based on the assumption that the only truly free man is he who acts consistently with his reason. As St. Thomas put it, everything is that which belongs to itself naturally. When it acts through a power outside itself, it does not act of itself, but through another—that is, it acts as a slave. But man is by nature rational. When he sins, he acts in opposition to reason; then he is moved by another, and is a victim of foreign apprehension. Therefore whoever commits sin is a slave of sin. Or, as the heathen philosophers put it, the wise man alone is free. This encyclical, *Libertas,* went on to castigate those supporters of liberalism who declare that the State's authority comes from the people only, and that just as in every individual man reason is his only rule of life, so the collective reason of the community should be the supreme guide in the management of all public affairs. Hence the doctrine of the supremacy of the greater number, and that all right and all duty reside in the majority, which makes, as the encyclical suggests, for a tyranny of the majority. In fact, the Pope states abruptly, this is simply a road leading straight to tyranny. And he repeats St. Thomas's declaration regarding tyrants: whenever there exists or there is reason to fear an unjust oppression of the people on one hand, or deprivation of the liberty of the Church on the other, it is lawful to seek such a change of government as will bring about liberty of action. This was very much the case in Hitler's Germany, of course, when the Church did not acquiesce in the will of the majority. The Germans voted 99 per cent for Hitler, yet the Church held that the will of this majority was unjust.

Leo XIII goes on to declare that the modern liberties of thought, speech, writing and teaching must consist in the firm resolve only to think, to say, and to write that which is true, and to will only that which is good according to natural law—otherwise such liberties cease to exist; and that though a man is politically free to think as he pleases, and to profess what religion he pleases, he is not morally free to do so, since such behavior is not consistent with reason.

The basis of the social doctrine of the Church is that no authority is the end of man, but one of the means he uses to attain salvation. Nature did not fashion society with the intent that man should seek it in his last end, the Pope wrote, but that in it and through it he would find suitable aids whereby to attain his own perfection. Yet even as he wrote, Pope Leo was aware, as are indeed all social reformers, that society was not, then, providing suitable aid to man's perfection. For some, of whom Marx is the representative, the answer was—and is—to change society drastically. Others sought to alter it less radically. In England many of the early socialists, like Charles Kingsley and Percy Widdington, were ordained members of the Church of England, while at the same date in the United States the President of the Knights of Labor, forerunner of the American Federation of Labor, was a Catholic. In France, a number of the Catholic reformers, such as Albert de Mun and Lacordaire, remained in the Church while Fathers Tyzzell and de LaMennais left it. In *Sapientiae Christianae* (January 10, 1890), the Pope had defined the nature of Christian citizenship: the natural love of country and the supernatural love of God both proceed from God who is their common Author. There can be or should be no conflict of loyalty. But if the state commands things contrary to the divine law, those commands are not lawful, and there is no sedition in refusing to obey them. For it is the essential duty of Christians never to set human laws above the divine. This confrontation occurred in Nazi Germany and occurs in the Communist countries.

The stage was now set with these two encyclicals, *Libertas* and *Sapientiae Christianae*, for what all the preliminary encyclicals had been leading up to—*Rerum Novarum*, probably the most famous of all encyclicals until *Mater et Magistra*. It was issued on the 15th of May, 1891, and its main objective was to set down the Catholic position on the condition of the working class. This great encyclical is generally supposed to have been drafted by Cardinal Manning, who had deep knowledge and the practical experience of the workers. It was Cardinal Manning who had negotiated the settlement in the 1899 London dock strike. The directors of the dock companies had agreed to negotiate terms only if they came through Cardinal Manning. The Archbishop of Canterbury had spoken harshly against the men and even preached against them, but the Cardinal had waited hour-long, day-long at the Mansion House on sultry August days, in the hope of being able to bring about a settlement. He finally did so. The magazine *Punch,* which was by no means specially pro-Catholic, printed a very fine poem beginning "A dying man went down to a dead city", commenting on the Cardinal's achievement. Whether it was Manning who wrote the text of *Rerum Novarum,* or someone else, the text is a magnificent statement which embraces the whole social problem in its context, as part of religion, politics and the right order in society, and has provided the basis for Catholic teaching on social justice ever since.

Nothing is more useful than to look upon the world as it really is, and at the same time to seek elsewhere for the solace to its troubles, wrote the Pope in Article 18. The revolutionary spirit has invaded all departments of human life, and the practice of usury has reduced the masses to a condition little better than that of slavery. Socialism's remedy, to transfer all private property to the state, is against justice, since private property is a natural right, and without this right parents cannot provide for their children. The family precedes the state and has at least equal rights with it. The state must supply public aid to families in exceeding distress, since each family is part of the commonwealth. That, by the way, is the basis of the Catholic position on the bus transportation issue in the USA; the state has an obligation to provide each family, whatever may be its religion, with what is necessary to its welfare.

The employer's duty is to give a worker what is just. Each needs the other. Capital cannot do without labor, nor labor without capital. The two classes should run in harmony. But it is one thing to have a right to the possession of money, and quite another to have a right to use money as one wills. As St. Thomas Aquinas put it, man should not consider his material possessions as his own, but as common to all. Thus

182

the regulation of working hours and conditions, the control of women and children's labor, the right to a minimum wage, and the right and extremity to strike, all these are sanctioned and given support. Although *Rerum Novarum* was the greatest of his encyclicals, Pope Leo XIII continued during the remainder of his long papacy to be occupied with the condition of the working class. In *Permoti Nos* (July 10, 1895) he wrote to the Belgian Bishops on social problems, and in *Graves de Communi* (January 18, 1901) he discussed Christian democracy.

One result of *Rerum Novarum* was the formation of groups of Christian democrats, taking their stand on the papal directives and programs. These challenged other political parties. The Pope insisted that if democracy is not Christian, it ceases to be a political form of government. He wrote that the laws of nature and of the Gospel are superior to all human contingencies.

And they are necessarily independent of all particular forms of civil government. At the same time, they are in harmony with all that is not repugnant to morality and justice.

Pope St. Pius X, in his encyclical *Il fermo proposito,* (June 11, 1905), laid down the norms for lay Catholic action, which should prudently and fearlessly train lay Catholics for political life. During his papacy anti-clerical legislation in France was at its most virulent, and his encyclicals *Gravissimo officii* (January 6, 1906), and *Vehementer Nos* (February 11, 1906), both refer to this sad state, while *Pascendi,* (September 8, 1907), deals with the heresy of modernism. Among the tenets condemned as heresy, is the theory that "the state must therefore be separated from the Church and the Catholic from the citizen, for the Church to take out and prescribe to the citizen any line of action on any pretext whatsoever, is to be guilty of an abuse of authority." To believe this is to be a heretic.

Benedict XV spent his brief reign, 1914-1922, in appealing for peace.

Pius XI roundly condemned Facism in *Non abbiamo bisogno* (June 29, 1931), Nazism, in *Mit Brennender Sorge* (March 14, 1937) and Communism, in *Divini Redemptoris* (March 19, 1937). In this last encyclical, after demonstrating the errors of Marxism, the Pope again sets out the mutual duties and rights of man and of society, and discusses the social and economic order. In *Caritate Christi* (May 3, 1932), he wrote of the crises of international relations, of the menace of new wars, of famine and misery, of the class struggle and of the rancor between conqueror and conquered. He called to account immoderate nationalism and the materialistic ethos of society, and the inclination to incite political parties to civil war.

On the occasion of the fortieth anniversary of *Rerum Novarum,* Pope Pius XI issued *Quadragesimo Anno* (May 15, 1931), the second of the great labor encyclicals, which was essentially a restatement of the first. Individualism and collectivism are both seen as dangers and the right to form labor unions is emphasized. The Pope notes that "the right order of economic life cannot be left to a free competition of forces."

Pope Pius XII, in his first encyclical, *Summi Pontificatus* (October 20, 1939), at once revealed his awareness that one of the chief problems of the Church today is its relation to civil society. To consider the state as something ultimate, he says, to which everything else should be subordinated and directed, cannot fail to harm the true and lasting prosperity of nations. This may occur when "unrestricted dominion comes to be conferred on the state as having a mandate from a nation, people, or even a social order, or when the state allegates such dominion to itself as absolute master without any mandate whatsoever." The Church, he notes elsewhere, reproves none of the different forms of government, provided they be in themselves suitable to securing the welfare of citizens. He also made the useful distinction between the people and the masses. As he said, "A people move and live, have vitality. A mass, or the mass, or the masses is inert in itself and can only be moved from without." Pope Pius XII was the first Pope to insist on the obligation under the pain of sin of every citizen vote.

In his second encyclical, *Sertum Laetitiae* (November 1, 1939), addressed to the Bishops of the United States, the Pope affirmed the absolute need for "wealth created by God for all men, to flow fairly to all, according to the principles of justice and charity."

During the Second World War in his Christmas radio messages of 1941 through 1944, Pius XII repeatedly stressed the necessity of basing peace on order, on the dignity and duties of the human person, on social unity and the rights of labor. He advocated the internationalization of private law and stated that the United Nations "ought also to have the right and the power of forestalling all military intervention of one state in another, whatever the pretext under which it is effected, and also the right and power of assuming by means of a sufficient police force the safeguarding of order in the state which is threatened." "We desire," he also said, "the authority of the United Nations strengthened, especially for effecting general disarmament which we have so much at heart." He also commended the European union, and noted that in the case of atomic, biological or chemical aggression "defending oneself against any kind of injustice is not sufficient reason to resort to war. And the losses that such war brings are not comparable with those of the injustice tolerated. One may indeed have the obligation of submitting to the injustice."

On the seventieth anniversary of *Rerum Novarum*, (May 15, 1961), Pope John XXIII issued *Mater et Magistra.* This reviews the whole relationship between the Church and society, between the Church and labor. Yet, while the earlier encyclicals are recalled and re-affirmed, John XXIII went much further than his predecessors in condemning *laissez-faire* capitalism, and in declaring it hardly less a menace than communism. And though perhaps not the last word on these great themes of the Church's social doctrine, it is the latest.

What Cardinal Newman called the development of doctrine is evident in all these encyclicals, from *Rerum Novarum* to *Mater et Magistra.* The Church has really had to tack, like a ship, three times. In *Rerum Novarum* she had to come out against *laissez-faire* capitalism in favor of the workers. In *Quadragesimo Anno* she had to come out for the workers against the state, against the Fascist or the Communist state. Finally in *Mater et Magistra,* she has again to right the balance, by declaring that the obligation of labor is not merely to oppose the state. This encyclical really confirms the authority of the state, for in the past seventy years the Church has always to redress the balance of society in her pronouncements.

And today the balance is again threatened. That always teetering balance between capitalism, workers' rights, and statism, that balance must always be precarious, because of the dichotomy between man's freedom and his nature as a social being. Man is by nature free and by nature social, and the limit of the freedom of my elbow, as a wit once said, is my neighbour's nose.

Nor, for us Catholics, is man born free. He is *created* free. Just as man's only equality is spiritual—there is no genetic or environmental equality between the umpteenth moron child of starving South African or United States Negro parents and the fourth child of Queen Elizabeth and the Duke of Edinburgh. But there is total spiritual equality. No one is born free—free of heredity or environment, of the laws of chance and causation. But man is created free. This sounds like mere semantics, but it is much deeper than semantics. This point was early made at the United Nations —and is pertinent to any discussion of the relevancy for today of the Encyclicals. Brazil, in a discussion on the wording of the Charter, introduced the phrase "Man is created free." The Soviet Union insisted the word be changed to "born" and was seconded by the United States, alas! So the statement "Man is created free" was changed to "man is born free"—which is completely untrue.

This is a fact the encyclicals emphasize: that man's essential (and only!) freedom stems from his creation. Before Christianity, there was no consensus about man's freedom. As Lord Acton put it: "When Christ said 'Render unto Caesar the things that are Caesar's, and unto God the things that are God's', He gave to the civil power under the protection of conscience a sacredness that it had never before enjoyed, and bounds it had never before acknowledged, and He took the charge of human freedom out of the hands of pale, ineffectual philosophers and gave it to the perpetual charge of a universal Church."

Now what can the ordinary, average, individual Catholic do about these things personally? One of the first things is to remember that (as the Chilean Bishops have said) the Church today is a minority in the world. Not only the Church, but Christians. There are only 900 million Christians in the world. There are only 500 million Catholics—not as many as there are Chinese. There are 700 million Chinese, 200 million more Chinese than there are Catholics anywhere. And in the world today, Christianity as a whole is a minority. Less than one quarter of the human race is Christian—less than one eighth is Catholic. Catholics have got to live in a society in which they are a minority, and must learn to behave themselves as a minority. As the Chilean bishops put it, "Christendom, that is a society in which the various associations of the public and temporal order incorporate constitutionally the norms and practices of the Church, and everything temporal becomes denominational, even if not by law, and society is monolithically Christian—Christendom in that sense is dead. On the contrary, the whole world is now what Catholics call a state of mission, in which Christianity is represented by a minority, not only in numbers, but also in real influence on various social structures and on the national community as a whole."

In medieval times, when Christendom was a reality, there were very few relations between Christians and other non-Christians. Pagans were strange, extraordinary beings, met only by Christians when killing them in a Crusade, or perhaps if a man were a Franciscian Friar and traveled over to Nigeria or somewhere like that. In Europe there were very few pagans. When Columbus discovered America, and the Spaniards settled there a great question arose as to whether the pagan Indians were human beings at all. The king of

Spain and the king of Portugal, and the powers that be, wanted to consider them as animals, some kind of pre-Darwinian monkey. So considered, they could be killed with impunity and could have no rights.

One of the chief problems for today's Christians is how to behave as a loyal minority, and not as His Majesty's loyal opposition, in the construction of a world which will not be built according to Christian principles. For whatever way this new world is built, it won't be Christian. Here the leadership given by the Popes in the social encyclicals is tremendous. Especially the leadership of Pope John XXIII when he says that he agrees with St. Augustine that "truth, wherever it is to be found, we must accept hungrily." That is, we have to accept truth wherever it is found, whether it be Muslim truth, or Hindu truth, or even Communist truth: we are obliged to accept it "hungrily." Finally, as Cardinal Suenens of Belgium, speaking on *Pacem in Terris* before the UN, put it, the onus is individual. He said: "Our century has discovered interplanetary space, but it has hardly discovered the space which separates men from each other. Our century has discovered nuclear energy, but it has yet to discover the creative energy of space and concord. It is for qualified and wise statesmen to determine the stages, the means and the extent of reconciliation among people, but it is for each of us, starting now, to create the atmosphere therefor. International peace will begin in the souls of each one of us. And only when peace has begun, continued and completed, will Christianity be adequate to starting its responsibility to match Christian answers to the world's questions."

Justice and the Spirit of
Social Responsibility [1]

BROTHER LEO V. RYAN, C.S.V.

Whether we consult the Old Testament, the New Testament, a modern management text, or the Encyclicals, Justice is portrayed as the virtue expected of all persons—and a characteristic especially required of all persons engaged in business and commerce. Justice is that constant disposition to render to each his due; the role of justice in the development of a social responsible citizen is a major point of emphasis in the latest social encyclical, *Mater et Magistra.*

In Leviticus we are warned: "Do not any unjust thing in judgment, in rule, in weight or in measure. Let the balance be just and the weights equal, the bushel just and the sextary equal." (Leviticus 19:35-36) St. Paul in his Epistle to the Thessalonians admonished them as follows: "None of you is to be exorbitant, and take advantage of his brother in business dealings . . ." (I Thess. 4:6).

The late Harvard Professor of Labor Relations, Benjamin Sekelman, in his book, *A Moral Philosophy for Management,* pointed out that "What one should expect and, indeed, demand of business, in my opinion, is justice. Management must so organize its corporate operation as to insure justice to the various individuals and groups associated with the enterprise."[2]

Walter Gast in his *Principles of Management* lays great stress on the fact that business is a society—a union of persons pursuing a common purpose. He emphasizes the role of justice as the fundamental, underlying principle of every society and therefore identifies justice as the fundamental underlying principle of a business.[3]

Every social Encyclical places repeated stress on the urgency of justice serving as the correcting and unifying force in our society. The Encyclical of Pope John XXIII, *Mater et Magistra,* repeatedly emphasizes the matter of justice and equity as essential to resolving the ills that beset our social structures.

It was significant that in 1961, to commemorate the anniversaries of two great Encyclicals—the seventieth anniversary of *Rerum Novarum* and the thirtieth anniversary of *Quadragesimo Anno*—and to focus world attention on these anniversaries, that Pope John XXIII should issue his vibrant social message, *Mater et Magistra*—a truly extraordinary document related to Christianity and social progress. Throughout *Mater et Magistra,* the emphasis is on justice, and the prudent application of the principles of justice to the social issues of our times.

Mater et Magistra is divided into four major discussions:
(1) The teachings of *Rerum Novarum* and later doctrinal developments by Pius XI and Pius XII.
(2) Development of the teachings contained in *Rerum Novarum.*
(3) New aspects of the Social Question.
(4) Reconstruction of social relationships in truth, justice and love.

192

In this discussion, we will examine briefly some of the high-lights expressed in each section of the Encyclical with special reference to the question of justice.

The opening section on Christianity and Social Progress forms a historical backdrop and a valuable preface to the later sections of the new Encyclical. In reviewing the principle efforts of Popes Leo XIII, Pius XI, and Pius XII, the late Holy Father establishes a continuity of thought and brings into focus the relationships between and among the social Encyclicals.

He begins by acknowledging the debt of the Christian world to Pope Leo XIII, declaring that *Rerum Novarum* contained norms and recommendations "so momentous that their memory will never fade into oblivion." (8)[4] *Rerum Novarum* presented an organization of principles and a singleminded course of action which formed a summary of Catholic teaching in the economic and social fields.

Rerum Novarum noted that: (1) work is not a mere commodity and that remuneration for work is subject to the laws of justice and equity; (2) private property is a natural right possessed by all; (3) the State must safeguard rights of citizens and better their living conditions; (4) labor agreements must be entered into according to the norms of justice and equity; (5) there is a natural right of corporate association for both workers and management; and (6) that mutual relationships should be regulated in a spirit of human solidarity and in accordance with the bond of Christian Brotherhood. *Rerum Novarum* is truly the Magna Carta for a reconstruction of the economic and social order.

During 1961, we commemorated the thirtieth anniversary of *Quadragesimo Anno* by Pope Pius XI. The contribution of this Encyclical to the body of social doctrine can be identified through a brief examination of the purpose for which it was written, the additional principles it presented, and the fundamental points it stressed. These purposes, principles and points are repeated in the new encyclical. In *Quadragesimo Anno,* Pope Pius XI confirmed the right and duty of the Church to act in social issues; reaffirmed the principles of *Rerum Novarum;* and clarified various points of the social doctrine. *Quadragesimo Anno* established four special principles: (1) The organization of economic affairs must be conformable to practical morality; (2) Economic affairs must be harmonized with the common good; (3) Civil authority should resume its proper function and not overlook any community interest; and, (4) Government should seek the economic good of all peoples. The entire Encyclical places emphasis on two fundamental points: (1) Economic undertakings governed by justice and charity as the principal law of social life; and, (2) Within countries and among nations, the juridical order must be inspired by social justice and economic activities and must conform to the common good.

In acknowledging the fiftieth anniversary of *Rerum Novarum,* Pope Pius XII took occasion "to explain in greater detail what the Catholic Church teaches regarding the three principal issues of social life in economic affairs, which are mutually related and connected one with the other, and thus interdependent: namely, the use of material goods, labor, and the family." (42) It is interesting in the light of our discussion on justice, to note that Pope Pius XII in discussing the fact that the right to own property should in no way obstruct the flow of "material goods created by God to meet the needs of all men . . . . ." stresses these needs to be "as justice and charity require . . ." Pope Pius XII, through letters and broadcasts, contributed a number of social messages of significance.[5]

Mater et Magistra concludes the first section with an identification of contemporary circumstances in science, technology, economics, the social and political fields that prompt a review of the earlier Encyclicals and an updating of an applied social doctrine.

Pope John XXIII then affirms the primacy of "the private initiative of individuals" in economic affairs; reaffirms the principle of subsidiarity; stresses the complexity of our social structure—reviewing, then evaluating this trend. The standards of justice and equity are reaffirmed as essential considerations in the determination of remuneration for work. "In determining what constitutes an appropriate wage" the Holy Father points out that "the following must necessarily be taken into account: first of all, the contribution of individuals to the economic effort; the economic state of the enterprises within which they work; the requirements of each community, especially as regards over-all employment; finally, what concerns the common good of all peoples, namely, of the various States associated among themselves, but differing in character and extent." (71)

This section of the new Encyclical also draws "the attention of all to a strict demand of social justice, which explicitly requires that, with the growth of the economy, there occurs a corresponding social development." (73) Speaking about the "common good of human society as a whole," the Holy Father points out that "the following conditions should be fulfilled: that the competitive striving of peoples to increase output be free of bad faith; that harmony in economic affairs and a friendly and beneficial cooperation be fostered; and, finally, that effective aid be given in developing the economically under-developed nations." (80) Later in the discussion, the social issue selected for some analysis will be this matter of aid to developing countries.

Justice is stressed as the guide to determining whether or not the institutions of society conform to the dignity of man. The sense of personal responsibility is likewise stressed. Note: "Justice is to be observed not merely in the distribution of wealth, but also in regard to the conditions under which men engage in productive activity. There is, in fact, an innate need of human nature requiring that men engaged in productive activity have an opportunity to assume responsibility and to perfect themselves by their efforts." (82) Also note this passage: ". . . . . if the organization and structure of economic life be such that the human dignity of workers is compromised, or their sense of responsibility is weakened, or their freedom of action is removed, then we judge such an economic order to be unjust, even though it produces a vast amount of goods, whose distribution conforms to the norms of justice and equity." (83)

The task of the business employer or employee lies in translating principles to the problems of our age. This is not an easy assignment. It "is indeed a difficult, though lofty task" (121), the Holy Father reminds us. Answers to social problems are not easy to develop; categorical answers are often demanded by people to questions which cannot be settled so definitely. In economic affairs, the Holy Father reminds us that it is not possible "to determine in one formula all the measures that are more conformable to the dignity of man, or are more suitable in developing in him a sense of responsibility." (84) However difficult the task of the business leader may be, it is only by accepting the challenge that we can begin to demonstrate the relevance of social principles to the daily problems which face all of us in the busy market-place.

The second section of the Encyclical then continues by detailing the demands of justice among artisan enterprises and cooperative associations, including worker participation in productive enterprises by size and at various levels. This section concludes with an important discussion of private property—the changed conditions affecting the exercise of the natural right of property ownership, the question of effective distribution of property, the rule of public property and its social function. The transition sentence linking this section with the subsequent discussion of specific social questions reflects the spirit of the Encyclical: "The progress of events and of time have made it increasingly evident that the relationships between workers and management in productive enterprises must be re-adjusted according to the norm of justice and charity." (122)

With the third section of the Encyclical, Pope John XXIII approaches four specific problem areas confronting Catholics in contemporary society. He asserts that "the progress of events and of time have made it increasingly evident that the relationships between workers and management in productive enterprises must be readjusted according to the norms of justice and charity." (122) But the problem is more deep than that. He notes ". . . many nations with varied endowments have not made identical progress in their economic and social affairs." (122) With these expressions, the Encyclical considers the problems of agriculture, aid to less developed areas, the population explosion, and international cooperation. Each of these problem areas provides fruitful material for study. To illustrate the role of justice in this presentation, it is sufficient to examine only one problem area: the question of aid to less developed areas.

Within a given country as well as between and among nations, economic growth may vary considerably. The Holy Father notes that "perhaps the most pressing question of our day concerns the relationship between economically advanced commonwealths and those that are in the process of development." (157)

In what way does justice dictate action in the field of aid to less developed nations? There is considerable evidence of variations in the distribution of wealth and social advancement between and within many nations. ". . . . . Justice and charity demand that the government make efforts either to remove or minimize imbalances of this sort." (150) Certainly, emergency assistance (161-162), scientific, technical and financial cooperation (163-165), and the fostering of commerce and skills (173), are all forms of aid demanded by justice. The necessity for these aids also prompts a caution. Any assistance to less developed nations must respect the individual characteristics of those countries; it must be disinterested aid without thought of political exploitation or economic domination ("another form of colonialism") and with respect for a national sense of values. "Justice requires that whenever countries give attention to the fostering of skills or commerce, they should aid the less developed nations without thought of domination . . ." (173)

This area of the Encyclical has been selected for analysis because of the impact made on the author during a recent trip to West Germany. At the invitation of German Volunteer Agencies engaged in projects in development countries similar to projects undertaken by the Peace Corps, this writer spent time in West Germany gathering information on programs in the socioeconomic fields sponsored by lay groups.

The efforts of German Catholics through *Misereor* (German Episcopal Program Against Hunger and Disease in the World) to support community development is an outstanding example manifesting the personal commitment of individuals to the doctrine outlined in the Encyclical. Their annual collection of funds during Lent is directed to socio-economic community development projects throughout the world. This program exemplifies the idea expressed by the Holy Father when he notes "that Catholic citizens . . . are making extensive efforts to ensure that aid given by their own countries to needy countries is directed increasingly toward economic and social progress." (183) Examples of the spirit of the Encyclical are not limited to this illustration alone; there are many others, but *Misereor* is an outstanding European example. Discussing the contribution of the Church and Catholics in the area of economic and social aid to development of countries, the 1961 Bishops' statement likewise places stress on this responsibility: "All these things we must do, not as mere counter-moves against Communism, but for their essential rightness, as expressions of our highest principles: love of God and love of neighbor." [6]

The real challenge to the thinking business leader is contained in a very important message proposed in the concluding section of the Encyclical. The task has been identified by Pope John as follows: "Principles . . . must not only be known and understood, but applied to those systems and methods, which the various situations of time and place either suggest or require." (221) Again: "The role of the Church in our day is very difficult: to reconcile man's modern respect for progress with the norms of humanity and of the Gospel teaching." (256)

To meet this "difficult, though lofty task" (221) thoughtful consideration, reflection, study and application are required. ". . . More and more attention [should] be given to this branch of learning" (social matters) and this attention should be given the Holy Father urges "in Catholic schools at all levels." (223) The task of applying principles to a specific problem is not easy. ". . . It is difficult at times to discern the demands of justice in a given situation." (229) Yet, each and every day we must face the complex and difficult situations common to the market place, making decisions that are just and prudent. We must show by action that we are indeed aware "of the Church's teaching on social matters, which has truth as its guide, justice as its end, and love as its driving force. . . ." (226)

The results of a serious application to the challenge of *Mater et Magistra* will have beneficial results for all. In the words of the Psalmist, "Justice and peace shall kiss; Truth shall spring from the earth and justice shall look down from heaven." (Ps. 84:9ff.) For the teacher there is the special promise recorded in Daniel (12:3) that "They that are learned shall shine as the brightness of the firmament; and they that instruct many to justice, as stars for all eternity."

References

[1] This article is an adaptation of an address delivered February 27, 1962 at *Gonzaga University,* Spokane, as one of its series of Diamond Jubilee Convocations.

[2] Benjamin M. Sekelman, *A Moral Philosophy for Management* (New York: McGraw-Hill, 1959), p. 165.

[3] Cf. Walter Gast, *Principles of Management* (St. Louis: St. Louis University Bookstore, 1953), p. 10 ff.

[4] All quotations from the Encyclical are quoted from *Mater et Magistra*: Encyclical Letter of His Holiness Pope John XXIII on Christianity and Social Progress (Washington, D.C.: National Catholic Welfare Conference, 1961). Numbers following quotations from the Encyclical refer to the sections in the above edition of the Encyclical.

[5] See *Six Social Documents of Pope Pius XII* (Huntington, Indiana: Our Sunday Visitor Press, 1953), 60 pp.

[6] "Unchanging Duty in a Changing World," Statement of the Administrative Board, National Catholic Welfare Conference, 1961, quoted from *The Witness* (Dubuque, Iowa), November 23, 1961, p. 3.

The Church, Management, and Labor

MSGR. GEORGE G. HIGGINS

There's a cartoon on the bulletin board which pretty well summarizes my feelings as I begin this discussion. It shows a man and a wife driving up in the mountains, about to go off a precipice, around a winding road, and she said "Well, it looked flat on the roadmap."

When I was foolish enough to accept the Bishop's invitation, it looked very flat, it looked fairly easy, and then I came into a very profound discussion at the end of Msgr. Pavan's lecture and that scared me a bit.

I'm not going to talk very much about Catholic social theory and its relevance to labor-management relations. What I will talk about are a few notions in the field of labor-management relations in the United States at the present time, rather than any abstract theory.

Let me begin by saying a word about the relationship of the Church in the United States to the labor movement and the Church's approach to the field of labor-management relations. Those of you who know Washington, who have spent any time there, will recall that among the many statues that we have in the city, public statues, there are two in rather out-of-the-way places which are of some importance in this field. One is the statue of Samuel Gompers, the first head of what we now know as the American labor movement, the first President of the old American Federation of Labor, which is on Massachusetts Avenue in what is today kind of a run-down neighborhood. And the other is a statue of Cardinal Gibbons in front of the Sacred Heart Shrine on 16th Street. These two men were contemporaries. They died within a year of one another, I think. As far as I know, they never met personally, but there's a striking parallel between their approach to the problem of labor-management relations in the United States which may help us to put this thing in some kind of focus.

But let me come around to this parallel in a rather circuitous way by referring first of all to the history of the labor movement and the history of labor-management relations on the continent of Europe during the past hundred years, roughly speaking. I touch this subject with diffidence in the presence of Msgr. Pavan, who knows much more about it than I do, but he will correct me if my generalizations get too far afield. I cite it only to contrast it with the situation that we had experienced in this country.

As you know, for a good number of generations—I'm not speaking of today; let's stop at World War II—and for a variety of historical reasons, of which the average American, in my experience, is totally unaware, there was a rather serious cleavage between the Church and the dominant labor unions on the continent of Europe which tended to be Marxist unions, collectivist in their economics and often more than anti-clerical, but anti-religious in their philosophy. As a result, many sincere Christians, Catholics and non-Catholics as well, found it difficult to participate in these unions and therefore tended gradually to segregate themselves into specifically denominational or confessional unions. The rather tragic history of this unfortunate conflict in the field of labor-management relations between Marxism and Christianity, and between socialist and Christian unions, is of course of no immediate concern to us today. There is no point in going into it in detail. The important thing to bear in mind is that this conflict between religion and labor has never existed in the United States. I think it's almost impossible to understand the labor situation in the United States unless we keep that fact in mind, namely, that in a country where Catholics, rightly or wrongly, have been accused of living in a ghetto, whether in intellectual areas or in social and cultural fields, in labor-management relations there has never been a ghetto mentality among American Catholics. The significance of this to me is very profound. I hate to think what the situation would be like in the States today if in the economic field, Catholics were segregated into separate economic organizations as they might well have been if the situation had taken a sudden turn for the worse around the end of the last century.

By and large then there has always been a reasonably cordial relationship between the Church and the labor movement in this country, so cordial that, in my experience, European labor and management representatives, who come to our country in great numbers these days, almost always single this out as one of the most significant things that they've seen here. From their point of view it is one of the most striking characteristics of our national tradition.

The reasons for this reasonably wholesome relationship between religion and labor in the United States are numerous. It would be a rash and foolish historian who would try to pick out any one single reason to explain it. But I think it would be accurate to say that if any two men were more responsible for it than others, they were Gibbons and Gompers, and that's why I've mentioned the coincidence of their statues being nearby in Washington. I say this because in the labor field, as Gompers was coming along, there was a critical moment when it was theoretically possible for the American labor movement to go in the direction of Marxism. Gompers himself had grown up in London, in the slums. He was a Jew. He came to this country as a young man, as a convinced socialist. All of his early training, his early reading and studying, was in German socialism, and he could easily, given the right set of circumstances, have tried to move the labor movement in that direction, but he was a great realist. He had a great sense of reality and he sensed quite early in his career that, whatever the theory might be, in practice it would not be feasible in the United States to try to develop this kind of labor movement. And therefore, he opted for a rather pragmatic type of collective bargaining, for a labor movement which would make no distinction on grounds of race or religion, and would not involve itself in philosophical or religious matters, but would leave that to the conscience of the individual worker.

Gibbons, on the other hand, significantly affected the attitude of the Church toward the labor movement and toward the field of labor-management relations. You may recall that the old Knights of Labor, which was the forerunner of the American Federation of Labor, had been condemned in French Canada, and had been condemned by Rome at the request of the French Canadian bishops, as a secret society— secret in the sense of being covertly anti-religious. There was great danger that this condemnation would also be applied to the United States. Surely one of the greatest things that

Gibbons ever did—although he didn't do it alone; he was probably pushed into it or nudged into it by Archbishop John Ireland and by others—was to go to Rome with a very historic document. In it he told Rome very plainly—much more plainly, I might say, than we'd been accustomed to speak to Rome—that this simply would not do, that the Church in the United States could not live with this kind of policy, that it would mean the loss of the working man to the Church, if this decision prevailed. He even went so far as to suggest that it might affect the Peter's Pence—which was rather odd for Gibbons, who was a gentle man. But in any event, as a result of the general trend towards a pragmatic but rather sound type of unionism on the part of Gompers and a general spirit of friendliness or at least openness towards the labor movement on the part of Gibbons and the American hierarchy, we then moved into a period when the question of confessional or denominational unions became purely academic. There has never been any serious discussion of it from that day to this, and so far as anyone can see, there never will be. I think we can count ourselves very fortunate that this has happened.

This has been a rather long introduction to a simple conclusion, and perhaps too simple a conclusion, but it's mine and I'll stick with it. My conclusion is that the labor movement in the United States, in spite of a good number of mistakes and a good number of faults and imperfections, including at the moment a certain amount of dragging of the feet in the field of race relations, a certain amount of racketeering, and a certain vagueness of philosophy, is a basically sound and wholesome labor movement. I would say, at the risk of being considered a chauvinist, that it's probably the soundest labor movement in the world, even though the average person who comes to my office from France or Bel gium or Latin America, or even from French Canada, from traditions where people are more accustomed to look at these matters philosophically, is inclined to write off the American labor movement as reactionary. I had two Canadians in the office the other day, not from French Canada, but from Nova Scotia, where great things have been done in the social field. They had a very abstract approach to the American labor movement. They were Catholics from St. Francis Xavier University, in Antigonish. They told me quite plainly that, in their opinion, the American labor movement, even Walter Reuther's section of the American labor movement, was reactionary. When asked why, they said because the American labor movement is in favor of capitalism. That's a matter of semantics. It's like the American labor movement saying that the Christian unions of Latin America are communist because they're against capitalism. The word "capitalism" means so many things to so many different people. I'm sure it must come as a shock to ideological trade unionists from Germany or Belgium, and those in the Belgium socialist tradition, to hear even a man like Reuther get up and say that he believes in private enterprise. The problem is under-standing what he means by this. In my judgment, he means something which comes reasonably close to the essential teachings of the papal encyclicals on the nature of property and the relationship of unions and management with one another and to the public.

Well, that's enough by way of introduction. It's quite obvious, I think, that neither Gibbons nor Gompers would be satisfied with what we have today. They wouldn't want us to waste much time in self-congratulations. But I think if American Catholics want to understand what's going on now, they would be well advised to try to understand what went on in the past, so that they will not feel that we can come in, or should even try to come in as Catholics in the '60's, with an abstract, philosophical or even theological approach to these problems, and try artificially to implant it as though the old system were all wrong.

In talking about the historical relationship between the Church and organized labor in the United States, you inevitably run the risk of appearing to say that the Church has taken sides in favor of organized labor and against management. I became conscious of this risk a year or two ago in preparing a paper on this subject. I went through all of the principal labor economic textbooks used by colleges and universities. For the most part these books covered the subject adequately. They were good workable textbooks. One or two of them were very good. But I was surprised to find that, with one exception, all of them ignored the relationship of religion to the field of labor-management relations and the attitude of religion toward the labor movement. Out of a total of some 3,000 or 4,000 pages, I found only one brief reference to the role of the Church in the field of labor-management relations. This paragraph reads in part as follows, and it illustrates the risk that I'm talking about: "In its contest for public support, organized labor can usually count upon the Churches. A feature of the depression and post-second world war years was the shift of religious influence to the side of organized workmen and criticism of managerial labor relations which have been aired in church conferences and pulpits. The Catholic Church is a leader in this respect, its representatives having demonstrated great sympathy with union labor on many occasions."

Well this is a capsule-like summary of the attitude of the Church with regard to organized labor. It's all right as far as it goes, but it could distort the picture if it were taken out of context. It is accurate if it means that, by and large, the official Church in the United States has defended the right of labor to organize and has encouraged the labor movement to organize the unorganized, and is still doing it. In fact, in some fields it is doing it more effectively than the labor movement is, for example, in the field of migratory labor, where we have perhaps a million or a million and a half workers untouched by social legislation, unorganized completely. So far as I can see, Church groups are doing more to try to solve this problem than the labor movement itself.

Secondly, it is accurate if it means that the Church has supported the labor movement in its demand for adequate legislation and the repeal or the amendment of discriminatory laws or that it approves of labor's request for adequate representation in the economy along the lines outlined in *Mater et Magistra;* that it is critical of those employers who refuse to bargain collectively in good faith, and critical of the philosophy of unregulated economic freedom in the name of which this refusal is usually rationalized. This is a problem here in the South. We're a long way from solving even the basic problem of the organization of the unorganized workers. It's foolish, it seems to me, to talk in hifalutin, academic terms about Catholic social theory in the labor-management field unless we take care of first things first. And we can't begin to have a structured program of sound labor-management relations until workers are organized. I don't know what the percentage is in North Carolina, but I dare say that it's still very low. Certainly, as one goes farther South, in Alabama, in Georgia, and Mississippi, one finds the great masses of workers still unorganized. One of the reasons, not the only reason, but one of the reasons that industries have come into those states is that they keep trying, very foolishly, to run away from the organization of workers.

We have many cases of mills which have closed in the North and have run down South. Some of them did it for market reasons, but my point is that until we agree on the basic principle that workers must have an organization of their own with which they can deal with employers in collective bargaining and move on to more formal forms of labor-management cooperation, we can't get very far.

Well, the author's statement, then, is correct if it means these, among other things. But it doesn't say enough. It doesn't say, for example, that unions cannot count upon the support of the Church when they discriminate against Negroes, and this is a serious problem at the moment. I attended a meeting the other day at the Labor Department in Washington, a committee meeting called by the Secretary of Labor, to come up with some recommendations on what to do about apprenticeship programs, some of which are run by unions alone, and some of which are run jointly by unions and employers. Many of these programs discriminate against Negroes, and I must say that it was a rather sad experience to find that the Churchmen present and the poor beleaguered bureaucrats who have nobody to back them up in case of a fight, were ahead of the labor representatives in facing up to this problem. It's a very difficult problem, a very human one. Labor leaders are involved in long traditions which they find it hard to break, but it's an issue on which the Church inevitably is going to have to differ with spokesmen for labor and differ very sharply in the days immediately ahead.

I think they will eventually get over the hump and will realize finally that they are not living up to their obligations, but for the moment the Church, it seems to me, must be very blunt in recalling to their minds the ethics of this situation.

The Catholic Church, in other words, is not lined up with unions that discriminate against Negroes, that are guilty of racketeering, or that engage in political strikes for their own purposes, but it is lined up in this country with any organization, whether it's a union or an employer's association, which is honestly trying to work out a better system of labor-management relations, using collective bargaining as the first step. And that's about where we are today. We have a widespread system of collective bargaining, which is not good enough, but is basically sound, I think. I think it has to be improved by the organization of more workers in industries where they're not organized. It has to be related much more—in a much more sophisticated way than it is today—to the problems of the whole community. How, for example, do the owners of the railroads and the railroad unions engage in collective bargaining to avoid paralyzing the entire country? We used to think that collective bargaining had within it all that was necessary to solve that kind of problem. Many people are beginning to wonder today. No one, except David Lawrence, and perhaps Walter Lippman in a weak moment, would advocate compulsory arbitration. But something like compulsory arbitration may come unless collective bargaining can develop in a more sophisticated way to meet problems which neither labor nor management contemplated at the time they first began to bargain collectively. By that I mean that because of the growing complexity of our economy today the whole notion of collective bargaining must be fitted into a larger picture and cannot remain static. But I personally am hopeful—perhaps overly optimistic—that we can keep developing beyond collective bargaining, relating the government more closely to collective bargaining, relating the public more closely to it, without going into compulsory arbitration. That I think would be a step backwards, and while I have profound admiration for Walter Lippman, nevertheless I think he was talking as an academician when he seriously proposed that we change our whole system and go into compulsory arbitration. I think it would be a great step backward, and one which would not be in harmony with the genius of the American system so far, nor in harmony with the basic trend of Catholic social teaching.

The fact that the Church is well disposed towards the labor movement does not mean that it is satisfied with the present labor-management situation in the United States. The Church keeps suggesting, as, of course, the encyclicals have done, that while we have made progress in labor-management relations in recent years, we still have a long way to go. And of course, Churchmen are not alone in this regard. We are in a sense at a turning point in the field of labor-management relations in the United States today.

In the sense indicated earlier: that our economy now is vastly different from what it was when Gompers lived, when collective bargaining in the simplest of terms seemed to be at least a satisfactory answer to most of the problems that labor faced. The technological changes in the economy have been fantastic since his time, and they're going to be even more fantastic, in the years ahead. We are faced with the apparently insoluble problem, of the richest country in the world still experiencing a dangerous rate of unemployment. And that is the seriousness, the real seriousness of the race

211

problem, in my opinion. I'm all for Civil Rights demonstrations or a legitimate expression of interest on the part of Negroes in legislation, civil rights legislation. But the frightening thing about the race relations problem today is that all of the statistics indicate that our unemployment rate is going to stay steady, and possibly even go up, and if it does, of course, Negroes are going to be the ones who will suffer most. Unemployment today is hitting the least skilled, and the Negroes are, by and large, the least skilled. So, I would hope that no one in the Negro community feels or thinks that a few laws are going to solve this problem. They will help, but the crucial aspect of the problem, I think, is in the economic field, and therefore much depends upon whether or not labor and management will have enough statesmanship to improve upon collective bargaining and enough statesmanship to cooperate with the government in ways short of compulsory arbitration to work on national problems, and stop thinking exclusively in terms of their own local or parochial interests. That's the great unsolved problem in the field of labor-management relations. Automation has dramatized it. It's quite obvious today that collective bargaining in the old sense of the word is no answer to automation in some industries, even though the experience in the steel industry within recent months, in the Kaiser section of the industry, has been rather encouraging in that regard. They are making an attempt at least to improve upon collective bargaining so as to meet problems which are beyond the normal definition of that term, and how good that is. It is also a fine positive way in which to end this discussion.

The Church in the City

JOSEPH H. FICHTER, S.J.

I should like to state two assumptions, the first of which is that this audience is made up of Christians who are apostolic, perhaps even charismatic, professional, prophetic, intellectual, and dedicated, who do not need exhortations or explanations after each secular remark I shall make as a sociologist. I would like to assume that you have the total vision of Christ in the Church—that you would not be here if you were not wholly dedicated people. My second assumption is that you understand the sociological approach to religion as empirical, secular, profane, scientific and natural. My assumption is that this group is sophisticated enough not to require a total explanation of fundamental and introductory concepts.

My subject is the Church in the city. A very handy way of characterizing modern American society is to feature the growth of urbanism, industrialism, and secularism. These three developments are certainly not synonymous, nor are they necessarily inter-related. There probably have been agrarian societies that are highly secular, and one can imagine the dispersal of industry into rural areas as automation makes this possible, or as perhaps the threat of saturation bombing makes it necessary or advisable. The fact is, however, that our secularized and industrialized western society has built up great concentrations of population in the urban and the metropolitan area during the past century.

Most Americans seem now to have accepted urbanism as a natural and logical way of life, but probably most of us have not yet really learned to live with it. We take cities and towns and suburbs for granted. When we study urban sociology we become aware of the startling recency of city growth in the history of mankind. It is only in the last hundred years that cities have become important in western civilization, and it is only in the last forty years that most Americans have been living in urban places. Before the 1920 Census the majority of Americans were still living in rural areas, and that was the first year in which the United States' population was more urban than rural. In the last census it was 67% urban. So the city looms large to the social scientist. Every social problems textbook has at least one chapter on urban problems. Demographers are entranced by it. The fact is that most social problems today are urban problems.

In spite of valiant efforts in city planning and urban renewal, western society has not kept up with urbanization, with its political graft and corruption, blighted areas, minority problems, congestion of traffic and transportation, inadequate schooling and sanitation. Man as an individual has not kept up with the explosion of the cities, and one can almost say that the more urban man becomes the more frustrated he appears to be. The human personality seems to have become more dependent, more complex, and more segmented in this process of adjustment to city life. And if society in general and man in particular have difficulty in adapting to urbanism, we should not be surprised if the religious institutions and organizations have failed to become smoothly urbanized.

There is a kind of anti-urban bias in our culture. Does all of this mean that we must flee Babylon and return with "bucolic nostalgia," as Peter Berger calls it, to God's own unspoiled rural fields? Truman Douglas complains about an anti-urban bias which has become almost a point of dogma in American Protestantism. Now as the story has it, once upon a time the United States was a land of militant, inner-directed, non-conformists—men who were as sensitive to the rights of others as they were fierce in the defense of their own autonomy. Then slowly over this green and pleasant land crept the miasma of orthodoxy, an enervating spirit of conformity which left in its wake an atomized population of other-directed status seekers, gibbering the slogans of the moment, terrified of the FBI, and finding ultimate consolation only in the narcosis of mass culture.

Underlying all this nonsense, of course, is the myth of bucolic virtue about which Richard Hofstadter talks in his *The Age of Reform.* It is the notion, profoundly Jeffersonian, that the rural yeoman is the paradigm of the democratic citizen and that cities are a source of civic degeneracy, a malignant cancer on the body politic. With this agrarian nostalgia is combined a heavy dose of sociological paranoia. A self-anointed intellectual elite has simply lost patience with the mass society that persists in spending its new-found leisure in bowling, or watching wrestling on TV, rather than reading Kafka. It is a society where the masses refuse to genuflect to their cultural betters. So the critics talk morosely of the "eclipse of the community," and the "lonely crowd," conveniently forgetting that a mere half century ago it was precisely the so-called "integrated" rural community and the

215

accompanying idiocy of rural life that set off the mad rush to urban anonymity. Few historians, political scientists, or sociologists seem to love cities. The medieval German aphorism, "Stadt Luft Macht Frei"—City Air Nourishes Freedom—has seldom been echoed by American students of the process of urbanization.

As a matter of fact, urbanism has been a major factor in the growth of liberty in the United States, by bringing about exactly the collapse of the "natural" community the Europeans like to talk about, and which brings nostalgic tears to the eyes of sociological critics of contemporary American culture. There have been observers who doubted that religion could survive in a city environment. Everyone knows that Sodom and Gomorrah were dens of urban iniquity, cesspools of sin. In 1915 a city priest who would not identify himself at first, stated without any ambiguity that "life in a large city invariably and inevitably tends to undermine the faith." At that time he went so far as to say that there were no city Catholics. "A population of city Catholics left for three or four generations without any recruits whatever from country districts would certainly be in the last stages of irreligion and indifference." Many Catholic pastors in the city vehemently rejected this pronouncement, but Father Kelly (as he later turned out to be), as late as 1931 still maintained his thesis and claimed, as so often happens, that his opponents were not really making the surveys he had.

Father Kelly's study indicated that city-reared Catholics were less religious than country-reared Catholics on all of the following items: they missed Mass more frequently; fewer of them attended parish missions; they had poorly behaved children in the parochial schools; they were not good members of parish societies; they did not produce vocations; and from their ranks came the professional city tramps. There is, however, a contradictory stream of data concerning the Catholic immigrants of the past. The national ethnic parishes were mainly concentrated in large cities, and today American Catholics, you and I, are mainly the descendants of these immigrants. Catholics clustered largely in the cities, and many of those who went down the Appalachian range, for example, in this direction, or out to the frontiers, gave up or changed their religion because the Church could not supply priests and parishes in the more sparsely settled areas of the country.

This seems to mean that the physical environment is not so important as the religious environment that the organized can provide. There was also the argument twenty-five years ago, put forth by people who favor rural life, that the urban population was not reproducing itself, and the Catholic population would thus dwindle. They said also that rural families were an important source of Church vocations. I might say in passing that in our studies of vocations we found that this was not true of Sisters, Brothers, or Priests. They are not represented in the seminaries and convents, monasteries, diocesan seminaries, in proportion to their percentage in the population. Our vocations are city vocations for the most part.

Russell Dynes remarks that there is no reason to assume that the city is the enemy of religion. Many cities, such as Rome, Jerusalem, Salt Lake City and Mecca, have been and remain great religious centers. On the other hand, the great Protestant sociologist, H. Paul Douglas, who did more research than anyone else on the American city Church, bemoaned the fact that as a consequence of violent urban changes, multitudes become religiously maladjusted and shaken out of a former Christian allegiance. He said that the unchurched were not those who never had any religion, but mainly those who had fallen away from a church.

A fairly thorough analysis of urban-rural religious differences was made by Sorokin and Zimmerman, and published more than thirty years ago. They found that the factors of urban heterogeneity and mobility apply also in general to religion. Beliefs change more rapidly in the city; there is a greater variety of religious organizations and denominations; there is more skepticism and sophistication in the urban areas. Their sobering tentative conclusion, with which I do not agree, was that the real menace to historical Christianity, once an urban or Roman development, is this same urbanization of society. The small churches, underpaid ministers, and the inadequate organization of rural religious life are the greatest bulwark for preservation of this historical Christianity.

At this point, I would like to speak briefly about the dynamics of adaptation. The central question of urban and suburban development in relation to religion involves the assumption that the city and the Church are both here to stay. Neither of them is or can be static. We can safely assume also that the city changes faster than the Church; that there is therefore a kind of culture lag between the two, and that the Church is seriously concerned about adapting itself to this change. American Catholics came mainly out of rural Europe and American Protestants out of rural America. Yet both now have sufficient experience to realize that they are facing relatively the same problems, and I would underscore this fact: that we are in a unique situation that the world has never seen before, and perhaps we need unique ways of adaptation. There are sociologists who feel that Catholicism has adapted itself better than Protestantism to the demands of the city. Wilbur Hallenback remarked that the Roman Catholic Church not only has a greater genius for adaptation, but "with centralized resources and some measure of administrative control has met the changing needs of the cities with greater success" than the Protestant groups. And Russell Dynes again said that the Catholic Church gave organizational efficiency to its urban parishioners without exhausting its energies on sparsely populated rural parishes. James Quinn, the urban sociologist, wrote that the Catholic Church which operates under a diocesan plan does not exhibit the variety of local congregations characteristic of Protestant denominations and sects.

The data demonstrating the adaptability of the Catholic Church to the city can be inferred from the writings of those social scientists and from the small but significant amount of research that has been going on in urban Catholicism. Quinn was probably right when he said he knew of no systematic studies of adaptations of Roman Catholic Churches in contrasting urban neighborhoods. From the beginning of my own research experience, men like Douglas, Kinchenlow, and Sanderson, all of whom were Protestants, provided genuine models of careful social science research in Protestantism. Father Schuyler's book is one study of a Northern parish; Father Connor Ward studied a parish in England, and with a couple of studies that I did, that just about exhausts what we have that is worth reading.

The first range of evidence is that the mortality rate of Catholic urban parishes is inconsequential when compared with that of Protestant congregations. Sam Kinchenlow found that during one period in Chicago alone, about 300 Protestant churches closed their doors, while during that same period only three Catholic parishes died out. In discussing these materials, Hallenback called the city the graveyard of churches. No statistics are available on the shutting down of city parishes, but everyone of us has observed the parish churches that were once crowded at five Masses on Sunday mornings, and now have fewer people at fewer services. The number of parishioners shrinks in one part of the urban diocese and expands in another part, particularly the suburbs.

Perhaps a comparative picture of rural-urban change will show better what is happening among Catholics. During the decade ending in 1962, the New York parishes increased from 389 to 402. The average number of parishioners increased from 3,391 to 4,107. This was a 3% increase in numbers of parishes, but a 25% increase in numbers of parishioners. During the same period in the rural diocese of Crookston, Minnesota—probably none of you has ever heard that there is a diocese at Crookston—the parishes increased from 53 to 54, and the average number of parishioners from 608 to 660. This was a 2% increase in the number of parishes, and a 10% increase in the number of parishioners.

The second comparable evidence of urban adaptability is that every study of Church attendance in the city shows that Catholics go to religious services more frequently than Protestants and Jews. There is a remarkable consistency in this area. Father Greeley found that in five national surveys, about seven out of ten of the Catholic respondents said that they attended church regularly or weekly. We have confirmed this ourselves in a national representative sample of over 4,000 Catholic young men in the armed services, of whom three-quarters (74%) said that they attended Mass every Sunday. The range is considerable, however, among

220

city-bred boys. From places like Cleveland and Scranton, where 83% attend Mass regularly, to cities like Los Angeles, where it is 58%, and Corpus Christi, where it is 54%.

Most studies indicate that rural people are more faithful than urban people in church attendance and that this is true for both Catholics and Protestants. This differential shows up in our recent national sample of Catholic young men, with eight out of ten rural boys and seven out of ten city boys attending Mass every Sunday. Such findings were called into question, however, in a recent report by Bernard Lazzerwitz who shows that rural Protestants are more regular in church attendance than urban Protestants, but that rural Catholics are considerably lower in attendance than urban Catholics. Lazzerwitz suggested the sizeable distances from the church is one of the explanations of lower regularity by rural Catholics, but we have found that about the same proportion of those who go to church regularly as of those who hardly ever go to church live two miles or more from the church—so this is one factor that probably is not important.

The third indication of Catholic urban stability and adaptability is said to be the fact that the Catholic Church has not been fragmented by the establishment of numerous lower-class Catholic sects. Thomas Hoult thinks that the strength of the religious sect in urban life is perhaps the greatest challenge facing the Protestant churches, and to a lesser extent, Catholicism and Judaism. Hoult goes further in asking this question, which I think is rather significant: Now that its American functionaries are influential and its members are becoming more fully acculturated in urban values, will Catholicism in the United States experience the type of lower class sectarianism found among the larger Protestant groupings?

In this context, sectarian attitudes are consistently more common in lower socio-economic groups, and sectarianism is thought of as a lower-class phenomenon. One of the most significant demographic shifts occurring in our times is the evacuation of the lower urban social strata by American Catholics. As city Catholics move socially upward and physically outward, the lowest economic classes of the city are filled out by Protestants, mainly rural and often southern, both Negro and white. Puerto Rican Catholic immigrants constitute a large exception to the so-called "hill-billy" migrants and the Negro migrant. The establishment of Puerto Rican storefront churches of the fundamentalist-holiness type may indicate a Catholic failure to meet these people at their own level. Or it may indicate a successful venture by Protestant Evangelism.

Catholic territorial parishes, ideally embracing all Catholics within the designated area, are social-class parishes only if the particular area is predominantly inhabited by one social class. The more pregnant hypothesis, yet to be established by solid research, is that the large Catholic diocese has room for and actually contains every level of religious organization from the sect type to the ecclesia type. This is a significant aspect of urban adaptability that has been largely overlooked up to now by sociologists of religion. We found, for example, that the fundamentalist type of religious sect that is developing in Chile among the poverty-stricken rural workers is indigenous. It does not appear traceable to North American Protestant influence. It is a kind of revolt against the highly organized formalistic ecclesiastical type of church.

Religion has a mission in the city as it has elsewhere in the world, and it may be well to recall that the urban religious relationship is a reciprocal one. The question therefore is not only what does the city do to the Church, but also what does the Church do to the city? Adaptation to urban change is not simply a negative reaction. It is meant also to be a positive influence over the urban environment. This reciprocal relationship may be discussed briefly in three general areas. First, the structure of the Church; secondly, clergy-lay relations; and thirdly, the parish as a community. Let us look briefly at each of these.

I have argued elsewhere that the need for structural reform of the city parish constitutes one of the major research issues in the sociology of the parish. Of course, Michenneau's book on the French city parish brought this strongly to the attention of Catholics. Martin Marty made the same kind of point for Protestants when he contrasted two neighboring churches in Chicago—the one, a paragon of agonizing adjustment on the part of a long established congregation; and the other a frontier experience of beginning all over again.

Much has been said about the need for restructuring the parish and for reforming urban religious institutions. Most of it has been a concern about the inner city and the so-called blighted areas where masses of underprivileged people live. There is probably also a case to be made out for the middle-class neighborhood, since these people have also altered their behavioral patterns. These concepts remain relatively vague as long as they are discussed in the abstract conceptual order. Yet there are certain concrete manifestations of adaptation that spell this out. One of the most penetrating and sobering analyses of lower-class areas has been made by Nicholas Von Hoffman in Chicago. Heretofore, he said, we have had national enclaves, voluntary and involuntary ghettoes in our big cities. Now we are menaced by the ripening of Casbahs, where the rich do not run, where outsiders dare not go, and where a dangerously separate world is coming into existence.

Yet, he notes, that even in these areas, churches that have not had their incentive sapped by debilitating denominational subsidies, develop organization and substance. These people literally live in another world, where a nice clean democratic ideology has little day-to-day meaning, and where organized Christianity tends to be a part of the "outside system." The Catholic Church has always maintained parishes and missions in these urban areas, but the apparent hardcore permanence of this situation has forced a rethinking of functions of human relations, of sub-structures, and even of the physical setting of the religious apostolate. The recent publicity given to Episcopal priests in the slums indicates this attempt at adaptation, and you may have noted the wide publicity given to such ventures, starting with a *New Yorker* article about poverty in the cities and what is happening there. *America* has had it; *Commonweal, The Reporter, Harpers*—almost every worthwhile magazine has been talking about this recently.

The adaptations of functions refers to the refocusing of activities in the parish. The image we have of the urban parish is one of a sacramental service station. It is the place where parishioners come for Mass and other services; to get married, to have their children baptized and their old folks buried; where they hear the word of God. As the number of Catholic parishioners shrinks in an area, or as the number of people who are not seeking these services increases, the parochial activity can either decrease or it can change to something else. This "something else" depends on the needs of the people. The kind of help these people require is only indirectly sacramental. It is primarily at the level of physical, material, social, and psychological redemption. This type of function can be conceived as a kind of doorway to the Church, rather than as the sanctuary of the Church.

The second adaptation is that of human relations between the Church representatives, clerical and lay, on the one side, and on the other the masses of people they are trying to reach. The direction of the relationship has changed; instead of the people coming to the Church, the Church is going to the people. One can make cooperative demands of the parishioners in a stable, urban, middle-class parish, but this does not work where there are few parishioners or many disinterested unchurched persons. Father Furfey made a strong plea for the missionary aspects of the city parish. Using mainly French material, he suggests that the relationship between a missionary and a potential convert is quite different from that between the pastor and his regular parishioner.

The third adaptation is that of the physical setting of church activities, relations and groups, and this too tends to weaken the traditional adherence to strictly parochial limits. The notion here is that a Catholic center, which may or may not be adjacent to the old church building, can act as an attraction for people who may otherwise never go near a church: Paulist information centers, Chapels of Ease in the large cities, Friendship houses, Catholic Worker Centers, St. Vincent de Paul stores, and so on. There are many examples of this kind of urban religious setting.

Now the question of clergy-lay relations logically comes out of this whole matter of parish and church structure. The fact is, of course, that there are other important relations besides that of the pastor and the parishioner, and other important associations of Catholics besides those on the parochial level. The urban supraparochial groupings seem to be drawing more and more persons from the established parishes, while the trend in the suburbs is in the opposite direction. People there tend to focus greater attention on the parish itself. This is particularly apparent in the newer suburban parishes where building is going on and the parochial school tends to be the focus of solidarity.

People who suspect a lurking anti-clericalism among American Catholics are involved in a kind of anomaly. They observe that the American Catholic laity has been upwardly mobile, but they suppose that the status gap between the clergy and laity is narrowing because the priesthood and Sisters and Brothers have not made a comparable upward shift in social esteem and prestige. Actually these professional functionaries of the Church have not stood still, and their training in many instances is developing according to the adapted prescriptions of Pope Pius XI and Pius XII. Nevertheless the status of the laity is changing, and this poses two important questions: Must there necessarily be a low ceiling for upward lay mobility within the Catholic lay structure? And is there opportunity for lay participation in any of the prestige-ful functions of the Church?

One way of approaching these questions is to look at the authority system of the Church. Researchers in large-scale industrial organizations talk about span-of-control theories. They distinguish between the long narrow structure in which there are many supervisors up and down the line, and which operate on the assumption that people need to be closely supervised in order to perform well. This is contrasted to the broad flat structure in which supervision is relatively loose, and which makes the assumption that people perform best when given a large area of freedom to make their own decisions.

It comes as a surprise to Protestants—who have an image of the authoritarian Catholic Church—when I say that the ecclesiastics in the Catholic system function generally on a broad flat structure in the sense that there are only three levels of authority—Rome, diocese, and parish. There is little supervision over the Bishops, and not much more over the pastors. The closeness of Episcopal supervision over the pastoral role depends partially on the Bishop's interpretation of his own role of authority, but mainly on the development of the diocesan bureaucracy which is common to all large-scale organizations. We have found in a recent study of clergy-lay relations that personal relations between the Bishop and the priests, and between the priests and the parishioners, are much closer, less bureaucratized in a smaller diocese like Raleigh than in a larger diocese like New York.

In the large city diocese the relationship between diocese and parish tightens up more formally and rigidly. Thomas O'Dea sees this as one of the dilemmas of the institutionalization of religion. The elaboration of offices tends to minimize rather than improve organizational effectiveness. Bishop Wright of Pittsburgh has a different view of this relation. He thinks that the diocese is replacing the parish as an administrative unit, so that the parish can improve as an educational, liturgical, and sanctifying unit of the Church.

The fascinating aspect of this span-of-control theory is that the lay person has often been dealt with as a client or a consumer, rather than as a cooperator and fellow-functionary. Up to recent times he has been outside or underneath the broad flat structure of Church authority. Yet there is a level on which the clergy and the laity have the relationship of peers and colleagues. Both Bishops and pastors turn to lay advisors on occasions, as for example in legal, financial, and architectural matters, and this lay function is quite clearly consultative. It is a preliminary participation in decision-making. It is not a sharing of authority. Lay persons who are parish trustees, or who serve on diocesan school boards, usually are pretty well aware that important decisions and ultimate responsibilities do not rest in themselves. The number of specialists and the need for their advices are naturally limited to a very small proportion of the Catholic laity.

On the other hand, we must not form the impression that the typical urban or suburban pastor treats his parishioners gently but firmly, like a flock of sheep. Most of the success of the vigorous suburban parishes has been due to the extension of lay initiative and responsibility. At this informal level of face-to-face relations, the participation of the laity is apostolic and parochial in a non-specialist sense. It is a kind of function that friends and parents and neighbors can do together for the welfare of the group. It is this, perhaps, rather than the specialized contribution that constitutes the tremendous potential of lay manpower in the American Catholic Church.

Looked at from this point of view, the informal organization of clergy-lay relations is something quite different from the formal, juridical structure of mutual rights and duties between priests and people. This is indeed the point at which the culture makes human relations visible. The traditional American relation between priest and people has been personal, friendly and cooperative. There does not seem to be a prospective rift in this relationship, even though occasionally one hears lay people complain of clerical lack of cooperation and priests complain of lay lack of cooperation. Like every other relationship, this is reciprocal, but more than in other types of relations, the initiative here tends to lie with the priests and the parochial situation is largely what the pastor wants it to be, or what he allows it to be.

The CHURCH

Clergy-Lay Relations

Joseph H. Fichter, s.j.

The thesis about which I would like to speak in clergy-lay relations depends to some extent upon the generalization one would make concerning the state of religion in America today. This practical situation involving the professionals in the Church and those who are served by the professionals must be understood, I think, from the point of view of whether we are a religious society or whether America is going materialist and secularist, and if so, what these concepts mean. Where do Americans stand on religion, and how do Catholics understand religion?

American society is full of surprises for Americans who do not study it clearly—and there are many who do not really understand our culture and society—as well as for foreigners who do not understand it at all. For instance, we still have a tremendous problem of poverty in the midst of the most affluent and prosperous society the world has ever seen. Henry George was concerned about this at the end of the last century and it is still hanging on. We are most productive in private luxuries in which there is a profit, and least productive, comparatively speaking, in public services, as Kenneth Galbraith has pointed out so forcefully in the last couple of years. We are popularizing our moral values, as

Sorokin constantly proclaims, so that the good get better, and the bad get worse, as he says.

What is happening here is what must happen in every open and dynamic society. The free and fair pursuit of contrasting goals challenges the attention and the energies of our people, so that we seem to be moving in several different directions at the same time. This is still part, at least, of the price we are paying for what the sociologists call a pluralistic society.

Now the subject we want to discuss at this point is not free from such confusion. There is sufficient evidence to hold both propositions—that America is becoming more religious and that America is becoming less religious. My own thesis is that the material and the spiritual, the religious and the secular were never meant to be opposites. The Incarnation implies, to me, that the human being and human society serve God in and through this world.

Yet it comes as a surprise to some people that a materially successful society like America is becoming more conscious of its religious principles and obligations. Even in materialistic, communistic Russia, religion has not disappeared; at the Fourth World Conference of Sociology in Italy I listened to a Soviet delegate say that there still is religion in his country, where social enlightenment and progressive materialism had achieved so many other goals.

Several American sociologists still retain the thesis that a scientific and secular society has no need for religion. They say that the appeal to the supernatural for the explanation of our problems becomes less urgent as we learn by scientific break-throughs to solve our own problems. Obviously, if religion has lost its utility, the professionals in the field of religion, clergymen, sisters, brothers, ourselves here, are functionally useless. This hypothesis is perhaps the most sophisticated form of anti-clericalism you can find. It does not suggest that parsons be hung and quartered or that rabbis be put in concentration camps or that priests be sent back where they came from. To ignore the clergy as useless members of society may be the most insulting kind of anti-clericalism. You despise your opponent but you do not think he is worth fighting. The French intellectual and the Latin-American politician have sometimes exhibited this kind of distaste for the clergy. The working-class Italian communist and the Cuban leftist may hate the priest enough to spit upon him and vilify him. He thinks the priest is so dangerous that he must be attacked physically.

All the studies that we have had show that religion is neither dead nor useless in America. More than that, they show that during the last century and a half, the percentage of religious affiliation and of attendance at religious services has steadily increased. More people are buying and reading the Bible than ever before. There is a great deal of evidence along this line. It has been a long upward curve that was not seriously affected in this century by the catastrophe of two world wars, nor by the depression of the '30's, nor by the affluence that we are now experiencing.

Research into the quantity of religion has little to say about the quality of religion. Will Herberg holds the thesis that we are developing a kind of American-culture-religion that is more natural than supernatural. He and others think that some of the distinctive elements are being rubbed off Protestantism, Catholicism, and Judaism and that the common denominator is becoming a vague national religion. Gerhard Lenski, in his book *The Religious Factor,* disputes this; and he argues that the kind of religion involved makes a large difference in the lives of people. Father John Thomas, who is an expert in family sociology, also argues this way, saying that Catholicism not only should but does affect family life. These are important speculations emerging from acute close observance.

Perhaps the same criticism can be made about recent generalizations concerning the increase of anti-clericalism, or the break in the clergy-lay relationship. Like the speculative deduction that religion must decrease when society becomes more rational and scientific (which of course I do not hold), the deduction is made that a rise in the status of the laity must be accompanied by a decline in the status of the clergy. Assumptions of this kind are always suspect, sometimes harmful, and frequently erroneous.

The latest fad among Catholic intellectuals and liberals seems to be the warning that priests are not doing their job and they had better watch out. The fact is that lay people in America are generally demonstrating an increasing respect and appreciation for their clergymen. Perhaps this is an effect, perhaps it is a cause, of growing religiosity among Americans. If medicine is valued, physicians are held in esteem. If science is important, scientists are considered important. If religion is esteemed, the ministers of religion share in that esteem. Even in an earlier period when America was less religious than it is today, clergymen enjoyed high social status. The man of the cloth generally had the respect of the American community. Even the fictional story, and the more recent movie, about Elmer Gantry, which does not have to be spelled out here, seemed to have no negative effect on the clergy's prestige.

There are probably still isolated places where rabbis are disliked by Christians and where priests are disliked by

Protestants, but these cases tend to be vestiges of ethnic rivalries and conflicts, and are not a direct expression of religious anti-clericalism as such. Elmer Roper ran a successful poll—I myself have used the same kind of approach in at least five or six studies, not only here but in Germany and Chile—which asks the question: who of the following are contributing the most to the good of this society? Then follows a list of religious leaders, politicians, labor leaders, military men, scientists, educators, and so on. In every case, without exception, clergymen are placed first. Usually educators are second.

One of the arguments employed to show that the status of the clergy is declining, or that the people are not so favorable to the clergy, is the so-called "vocation shortage." In our nationwide survey, we found that both priests and people consider this one of the most serious problems facing the Church in America today. Now the simple demographic fact is that the child population increased tremendously after the war, and these children have not grown up yet to be ordained or to become functioning Sisters or Brothers. Another fact is that the minor seminaries are booming right now. In other religious denominations, they are also reporting a satisfactory increase in the number of trainees for the ministry. When we look at the long-term trend and standardize the rise and fall in the birth rate, we find that there has been no effective change in the ratio of clergy to total population during the past century.

Meanwhile the proportion of men in all professions has increased sharply. You must remember that professions have multiplied. In early America the ministry was one of seven recognized professions. Now there are about 300 different professions. Sociologist Seymour Lipsit points out that the proportion of ministers has failed to rise with the increasing wealth of the American people, who in this respect do not appear to be "buying more clergymen." In one sense this is an amusing argument and would have validity only if people were becoming more sinful and therefore needed more clergymen to save them. Now even if you can measure appreciation of clergy in terms of this buying power, this consumer's approach, or in terms of money, there may be a hopeful sign in a recent *Time* article which shows that pastoral pay is on the increase in Protestant urban parishes. The man in black has often been in the red; now that is changing. I do not know whether the salaries of diocesan curates is going up, or to what extent this differs from one part of the country to another, but generally speaking where you can measure this they are getting a better salary than they used to.

It seems reasonable to say that people are willing to pay for the things they value highly. A tremendous outpouring of money for religious purposes in all the American churches and religious denominations indicates a rather enthusiastic promotion and support of clergymen and their work. The fact that the very nature of the clergyman's position and calling logically places him at a level of importance to the people he serves. As Lenski remarked, laymen in general and more devout laymen in particular expect the clergy to be leaders and are prepared to accept their ideas and proposals seriously. The clergyman can dispense something of value that the people want, whether it is the preaching of the Protestant minister, the spiritual advice of the rabbi, the sacramental administration of the priest. As long as people continue to want these things, the religious professional is going to be valued because he is the one to dispense them.

236

In any well ordered church or denomination, the laity must depend upon the clergy for those functions in which the clergy has specialized. When we talk about the rise of the laity, we mean that the laity is no longer dependent upon the clergy for the many non-religious functions once performed in ethnic and immigrant parishes. I read in a recent book on the Church in Africa that missionaries sometimes treated natives as though Colonialism would last forever. I suppose there are still some priests who act as though the American laity will remain immigrants forever.

In other words, what is happening more and more now is that lay people no longer need the clergy to help them in areas where they have become independently competent. If this is anti-clericalism, then I think we ought to have more of it. Certainly the Catholic laity differs greatly from its predecessors of a generation or two ago, and its status vis à vis the clergy is necessarily different. Social status is a relative concept. Each position in the social structure is related to all others. This does not mean that there is only so much status to go around, so that when one person gains another person loses. The fact is, of course, that as the total American Catholic population rises into the middle and upper middle classes, the gap between the layman's status and the clergyman's is narrowing.

Our era has been called the century of the laity. Books and pamphlets, speeches and articles are being produced and distributed by the thousands, all of them dealing with the problems and prospects of the laity. I get the feeling sometimes that they deal with the layman as though he were a novelty, some fascinating creature they had just discovered lurking in the underbrush. The title of Donald Thorman's popular book, *The Emerging Layman,* gives you the impression that the laity has just come up out of the underground, out of some prehistoric cave. He is shaggy and unkempt, but ready and eager for civilization. As a matter of fact, Joseph Folliard, in his book *World Catholicism Today,* provides the image of the laity as a beast, a lion with immense and undisciplined strength. Perhaps this lion must be drugged into submission; it ought never to have been awakened at all. If it must always be fettered, it will never test its strength; but if it is allowed to run uncontrolled, God alone knows what damage it can do, even with the best of intentions.

These are caricatures that draw attention to the fact that the functional relations within the Church between priests and people are becoming more significant. The whole notion of the lay apostolate, of Catholic action, the cooperation of the clergy and the laity in the work of the Church, is taking on new meaning. This does indeed indicate that priests and people are closer, not only in their relative status, but also in their roles. There is a growth of functional cooperation between them. The factors that have worked toward this cooperation, or that are at least symptomatic of this functional change, are threefold.

First, the growth of religion both in numbers and in activity has reached the point where the clergy alone cannot cope with it. This does not mean trying to pile more work on the parish clergyman. The laity and the clergy cooperate in these things, and much of what was assumed to be the function of the clergyman only is largely, in many cases at least, the potential of the laity. Priests need help in many areas other than simple financial contributions. We must be careful not to say that the layman is just doing a residual and temporary job, filling in until enough clergy are trained to take over. Some people think this way about lay teachers in the parochial schools—that they are just a passing kind of thing until we get enough sisters to fill in for them.

The second factor is that religion is permeating life in a way that was not the case a generation or two ago. This is a demonstrable fact which is challenged by a lot of people who, I think, are mainly wrong in their interpretation of religion in America. The alert and progressive layman is no longer just a Sunday Catholic, practicing what some have called departmentalized religion. One sees this in many Catholic programs and activities: pre-Cana conferences, solemn engagements, the work of the Confraternity of Christian Doctrine, the introduction of seasonal prayers in the homes. This diocese here has an excellent program called the Mary Missions. There are so many people involved in so many of these programs around the country that this is a serious symptom of what I am saying—that religion means a lot more to a lot more people than it ever did before. We are coming of age.

Thirdly, perhaps of greatest importance, is the fact that as the laity becomes more educated it also becomes more appreciative of religion. At least there is strong evidence that the laity wants to participate more in religious activities. We have had a hint of this in several studies when we asked parishioners what kind of group activity they would prefer to do in the parish. The strictly secular functions, traditional things, like planning socials and raising funds, were the least preferred. They wanted to do things that would revitalize dormant Catholics: to Christianize the community, to clarify religious issues, to bring non-Catholics into the Church, to study the Bible, to have religious discussions.

Some outstanding examples of increasing competence have come out of research on the laity. In several studies we have asked the laity to make a judgment about sermons they have heard in the past year. We measured their responses against the amount of education they have had, and we have found invariably that the more educated are also the more critical of the sermons. It should be added that priests are more critical of their own pulpit endeavors than the laity, which was an interesting by-product of this study. Priests are more critical of their own sermons than the people are critical of priests' sermons.

On all the measurable items in this study, the laity thought more highly of the clergy than the clergy thought of themselves. Yet there was also always the difference that the better educated made the sharper criticisms. Not only can the laity now make better judgments than before; they also have demonstrated their ability to run organizations that are important to them. One of the best examples I know, and have had some contact with, is the Christian Family Movement. This is the first instance of a large-scale organized lay maturity in this country. But even this is an uneven picture. Wherever the CFM is run by the laity with the clergy's help it is successful. Wherever it is run by the clergy with the laity's help it is floundering.

What can be said about clergy-lay tensions? Let us look now more specifically and analytically at the relationship between the clergy and the laity. This is not merely a relationship of status, the relative prestige that each party enjoys, and the extent to which they esteem or disesteem one another. It is also a process of human relations, and our studies show that social processes can be negative in the sense that they drive people apart, and they can be positive in the sense that they draw people together. To get to the point here we might ask, are there other areas in which clergy and laity are in conflict or in competition? Are there other areas in which they are in accommodation and cooperation, and to what extent do the negative and positive processes balance or outweigh each other?

Strongest of the negative social processes, of course, is open conflict, which we might define as a form of mutual interaction through which two or more persons attempt to remove each other, either by annihilating the other party, or by rendering him ineffectual. Prize-fighting is a good example of this. Warfare is conflict in which the opponents are trying to destroy each other. Sports like tennis and golf are games of competition, not of conflict.

Pure conflict between clergy and laity would mean anti-clericalism on one side and anti-laitism on the other, in which the clergy and the laity deliberately attacked one another. The clergy is the victim of the laity's attack, as happened in Nazi and Communist countries. This is anticlericalism, and martyrdom, but it is not conflict. The Judaeo-Christian West and the Atheistic-Communist East have been fighting over forty years to destroy each other's system. This is a conflict of ideas and behavior patterns, even if it is not physical warfare. This is probably the main reason why co-existence is an essential problem to both West and East.

There is an important distinction to be made at this point. The incompatibility of values and interests and goals may well exist between two groups like the East and West, but there is no conflict between them unless one group tries to impose itself upon the other. There is incompatibility between Christians and Jews, between Catholics and Protestants; people talk about "tensions" in this area. We are able to differ basically, but at the same time, we can avoid conflict because incompatibilities can co-exist in our American pluralistic system.

Leaving aside the cruder notion of mutual conflict between clergy and laity, can we say that there are areas of serious tension? You remember the incident in Puerto Rico showing that the voters' choice was incompatible with the episcopal attitude toward the winning candidate. This was a measurable example of the laity's successful dissent, and insofar as the Bishop represented the clergy—which is sometimes questioned in this particular case—it was a clear case of anticlericalism. I have sometimes remarked that you do not have anti-clericalism except in those places where you first have clericalism. Thomas O'Dea writes that clericalism implies that those who make ecclesiastical decisions often tend to see the problems, tasks, risks and achievements of the Christian life solely from the professional perspective of the priest as an ecclesiastical official. Clericalism, he says, combines with formalism and authoritarianism to impose its own view upon the laity, who, trained under clericalist influence, are passive although often demurring in the face of such attitudes.

When we use terms like these—clericalism, formalism, authoritarianism—we may be inclined to picture the Church bureaucracy on one side, traditional, conservative, resistant to change, lined up in solid ranks against the Catholic laity on the other side, progressive, dynamic, alert, straining, and eager for change. In fairness to Professor O'Dea, this is not his inclination. He concludes his book, *The American Catholic Dilemma,* with the statement of the Catholic Bishops in 1919 concerning the social problems facing the nation. The progressive recommendations of the Bishops at that time were far ahead of the laity, and far ahead of the nation, but practically all of them are now established and accepted aspects of our legal and social system.

Let us look at two other examples of a progressive and dynamic hierarchy that is having trouble with a conservative and tradition bound laity. The loudest and most prolonged objections to Pope John's encyclical *Mater et Magistra* came from a group of educated and articulate Catholic conservatives, willing to accept the Church as their Mother, they said, but not as their teacher. The Pope's recommendations for social justice, for distribution of wealth, and for international aid are too revolutionary for these dissenters. They refuse to accept the teaching authority of the Church, which is too dynamic and too liberal for them. The most notable and continuing example of opposition to the progressive hierarchy occurs in my own area of the country, Louisiana, where a minority of the laity have been in open and expressed defiance of the program for Catholic school desegregation. What is typical in this case is the refusal of the dissidents to recognize the race question as a moral and theological issue in which their religious leaders have the obligation to make a judgment that is binding on Catholics. Some of them, like other Southerners, continue to argue that this is merely a political issue, a matter of States' Rights, or of constitutionality.

If clericalism means that the clergy are meddling in things that do not concern them, and if the race question does not concern the clergy, then the organized opposition of Catholics in New Orleans must be called anti-clericalism. But many of these people are not really anti-clerical. In fact many of them try to avoid the anti-clerical label by maintaining that the clergy have been duped, that the priests are too "other-worldly" to recognize the Communist menace that

243

lies behind the integration movement. They argue strongly that segregation has become a sin only since the Second World War, that this had occurred only because of certain pressures and circumstances that have nothing to do with religion or theology.

The point that I want to make here is one that is seldom made, especially by liberal commentators outside the Catholic Church. These are examples in which the doctrine and the program of the Church, often criticized for being behind the times and slow-moving, are in fact much too progressive for some of the laity. But it would be a mistake to set this up as a typical instance of clergy-lay relations. It is probably safe to say that the overwhelming majority of Southerners, including Catholics, think of unjust discrimination as a matter of conscience. It is probably also safe to say that the overwhelming majority of the American Catholic laity take seriously the admonitions of the social encyclicals.

Now there are also some false dilemmas. Some people find tensions where they do not exist, and they discover anti-clericalism where there is none. Two of these areas are in dealings with the birth-control problem and the parochial-school problem. Sociologists who look for tensions within the Catholic Church have a favorite example in the use of artificial contraceptive devices. They find in hospital surveys that some Catholic women practice birth prevention and that others are in favor of limiting the size of the family. It is no surprise that people go against their conscience and their moral principles in this regard as they do in other areas of morality. It is, however, an illogical leap from this statement to the conclusion that because people commit sin, they are anti-clerical, or even that every Catholic who finds it difficult to keep the commandments and the Church's rules is automatically antagonistic to the priests and the Bishops.

Another area in which non-Catholic social scientists pretend to find clergy-lay conflict is that of the parochial school system. Blanshard is notorious in this. It is assumed that priests are forcing reluctant parents to send their children to Catholic elementary schools. The facts are quite the opposite, of course. Catholic parents are clamoring for more parochial schools and are demanding that the pastor build more schoolrooms. What little scientific evidence we have on this points to the conclusion that parents consider the parochial elementary school more important than the Catholic high school or the Catholic college and university. It shows also that parents prefer the parochial to the public or the private elementary school.

It ought to be pointed out that the parochial school system does not represent a complete and settled policy among the clergy and the hierarchy. Some Bishops put great stress on the building and maintenance of elementary schools. Others prefer to put their diocesan resources into other apostolic ventures. Statistics in the Catholic Directory reveal the uneven provision of parochial schools from one diocese to another, from one region of the country to another.

The only serious case of anti-clericalism that the United States has experienced was a century ago when the controversy over lay trusteeism resulted in a genuine incompatibility of policy. Some people wanted full control over the parish, not only in financial matters, but also with the right to choose and retain their own priests. This called for a showdown, and perhaps the American hierarchy then overreacted. To this day, the clergy retains even the financial management of the parish, and it tends to be a lurking fear, especially in older priests, that the laity may want "to take over." Here again there are different approaches to this problem. In French Canada and in some European countries, the management of the physical plant is entirely in the hands of elected committees of lay parishioners. The pastor has only one vote in the proceedings, and then even the Bishop of the diocese cannot change the territorial boundaries of the parish without the consent of his lay committee.

A final word on the progressives and the traditionalists. We might well summarize and conclude this discussion on lay-clergy relations by emphasizing the fact that the changing relationship between clergy and laity is occurring in a Church adapting to a changing world. Adaptation has been a kind of slogan of the Papacy during this generation. Even with the best of good will there can only be legitimate differences of opinion about the rate of change, and even to some extent about the kind of change. The problem then resolves itself to this: who are the reactionaries, the clergy or the laity? James O'Gara of *Commonweal* does not believe that reactionary laymen who refuse to accept the teaching authority of the Church are a major problem in America. What he does consider a "real and present danger" is in the stone walls that informed and apostolic laymen may run into and get discouraged about. Note that carefully. The obvious translation is that these stone walls are made up of the clergy. Even though the strongest anti-clerical denunciations are not coming from conservative or reactionary laymen, the assumption is made that the real future tension will come from conservative or stone-wall priests.

Now I differ with Mr. O'Gara on this and I think I have the evidence to support my position. In the nationwide survey of priests and people that we have just completed we found, as expected, that the proportion of conservatives is higher among the clergy than among the laity. This is the national picture. But everyone knows that there are important regional differences in this country. In the resultant comparison between clergy and laity, the picture looks something like this: In the Middle Atlantic States (New York, New Jersey, Pennsylvania) both priests and people are conservative. In the East North Central States—what we call the Middle West generally (Indiana, Illinois, Michigan and Ohio)—both clergy and laity are liberal. In the West North Central States (Minnesota, Iowa, the Dakotas and so on) the clergy is more liberal than the laity. In the Pacific States (Washington, Oregon, California) the laity are more liberal than the clergy.

It may also be more than a coincidence that the practice of the faith by the laity differs regionally; where both priests and people are liberal and progressive, the practice of the faith is high. By the practice of the faith, I mean the measurements that we take on frequency of attendance at Mass, reception of Communion, and so on. Where the clergy are traditionalists and the people are progressive, the practice of the faith is low. Where both clergy and people are conservative, religious practices are middling. Most important of the conclusions emerging from this nationwide research project, is the fact that the liberal laity has a tendency to be pro-clergy, while the conservative laity tends to be anticlergy. On every item that could be used in our study as an index of lay attitude toward the clergy, liberal laymen are more favorable to priests than are conservative laymen.

In my modest opinion, this is the most significant breakthrough we have made in research on clergy-lay relations to date. The kinds of lay people who are constantly cited as being restless and progressive and disturbed about the position of the laity are the very best friends the priests and the Church have. They have a positive and healthy approach to clerical-lay relations. There may continue to exist a healthy tension between laity and the clergy, but these people are in no sense of the term anti-clerical.

I think it ought to be emphasized that the real danger of anti-clericalism, if it really occurs in America, will come from the conservative and reactionary laity. These are the people who are already causing us trouble. They want to keep the status quo. They find the Church too liberal on race relations, on labor unions, on social justice, on freedom. The irony of it is that for them the Church is moving too fast, and all the while the vocal liberals have been afraid that the Church is not moving fast enough.

Christian Responsibility in Interfaith Contacts*

Sister Joan Bland, s.n.d.

It is bold indeed for me to speak about Christian responsibility, for I have come to suspect strongly that I only began
to have some grasp of what the term really means two
months ago when I heard Father Bernard Haring speak at
the Catholic University of America. Somehow, although we
have certainly always recognized the existence of Christian
responsibility, it seemed to operate in a framework so con-
fining as to exclude great blocks of human concern. There
were moments when we felt a certain frustration about specific cases of personal anguish which we longed to relieve,
but had no commission to deal with. But, for the most part,
and especially as we grew older, it seemed certain that our
often passive role was the best and most comforting. We
were glad, in all good faith, but also with the relief of the
weary, that the will of God for us tended to take relatively
predictable forms. We were willing to make genuine sacrifices, to work a great deal harder than anyone has a right to
expect, to pray long and sometimes unexciting prayers. But
these things we were accustomed to; we had reflexes to ac-

* Several paragraphs in this paper appeared in the *Records of the American
Catholic Historical Society of Philadelphia,* September, 1963, in the author's
"Christianity and the Enlightenment: An American Synthesis."

commodate them, as it were. They formed a neat and predictable pattern. They did not trouble us with ambiguities. Perhaps we were in a rut.

Now, suddenly, nothing human is foreign. We are responsible, responsible, responsible. Obedience? Yes, it is still there, as a means to solidarity, as a personal holocaust, as a corrective for egoism. But it no longer constitutes much of a protection; it has lost its anesthetic qualities. We owe God initiative as well as docility. We are expected to act creatively, existentially, viewing life in the dynamic context of the Holy Spirit's action. Into the tidy housekeeping of our personal conscience comes the new suspicion that we may fail by acting unimaginatively OR BY NOT ACTING AT ALL. Our obligations or at least the things love asks of us go beyond the law. We can never say "it is enough; I have observed every jot and tittle of the law and of the counsels (not too broadly interpreted); everything is in order; I can relax. I can dispense with creative tensions." Relaxation seems relegated to the next world, until we reflect that there we shall have no need of it.

Still it is clear that we can't have everything on our minds at once. We are all severely limited beings. If one's job is to teach mathematics, one will save souls by teaching mathematics. At the same time, one will take attitudes towards many extra-mathematical matters, and one's attitudes will matter. Sometimes they will matter very much. Always, in one way or another, they will affect souls. To come at long last to the subject of this paper—they will affect interfaith contacts.

Perhaps this is truer for sisters than for any other group in the world. Because, whatever else may be said of us, we are the world's most conspicuous Christians. No one wonders what faith we possess. No one looks at us without some reflection on what it is that we stand for. The most ardent of Catholic housewives can entertain the plumber who comes to fix her ailing sink without necessarily affecting his outlook on life. At least it is possible for her to avoid it. But it is simply impossible for the Sister Cook, should the plumbing fall apart in a convent. All human contacts produce some person-to-person impact; it is always at least somewhat negative or somewhat affirmative. In the case of a person who is as firmly and unambiguously identified as we are, the impact is for all practical purposes the impact of the Church, which is to say the impact of Christ in the world. We need not preach a sermon at the plumber, but we may not alienate him. We may not alienate anyone in the world, because we are Christ's and the terrible possibility always exists that alienation from us may lead to alienation from Him.

Merely to state that we must not alienate does not, of course, go far toward defining our relations with the non-Catholic world, either for our own guidance or for that of our students. What are the principles that can help us to make an effective apostolate of life in the pluralist society? Of course the answers are simply not all in. I can only give you the opinions I have reached, chiefly by what I hope was judicious shopping in such excellent sources as Fathers Murray and Weigel, and from Dr. John Meng, the recent Catholic president of Hunter College, who has had hourly experience of dialogue.

But to begin without reference to these admirable sources —I have personally been led, from modest, but deeply interested studies of the history of U.S. Catholicism to the conclusion that, quite aside from the body of dogmatic and moral teaching which we hold in common, American Catholics have usually tended in one of two directions. Privately, and sometimes publicly, I have called them the tradition of Thomas More and the tradition of Don Quixote. Thomas More stands for the spirit of mellow tolerance, cooperation, balance. He stands also for a loyalty to truth strong enough to motivate the most cheerful of martyrdoms. Don Quixote stands for another U.S. Catholic attitude, one which perhaps does not deserve the broad adjective "Catholic." It is defensive, bellicose, ultra-aggressive. It tends to scan the non-Catholic population in a nervous search for bigotry. Inevitably, we find what we look for and the discovery perpetuates the search. Such psychology is natural enough in a minority group, natural enough, no doubt, but not supernatural, not in conformity with the Sermon on the Mount. No doubt all groups have their Thomas More's and their Don Quixote's, with most of us somewhere between the two. As a Catholic, St. Thomas More is sufficiently recommended by his canonization. He was not an American, certainly, but some historians regard his *Utopia* as the source of the American Dream, the vision of a world of freedom and justice for all men.

So what we need in discussion with the non-Catholic world, after amicable relations on the level of ordinary human intercourse, is the dialogue, as defined by Father Murray, "orderly conversation." This enterprise is indispensable on two counts (later, we shall discuss the question of whether these two are one)—as pre-evangelization, to condition ourselves and our neighbors for the reception of truth, and because the pluralist society needs discussion. Society needs discussion because to survive it must form a consensus. No body of men can share a living civilization without a body of principles held in common. Political

252

society, like religious society, requires and is in fact maintained by articles of faith. Civil faith is certainly not identical with religious faith, but neither is it independent of religious conviction. A man's view of ultimate reality must provide the basis for all his value judgments. Our society seems to be proving, with some measure of success, that men may live together in reasonable peace without sharing all their religious beliefs. But, and this is essential, they cannot do so without sharing *any* beliefs. Actually, it is in great measure true that the principles essential for a working social consensus are firmly grounded in each of our major religious traditions.

Dr. John Meng, to whom I referred earlier, in an address at a Catholic-Jewish dialogue meeting held several years ago at Trinity College, enumerated three such principles: I shall borrow them quite shamelessly from him. The comments and interpretations are my responsibility, but the enumeration of principles is Dr. Meng's.

The first is respect for the intrinsic dignity of every man as a person in his own right. This concept goes to the heart of the Judeo-Christian ethic. Protestants, Catholics or Jews can, of course, fail to maintain this attitude, but only by being bad Protestants, bad Catholics, bad Jews. No one denies in theory at least that such a failure flies in the face of the moral imperative recognized by all three groups. Obviously man's basic rights spring from his human dignity, and disbelief in the one inevitably leads to neglect of the other. This recognition is the most important single aspect of democracy, the one real guarantee of human freedom. Majority rule, as such, is no guarantee at all. It is possible to have an utterly totalitarian democracy, in the sense of a state controlled by the will of the majority. We do not know whether a majority of the Chinese would freely vote to keep their present regime, but we do know that if they did their free vote would not make it a free society. Majorities can vote to keep dissenting minorities deprived of their rights. It takes little experience of human nature to see that this is always a possibility. The tyranny of the majority can be more terrible and more permanent and hard to escape from than the tyranny of the dictator who lacks majority support. The American legal sanction protecting those rights which spring from our human dignity is of course the Bill of Rights. We know by a hundred years of race relations that such institutional guarantees, useful as they are, cannot achieve much beyond what the consensus of society demands and supports. Obviously the major purpose of the building up of a consensus is to define and motivate those means by which men, in harmony with their own religious traditions, may bring the practical consensus of society closer to its own ideals, acknowledged as such in its own political institutions.

Dr. Meng's second principle is equality before the law—legal equality. What this means is simple justice, impartial, even-handed justice. "I have loved justice and hated iniquity," we pray in the psalm. God grant we may mean it in some of the harder tests of every day. Even three years ago we might have claimed that this essential minimum could be taken for granted in American society. Such a claim could be difficult to make today. Probably iniquities are not more serious than they were, are in fact rarer, but we have become much more generally aware of them.

Dr. Meng's third principle goes somewhat beyond this legal minimum. It is freedom of choice in all fields. This freedom seems to me to imply a reasonable equality of opportunity. Here responsibility passes from the courts to the market place, the social gathering, the cultural assembly, the Church, the school. Where these institutions are under public control, as for example, in the public school, the law may provide sanctions, but it can do so effectively only where it is supported by some measure of consensus. Surely the building of a social consensus which will willingly recognize this human right to freedom of choice is a task of highest priority for Church and school and family, and for all men of good will. Yet persons sincerely interested in justice will argue about what freedom of choice means in this connection. It is not quite so obvious as the meaning of equality before the law, for instance. Because, of course, one man's freedom of choice does have to balance against another man's right. A man is not free to choose another man's house or another man's wife. Human weakness being what it is, the twilight zones inevitable in making judgments along these lines invite rationalization. What we are obliged to do, I think, is to be aware of this tendency in ourselves and in others, be prepared to face the fact that in uncertainties about whether the right of a minority should, in a given case, yield to the prior rights of the majority, we shall probably tend to take the easy way out—and to see that we don't.

It seems to me that only the genuine desire to serve God in his creatures can guide us in all these contingencies, which is to say only love. To quote Dr. Meng once more: "The pulls and tensions of our social, economic, and political life together in this pluralistic society arise not so much from an absence of theological or philosophical agreement among organized religious groups as they do from the failure of the members of these groups to practice the principles they profess." Social injustice, economic iniquities, and political discriminations result from the failure of persons and not of institutions.

Our society needs a genuine consensus, solid as far as it goes, not merely a pragmatic arrangement designed to discourage mutual murder like Hobbes' *Leviathan*. The consensus is, in itself, a civil one, but it is not merely civil in its basis, in its origin or in its sanctions. It is rooted in the Judeo-Christian tradition which is first of all a religious tradition. A man who is not interested in maintaining the consensus is not only a bad citizen, he is also a bad Catholic or a bad Jew or a bad Protestant. But in the past it is chiefly we who have refused to talk.

And so the desire to bring about one fold and one shepherd is not the only proper reason for the interfaith dialogue, because there is also the need of building up the consensus. Such a basis of agreement is not merely social cement, it is also pre-evangelization. It is a preparation of our society for the full Christian message.

The consensus is necessary for many reasons. Father Murray calls it the "articles of social peace." It is a solid basis for law and social institutions, for the morals of the community, for the relations of men with one another. But it is also a place for genuine religious dialogue to start from. We cannot even disagree constructively unless there is an agreed point of departure. Refusal to talk with those who differ from us can only pull the two sides farther apart, making communications more and more impossible.

Related to but different from the need of communication for consensus is the route of communication by service, by charity, in the Christian idiom. We must show ourselves willing to work with all those who thirst for justice. In other words we must work to implement the consensus, to apply its principles in the real world. And we must not hold out for making our contribution from the ghetto. We must be willing to swim in the full stream.

Even with the staggering changes of the last few years, stemming from the impact of the two Johns, the Pope and the President, this kind of collaboration for justice and charity remains difficult, and at present the sphere of too small a minority. No doubt the civil rights struggle has provided the best evidence of the brotherhood of those who thirst for justice and are willing to make serious sacrifices to achieve it. But the sincere service of men can open ecumenical doors on a thousand other fronts, and it does not involve anything like the risks of ecumenical dialogue on the theological level.

Why then, by and large, are we so slow to take up this challenge? Why, for example, are the graduates of Catholic colleges under-represented in the Peace Corps and in many analogous activities? Here we encounter what I think is one of history's greater ironies, the relationship between Christianity and the more benign side of the Enlightenment. Many Catholics have a mortal fear of and contempt for what, with a unique variety of Pharisaism, they call "do gooders." The group the phrase refers to are usually not militant Protestants. They are secularists more often, with a remarkably strong social conscience, who have ceased to feel deep convictions about anything except human suffering. Their religion is sympathy. They are what Crane Brinton calls the chastened children of the Enlightenment. They know the millenium isn't coming, but they want to do what they can. Given the fact that faith is a gift of God, I have never been able to understand why these people should be regarded with anything but admiration, nor why we should not cooperate with their often very well conceived efforts, provided they do not violate Catholic ethics. Observing that opposition to such a course is so deeply rooted in the consciousness of most Catholics, I have tried hard to determine why. I believe the answer lies in the historic relationship between Christianity and the Enlightenment. By and large U.S. Protestants have ignored the cleavage, but U.S. Catholics have not.

The Enlightenment, in the opinion of Crane Brinton, "is a Child of Christianity." [1] No doubt the validity of this statement must depend in large measure on how one defines the Enlightenment. Few terms are more variously used, but for the purposes of this discussion we may concern ourselves chiefly with the heart of the great eighteenth-century dream, the belief that human life in this world can be brought to perfection by human effort.

Melioristic activism is no stranger to Christian ideology. Yet in the western world of the last two centuries, these two streams of thought, the legacy of the *philosophes* and the traditions of organized Christianity, have been regarded as mutually antagonistic. Much of the history of modern Europe is the story of the conflicts of their votaries, and the deep cleavage between them has still to be adequately bridged. A study of the complex relationship of these two strains in the American ideological heritage suggests that ours has been a historic melting pot for ideas as well as for men. Often the United States has been considered the promised land of the *philosophes,* the world where the dreams of the Enlightenment came true. There is no doubt either that Christianity has been a major factor in American development. Yet here there has been no clear and consistent record of tension between these two ideals.

Certainly reverberations of the perennial controversy

abroad in which the disciples of the Encyclopedists have engaged conservative religious forces have often reached our shores. Americans have sometimes taken sides with more or less enthusiasm, but not so often as they have merely wondered what all the shouting was about. Is it not possible to be both progressive and religious, democratic and orthodox?

American Protestants who were so disposed could tell themselves and each other that the problem in the old world was the Catholic Church, that nations still in thraldom to the obscurantist see of Rome had no choice but ignorance and oppression on the one hand or infidelity to the established church on the other. U.S. Catholics, unwilling to accept this explanation of a situation as mysterious to them as to other Americans, have often been unable to find any answer at all. But at times they have retained a vague uneasiness, a suspicion that the effort to improve human conditions by natural means involved some betrayal of the faith.

Clearly at some point the idea of progress took one path in Europe and another in the Protestant new world. Louis Hartz, in his brilliant study of the American liberal tradition, offered some clue to the nature of this dichotomy. "Despite the European flavor of a Jefferson or a Franklin," he wrote,

> the Americans refused to join in the great Enlightenment enterprise of shattering the Christian concept of sin, replacing it with an unlimited humanism, and then emerging with an earthly paradise as glittering as the heavenly one that had been destroyed.[2]

In fact, with little conscious consideration of the matter and with what looks like instinctive wisdom, the new nation made its great decision: to choose both Christianity and the Enlightenment and decline to find any incompatibility between them.

It is this positive side of the Enlightenment that has always appealed to Americans; it is especially the ideal of human equality. Pressed for a justification of this doctrine, no doubt many of our sturdy ancestors would have referred to the equal brotherhood of the sons of the same Father, would have remarked that all souls are equal in the sight of God. Rooted in such a soil, equalitarian concepts have shown more vitality and permanence than they have enjoyed abroad. In a sense, it has been the pragmatic Americans who were consistent.

Nevertheless there is an inherent incompatibility between the basic Enlightenment tenet of the perfectibility of man and the fundamental Christian dogma of original sin. The line of cleavage so sharply drawn in Europe was not an imaginary one, not so long as the *philosophes* held out for the absolute perfectibility of human nature. With the ideal of progress, in knowledge, in virtue, in the excellence of human institutions, there was no reason for Christians to quarrel. But most minds of the day seem to have seen only a hazy distinction between perfectibility and progress.

In the nature of things the promise of perfection was subject to the test of history. It failed, and today most liberal thought is still little disposed to accept the doctrine of original sin; neither has it retained the pristine hope of human perfectibility. R. H. Tawney spoke from the disillusioning experience of two hundred years when he wrote: "The Age of Reason, as far as the conduct of men in society is concerned, deserves much more than the thirteenth century to be described as the Age of Faith." [3] Crane Brinton referred more recently, with mellow realism, to the phrase I have already quoted, to the "chastened children of the Enlightenment," who no longer look for the millenium. In the form presented by Jacques Barzun, the once controversial concept would present few problems for theologians: "The perfectibility of man does not mean his transfiguration. It means his being given the means to be reasonably decent." [4]

Perhaps then Americans have failed to find incompatibility between the best ideas of the Enlightenment and the Christian tradition simply because there is none. Situated as they have been, away from the vagaries of the new European secularist state and from the Church's inevitable reaction to it, their vision has not been clouded by conflict. The impression which existed in some quarters from the earliest days of our history has continued to be a common one—that democratic institutions are actually dependent on a religious atmosphere for their successful operation. Franklin, deist that he was, contributed cheerfully to every church built in Philadelphia during his residence there. Of the revolutionary leaders, only Paine, the foreigner, was actively anti-religious. Already there seems to have been an intuitive comprehension of the relationship between the old faith and the ideals which the *philosophes* had somehow managed to present as new.

The purveyors of the Common Law who largely wrote our Constitution believed in the rule of law. They knew that a society which ceases to enjoy it must accept the rule of men, with all its fearful possibilities and they may well have suspected that positive law cannot long maintain its position in a philosophical vacuum, in a world which recognizes no ultimates.

The informal and unconscious alliance between the Enlightenment and Protestant Christianity in the early national period had its moments of tension, especially over the French

261

Revolution, but essentially the union held and proved fruitful beyond the dreams of men. This dual inheritance appears in almost every aspect of the American tradition. There are broad possibilities for rewarding study of the interaction of what Arthur Schlesinger calls "these two basic sets of ideas or ideals, the one stemming from the Christian religion and the other from the Declaration of Independence," which have "sustained and refreshed the reform impulse." [5] The question of how completely our political institutions derive from that outgrowth of medieval Christian ideals, the English Common Law, and how far they were inspired by the *philosophes* has been discussed rather widely. The double heritage has been fundamental also in the development of education, in recurrent reform movements, and in the basic structure of our society. At times the two traditions have acted together against inertia and vested interests, as in the abolitionist circles and in the fight for racial equality which is still in progress. The crusading progressives of the early twentieth century surely did not depend on uniform ideological motivation, nor is it likely that Harry Hopkins and John A. Ryan viewed the New Deal in identical philosophical contexts.

The amorphous outlook which has evolved from the synthesis of Protestant Christianity and the Enlightenment has at least the merit of simplifying the challenge to our powers of communication. We are no longer dealing with militant, virulently anti-Catholic Protestantism, or with Voltarian anti-religious attitudes on the part of secularists. We are dealing with a society which more or less consistently holds a Judaeo-Christian moral consensus in theory, and whose best members implement it in practice. These are our brothers; these are the men of our world by the dispensation of the Spirit.

262

With them today the dialogue of action has produced a new phenomenon, a new idiom of genuine communication. No doubt the civil rights crusade is not quite the same thing to the more sophisticated secularist leaders of the NAACP as it is to the Rev. Martin Luther King. But when Dr. Carson Blake and Father Joseph Connolly went to jail together they went for the same reason. They witnessed to a Christian unity which already exists, and perhaps they pointed out to us the most promising of the possible avenues to its final consummation.

References

1. *Ideas and Men* (New York, 1950), p. 377.
2. *The Liberal Tradition in America* (New York, 1955), p. 39.
3. *Religion and the Rise of Capitalism* (New York, 1926), p. 61.
4. *God's Country and Mine* (Boston, 1954), p. 17.
5. *The American as Reformer* (Cambridge, 1950), p. 18.

The End of Innocence

Sister M. Madeleva, c.s.c.

During the last three years we have had what moderns would call, "three great classics on childhood." *To Kill a Mockingbird, Catcher in the Rye,* and *Lord of the Flies.* This, I think, may not be an accident of creative life in America, but in a sense providential of the God "who can write straight with crooked lines." It is an interesting willful resurgence of childhood. There was a whole classical era of writings on childhood, I can remember, sixty years ago. I would say that the formula for the modern *Catcher in the Rye* sixty years ago was, "Nobody loves me; everybody hates me; I'm going out into the garden and eat worms." Now we have *Catcher in the Rye,* which I call a modern classic of regurgitation. I would call the first part of *To Kill a Mockingbird* a modern classic on the age of innocence, and *Lord of the Flies* a modern classic on the end of innocence; this is what Ralph wept over at the end of the book. Here I shall attempt only to skeletonize *Lord of the Flies* and try to state a few of its basic ideas.

The author, William Golding, was born in Cornwall in 1911. He was a scientist at Oxford for two years. At the end of that time he revolted against science and turned to English literature, particularly the Anglo-Saxon period. In

World War II he served in the Royal Navy. In addition to *Lord of the Flies,* he has written *The Inheritors, The Two Deaths of Christopher Martin,* and one volume of poetry. He still has possibilities for a further creative career. His hobbies are interesting. His first hobby is thinking. Next come sailing, classical Greek, archeology. His favorite author is Euripides, and his favorite writer in Anglo-Saxon is the author of *The Battle of Maldon,* who is, of course, unknown.

The theme of *Lord of the Flies* is the defects of society and of human nature. The book establishes the symbolism in nature and the nature of the human personality with its reflection in society. The central symbol and translation of the title *Lord of the Flies* is Beelzebub, the Greek name for the devil, derived from the Hebrew. There are in the book these developments: the decay and the demoralization, the hysteria and the panic that arise from a condition of society which has been almost set up in the age of innocence in a group of children.

These children have been dropped on a tropical island in the Pacific. They are there without any adults at all. They have nothing to guide them, nothing to direct them, except their own humanity, their own childhood, and their own sense of what should be established in order to make life viable as they had known it in England. They were evacuated, theoretically, to preserve them from a third world war, a nuclear war of complete destruction, annihilation perhaps. There comes during this evacuation, in the period of their floundering around to find what to do with themselves without adult direction, a progressive decay among them, demoralization, heightened by hysteria and panic.

The symbolic characterization in the book must be established rather carefully in any analysis of it. Ralph represents civilization, Jack represents anarchy.[1] Piggy, who is asthmatic, has hard work breathing; he's very near-sighted and has had to wear very thick glasses since he was three years old, but he represents the world of ideals and of the intellect. Roger is a sadist who induces cruelty for cruelty's sake. Ralph has the capacity for organization and leadership. Jack, the incipient anarchist, also has the capacity for leadership but with it an appetite for domination, so he cannot subordinate himself to the leadership of anyone else. Simon—little Simon—who's a sort of aborigine, is called a mystic. I think that he was, perhaps, an epileptic. I could substantiate that by one sentence in the book, but even so, it would not argue against the mission of Simon and his significance.

The only adult comes into the book in the form of a dead man whose parachute lands on the island. As it gets entangled in the woods, the parachute blows forth and back. When the children see this strange movement up on the mountainside, they don't know what it is. They call it a "beastie." It terrifies them until little Simon, the mystic, discovers that it is not a beast at all. It's an artificial introduction of civilization upon the island and it bears with it the dead body of civilization in the dead and decaying body of this parachutist.

The matter of the book is characterized by essential cleanness. There isn't a word in it that one cannot read aloud without the slightest embarrassment. It has Greek austerity of style, grim catharsis, classical perfection, and idyllic beauty of setting.

One of the notable excellences of the novel is its use simultaneously of the realistic and the symbolic. I might cite as an example the finding of the conch shell, a symbol of authority. Ralph, who was with Piggy, was pointing into the lagoon. "Something creamy lay among the ferny weeds. 'A stone.' 'No, a shell.'" Ralph took the shell from Piggy, who had grabbed it. "We can use this to call the others. Have a meeting. They'll come when they hear us.'"

"Ralph grasped the idea and hit the shell with air from his diaphragm. Immediately the thing sounded. . . . Ralph found his breath and blew a series of short blasts." Signs of life were visible everywhere along the beach, and boys in groups from every direction on the island began to gather.

Ralph and his party, as they make their way through the hot, dumb sand, are met by the second group of boys. They are dressed as English choristers and are under the leadership of Jack Merridew. As the two groups meet, Jack says, "'We've got to decide about being rescued.'" There was a buzz, and one of the boys says, "'A chief—a chief.'" "'I ought to be chief,'" says Jack, in simple arrogance, "'because I'm chapter chorister and head boy. I can sing C sharp.'"

"'Let's have a vote.' 'Vote for a chief.'" The boys all shouted, "'Ralph, Ralph.'" Jack was chagrined. What would they do with Jack? "'Jack's in charge of the choir. They can be—what do you want them to be?' 'Hunters.' Jack and Ralph smiled at each other with shy liking."

This is the beginning of the organization of the new settlement of boys. They have a signal for authority. Who-ever holds the conch has the right to speak, and Ralph is the chief. He and his group will provide shelter. Jack is the chief of the hunters who will supply food.

We see in the attitudes of the children in this first con-frontation of two groups an instinctive demand for order. Although there is no adult to help them or to hinder them, they recognize that even their liberty cannot exist except under law. Later when there is a repudiation of law, and the conch is smashed, the result is anarchy, despotism, sadism, orgyism, demonism. This happens to these children in the period in which they are waiting for someone to find their island, and to rescue them. Ultimately the naval officer finds them in his British boat.

An effective symbol of the change that takes place in the children is the mask worn by Jack, the leader of the rebels. In its hideousness it effaces his human personal dignity. Again, through graphic realism, Golding describes the symbolic incident.

There was a pool at the end of the river. Jack knelt by it and opened two large leaves which he carried. He had white clay and red clay in these large leaves of foliage, and he mixed them in water. He planned a new face for himself. One cheek and one eye socket he made white. Then over the other half of his face, he rubbed red and slashed with a black bar of charcoal from the right ear across to the left jaw. "He looked with astonishment, no longer at himself, but at an awesome stranger. . . . The mask was a thing on its own, behind which Jack hid, liberated from shame and self-consciousness. . . . He rushed toward the twins. 'Come on. I'll creep up and stab.' The mask compelled the children."

Gradually tensions build up between the two leaders, and one day Piggy tells Ralph that Jack hates him. This happens just before they start on a hunt for a pig.

" 'Jack, that time you went the whole way to the castle rock?' 'Yes.' " Ralph sighed, sensing the rising antagonism, understanding that this was how Jack felt as soon as he ceased to lead. Now it was Ralph's turn to flush, but he spoke despairingly of the new understanding that Piggy had given him. " 'Why do you hate me?' The boys stirred uneasily as though something indecent had been said. The silence lengthened."

I think this is rather interesting. To me it is the climax of the book, whereas the other climax pointed out by Mr. Epstein is one of animality.[2] This is a climax of personality —the open break between the two boys who are the leader and the potential leader, the representative of civilization and the anarchist on the island. Piggy had told Ralph that Jack hated him; that he would abuse Piggy, but if he didn't have Piggy he would abuse Ralph. So Ralph says point blank to Jack, "Why do you hate me?" This one line is so significant to me: "The boys stirred uneasily as though something indecent had been said." In the recognition of the children that this hostility between them and the lack of support of their elected leader was an indecent thing, I concur. There was something beyond indecency. Such recognition stops, perhaps, with childhood.

In the confrontation of little Simon with "the beast" and his discovery that the beast is only a parachute grasped by a dead man, is the symbolic revelation of clear-sighted discernment given to the innocent. Before Simon makes the discovery, however, he has an encounter with the Lord of the Flies in which the symbolism of evil challenged by good is obvious. This mysterious experience Mr. Golding said he did not write, and did not know who wrote it. It just wrote itself.

Just previous to this experience, Simon had witnessed the preparation of "a gift" the boys planned to give to the beast on the mountainside. They had killed and gutted a sow, thrown the offal into the woods, and brought the carcass into the camp to roast it. They put the head of the animal they had tortured on a spike. This was to be their gift. Simon does not participate, but reconnoiters on his own private expedition in the woods nearby. Evade it as he would, the after-image of the obscene sow's head kept returning to him. In fact, it is the flies that swarm around the offal that find Simon. The Lord of the Flies is the sow's head itself. "Gorged, [the flies] alighted by his runnels of sweat and drank. They tickled under his nostrils and played leap-frog on his thighs. They were black and iridescent green and without number; and in front of Simon, the Lord of the Flies hung on his stick and grinned. At last Simon gave up and looked back, saw the white teeth and the dim eyes, the blood, and his gaze was held by the ancient, inescapable recognition. In Simon's right temple a pulse began to beat on the brain.

" 'You are a silly little boy,' said the Lord of the Flies. 'Just an ignorant silly little boy.' Simon moved his swollen tongue, but said nothing. . . . 'There isn't anyone to help you. Only me. And I'm the beast.' [3] Simon's mouth labored, brought forth audible words. 'Pig's head on a stick.' 'Fancy thinking the beast was something you could hunt and kill,' said the head. . . . 'You knew, didn't you? I'm a part of you? Close, Close, close. I'm the reason why it's no go? Why things are as they are?' . . .

'Come now,' said the Lord of the Flies. 'Get back to the others. . . . You know perfectly well you'll only meet me down there—so don't try to escape!'

"Simon's body was arched and stiff. The Lord of the Flies spoke in the voice of a schoolmaster. 'This has gone quite far enough. My poor, misguided child, do you think you know better than I do? . . . I'm warning you. I'm going to get waxy. D'you see? You're not wanted. Understand? We are going to have fun on this island. Understand? We're going to have fun on this island! So don't try it on, my poor misguided boy, or else—' Simon found he was looking into a vast mouth. There was blackness within, a blackness that spread. '—Or else,' said the Lord of the Flies, 'we shall do you. See? Jack and Roger and Maurice and Robert and Bill? See?' Simon was inside the mouth. He fell down and lost consciousness."

Shortly afterward Simon falls asleep. When he awakes he sees the earth close by his cheek and gets to his feet. Painfully, slowly, he begins to climb the mountain. As the wind reaches the top, he sees a flicker of blue material against the brown clouds of a rising storm. Simon sees a humped object sit up suddenly on the top and look down at him. He hides his face and continues to climb. "Then, as the blue material of the parachute collapsed the corpulent figure would bow forward, sighing, and the flies settle once more. . . . The tangle of lines showed him the mechanics of this parody; he examined the white nasal bones, the teeth, the colors of corruption. He saw how pitilessly the layers of rubber and canvas held together the poor body that should be rotting away. . . . He took the lines in his hands; he freed them from the rocks and the figure from the wind's indignity."

When he turned away from the corpse of the parachutist and looked down on the beach, the fire seemed to be out; they had shifted camp away from the sow. "As Simon saw this he turned to the poor broken thing that sat stinking by his side. The beast was harmless and horrible; and the news must reach the others as soon as possible."

He gets down to the beach as Jack and his company are in an orgy of pig-roasting. The fierce thunderstorm is about to break. The children, all masked, all painted with red and black, are naked or half-naked. As part of the pig-roasting ceremony Roger pretends to be the pig, grinning at Jack and charging at him. A circular movement develops. As Roger

272

mimes the terror of the pig, the boys chant savagely, "Kill the beast! Cut his throat! Spill his blood." Soon Roger decides to change his role and become a hunter, leaving the center of the circle empty. "The dark sky was shattered by a blue-white scar. An instant later, the noise was on them like the blow of a gigantic whip. The chant rose a tone in agony. 'Kill the beast! Cut his throat! Spill his blood!' "

As the terror of the storm and the frenzy mount higher, Simon, viewed now as the beast, comes crawling out of the forest. The circle of boys becomes a horseshoe. "The beast" stumbles into it.

" 'Kill the beast! Cut his throat! Spill his blood!' The blue-white scar was constant, the noise unendurable. Simon was crying out something about a dead man on a hill. 'Kill the beast! Cut his throat! Spill his blood! Do him in'. . . .

"The beast was on its knees in the center, its arms folded over its face. It was crying out against the abominable noise something about a body on a hill." Finally struggling forward, Simon breaks the ring. He falls over the steep edge of the rock to the sand by the water. "At once the crowd surged after it, poured down the rock, leapt on to the beast, screamed, struck, bit, tore. There were no words, and no movements but the tearing of teeth and claws.

"Then the clouds opened and there was a great downpour of rain. The heap broke up presently and the boys staggered away. "Even in the rain they could see how small a beast it was, and already its blood was staining the sand."

Now "on the mountain top the parachute filled and moved; the figure slid, rose to its feet, spun, swayed down through a vastness of wet air. . . . The parachute took the figure forward furrowing the lagoon, and bumped it over the reef and out to sea."

When the storm had cleared, "the beast [4] lay huddled on the pale beach and the stain spread inch by inch. . . . The tide swelled in over the rain-pitted sand. . . . The water rose further and dressed Simon's coarse hair with brightness. The line of his cheek silvered, and the turn of his shoulder became sculptured marble. . . . The body lifted a fraction of an inch from the sand, . . . then it turned gently in the water. . . . Simon's dead body moved out toward the open sea." [5]

References

[1] Some critics hold that Ralph represents democracy, and Jack communism.

[2] Mr. Epstein, editor of the paperback Capricorn edition (New York, 1959), thinks the climax is the orgy at the killing of the sow, with its symbolism of sexuality.

[3] This refers not to the parachute beast, but to the sow itself.

[4] "The beast" here is the body of little Simon.

[5] The tape from which the transcription was taken ends abruptly shortly after this, and before Sister Madeleva had completed her commentary. She spoke from the text of the book without a manuscript. Before this volume was edited, Sister Madeleva had died. Since there is no conclusion to the talk, the editors judged it best to represent Sister by this fragment, since it contains much that is of value, and will give readers an insight into *Lord of the Flies*. Sister Madeleva, in addition to her own contribution, has given the views of other critics.

The Pleroma of the Christian

JAMES M. EGAN, O.P.

I hope that the use of pleroma may not seem an affectation; it is not meant to be one. Pleroma is a legitimate English word, with a basic meaning of fullness. To this basic meaning, Greek usage added two others, complement or supplement, and fulfilment. All of these meanings appear in the New Testament a significant number of times; in some cases the ordinary meaning is appropriate. But in Saint John and in Saint Paul the word and its cognates take on specifically Christian meanings. It is these meanings that are of special interest to us.

In Colossians 2:9, we read: "For in him dwells all the fullness of the Godhead bodily, . . ." This is the Pauline way of expressing what John formulated in his prologue in the well known words: "And the Word was made flesh." (1:14) These are the Biblical equivalents of the hypostatic union, the communication of the personal being of the Word to a perfect human nature. In the same letter to the Colossians, 1:19-20, St. Paul says: "For it has pleased God the Father that in him all his fullness should dwell, and that through him he should reconcile to himself all things whether on the earth or in the heavens making peace through the blood of his cross." This is the fullness of grace and redemptive power with which the Father has endowed the humanity of his Son.

It is only by our sharing in this fullness of Christ as man that we can share in the fullness of the Godhead.

That we can and do share in this fullness of the redemptive Christ is clear from the remaining passages in which Paul and also John use pleroma with clear reference to us. In Ephesians 3:19, Paul concludes a beautiful prayer for his readers (and for us): ". . . and to know Christ's love which surpasses knowledge in order that we may be filled unto all the fullness of God." In the following chapter (4:13), we read: ". . . until we all attain to the unity of the faith and of the deeper knowledge of the Son of God to perfect manhood, to the mature measure of the fullness of Christ." There are two phrasings that should be noted in this passage: first "we all," and then "to perfect manhood." Here there is the indication of a communal bond of perfection that finds, perhaps, its most perfect expression in Ephesians 1:22-23: "And all things he made subject under his feet, and him he gave as head over all the Church, which indeed is his body, the completion (pleroma) of him who fills all with all." It is in this context, although without the subtleties of meaning made explicit, that St. John says (1:16): "And of his fullness we have all received."

It is in the perspective of these texts that I intend to speak to you. I feel sure that I have sufficient scholarly support for seeing in the texts, of St. Paul especially, a distinction between the personal pleroma of the Christian and the mystical pleroma.

Finally, two remarks of general import. First, I wish to express my debt to the work of contemporary Scripture scholars, both within and outside the Church. Most specially, I have relied heavily on the Biblical dictionaries, in which the key words and the developing themes of the Word of

God are studied with much profundity and illumination. I must mention two in particular. The first is *Vocabulaire du Théologie Biblique,* produced by a group of French Scripture scholars under the editorship of Xavier Leon-DuFour and published by Les Editions du Cerf in Paris in 1962. The other is *A Theological Word Book of the Bible,* edited by Alan Richardson, and published by Macmillan in 1960. This work has been produced by a group of Protestant Scripture scholars, yet it is, in almost every detail, completely objective.

Secondly, I offer no apology for the general terms of my conferences; they are addressed to an audience of educated Catholics, Catholic "intellectuals," if you will. I am aware that there are pressing needs within every group belonging to the People of God, but I am also convinced that the mission of the Church is to all. Certainly the needs of the poor everywhere in the world are crying out for attention. There must be individuals, many, many individuals, who enter into personal contact with the poor in order to alleviate their suffering. Nevertheless, there is the more challenging task of eliminating it. And as recent Holy Fathers have made inescapably plain, it is to the leaders and in a special way to Catholics who are also leaders that the great task of eliminating poverty must be assigned. And so I feel quite justified in addressing myself to you who are educators, and through you to those whom you will educate, in such a way as to bring out the vocation of the intellectual and bring home to him the burden he bears in relation to all his fellow men because of the great privilege that God has given to him.

I. *The Christian "I" in the World*

Obviously, my subject is inspired by the contemporary concern, the very legitimate concern, with the human person, with the "I," and its relationships to the "thou's". And yet my approach will begin, as you probably expect, from an insight in St. Thomas.

In the five short treatises with which St. Thomas ends his lengthy second part of the *Summa Theologiae,* wherein he is concerned with the return of the creature, the human creature, the rational creature, to God and the complexity of this return, he reflects, as it were, over the whole path he has traced and discusses what the French translation of the *Summa* called simply *La Vie Humaine,* "The Life of Man."

These treatises contain a synthesis of Thomas' reflections on the states of man.

First of all, he notes the bent of man for either contemplation and theoretical understanding or for action and practical realization. Then there follows a discussion of the diversity of offices, dignities, and states that add variety to human life, both in state and church. Considerable attention is given to the states of perfection (for historical reasons that are well known to you); similar discussions are being carried on in our day. Perhaps, an awareness that in Thomas' discussion the emphasis is on the notion of "state" and that "perfection," at least in the context of religious life, should be translated "perfectioning" (*status perfectionis acquirendae*), might sharpen the areas of discussion.

In fact, Thomas's concern with the ratio of *state* is much broader, more profound and significant than with the particular ratio of *state(s) of perfection.* He first seeks a common ratio, that is, a notion that will find verification in many things which are nevertheless distinct. After all we use this word "state" even in English in many, many applications. The question is whether or not there is some basic note or notes to be found in every instance of *state.* In the pursuit of a common ratio of *state,* St. Thomas employs a linguistic analysis which might have been taken from Webster. He says: *"Standing* has two notes: first of all, upright position, therefore, not sitting or reclining; and stationary, not moving." This is clearly the first meaning of *standing;* if someone is standing, he is in an upright position and he is not moving.

In negotiating the metaphorical or analogical transformation of *standing* or *state,* as it is commonly used, to *state* with a special ratio, indicating a permanent condition of the human person, St. Thomas uses a commonplace of human wisdom, namely, that the upright position, which is the first note of the common ratio of *standing,* is the position which is most fitting for man. This of course may be disputed; most of our life is not spent standing. Can we agree, though, that when man is operating most as man, he stands? That, too, could be discussed. At least, standing is a fitting position for man.

Standing is, however, not a permanent position of man. Note, then, how the transposition is made to arrive at the ratio of *state* as a *permanent condition of man.* This is a most important step in the thought of St. Thomas. I feel that for St. Thomas, after the basic existential condition of a human being, namely, that he subsists, the ratio of *state* that he is seeking here, when rightly understood, is for him the deepest, the nakedest, the most existential consideration of human life—of man, of Everyman. In other words, he is looking for a note that expresses an existential mode of being that fits properly and neatly the nature of man. The note Thomas comes up with (and each will have to verify this for himself) is *obligation.*

When we speak of a state of the human person, we find there is one note that is absolutely universal, that is most proper, most fitting to the nature of man, and it is obligation. Now I admit when I first ran across this statement I was a bit startled. Not only does he say "obligation," but he spells it out this way—*obligatio personae hominis* (the obligation of the person of the man). The double genitive signifies a careful thought as well as careful wording. I think this can be translated adequately as "The obligation of Everyman precisely as he is a human person." This is the key to the ratio of *state* in its radical application to human powers.

To avoid a superficial understanding of Thomas's thought here, we must heed the warning of Cajetan. The point Thomas is making is not that obligation is *the* note of "state," but that the ratio of *state of a human person* must include a reference to obligation, and, specifically, *to its presence or absence.* That this is the thought of Thomas is clear from his own explication of the ratio he is looking for. Every man, he says, is either *sui iuris* or *iuris alieni.* In other words, every man is either a complete master of himself, or else he is bound to another. These are universal conditions distinguishing men as human persons. Looked at from this viewpoint, every man is either his own master, or he is bound to another. I think that the profound meaning of this distinction will be missed if we allow ourselves to be taken in by the historical experience of the distinction between free man and slave, although, as a matter of fact, this is a factor in Thomas's analysis. It is only now that we are beginning to realize that no man has the right to subject another man to slavery. We have not fully realized, though we must, that no man has the right to subject another man to conditions, social, economic, political, religious, that are equivalent to slavery. This is our problem today.

The phrase, *iuris alieni,* must be understood precisely as "the right of another." Every obligation of the "I" springs into existence at the presence of the rights of another. There is meaning also in the statement that the "I" has an obligation to its own complexity. The "I" must provide for the rights of its body, by prudent care; the rights of its intellect, by seeking the truth on all levels; the rights of its own greatest natural good, the common good of society, by fulfilling the obligations of citizenship; and the rights of the people of God, by fulfilling the functions of a member of that people. The most unfortunate thing would be to make too great a distinction between these two, e.g., if we were to say that anyone who is *sui iuris* has no obligation, is in no way *iuris alieni.* The *sui iuris* is preserved in its eminence when the "I" freely accepts the servitude that the *iuris alieni* imposes upon it. When the "I" is no longer *sui iuris,* its own, but totally *iuris alieni,* belonging to another to dispose of as he pleases, then the "I" is enslaved (with the one exception, which is an important exception of course, of the supreme dominion of God whose right we all are).

Here we have an analysis of human life in terms of the interrelationships of human beings. We know by faith that the supreme dominion of God is the only ground that makes us masters of ourselves, even though before God we can make no claims. But God Himself is the great Protector of the rights of men—of *all* men.

At the moment it is important to emphasize that the ratio of the human person, in so far as he is *sui iuris,* does not mean that he is free of obligation. It means that he freely accepts all the obligations involved in being a human person, an "I." And there are many. It is only when he is incapable of freely accepting his obligations, when he is compelled to be "the right of another," to act at the dictates of another, or impeded from acting because of situations set up by others, that he is no longer *sui iuris,* but *iuris alieni.*

We have now explored the meaning of the first note of the ratio of "state of a human person," a condition that is most fitting to human nature. We have found such a condition, affecting both existentially and universally the human person, namely, the presence or absence of obligation.

We must now turn to the second note, which will present a special difficulty to our contemporary mentality. In the common ratio of *state,* deriving from "standing," "upright position" came first, second came "not moving." The transposition of this in the ratio of *state of a human person* is stable, permanent, to which we can easily add the connotation of stationary, which belongs literally to "standing." Now, if anything annoys us, it is to be stationary. This is the age of progress. This is the age of forward movement. This is the age of accomplishment. And to designate anything as being stationary, pulls us up a bit. Actually, Thomas's transposition is more flexible. For a person to be in the *state* of freedom or the *state* of servitude, the conditions must be permanent, not transitory, not superficial, permanent and profound. This is an essential note of the ratio of *state.* Does this mean that, in any sense, the note of progress, movement, accomplishment, is ruled out? No, rather, the foundation for them is laid. This, it seems to me, is a crucial problem we have to face—how to put stability into life, how even to institutionalize it somewhat that more may be accomplished. Here, I think, we must all make an option, based on serious reflection on our own experience and on the nature of the universe in which we live. Is there no *stasis* in life, in the world, is there nothing but *dynamis?* Can we accept the extreme existential position that all is change, all is motion, all is progress, but without end? Have we the right to maintain a traditional, and certainly a Christian, position that there are elements of permanency, of stability, that in no way hinder true progress, but rather foster it. Are there elements, especially in human life, that are permanent, stable, sound, profound that actually open up and free us for the greatest conceivable accomplishments in every area of human endeavor? Personally, I opt for such a position and suggest that a further investigation of Thomas's thought on the universal existential conditions of the human person in terms of obligation will give us a glimpse of these possibilities.

The radical states of the human person are then the state of freedom and the state of servitude. And St. Thomas notes that they can be found in both the spiritual and the civil order. At the moment we are concerned primarily, and will be for the most part, with the spiritual, although there will be some consideration of the civil. It may seem to you that we have spent a lot of time getting—where? Is this just a neat Aristotelian formulation, rationalizing a sociological situation of its time, or is this perhaps the core of the much publicized message of some contemporary theologians that Christian man has been established in a state of freedom, impelled only by love, with obligation as an intrusion. True it is originally an Aristotelian formulation. But Thomas transposes it into a realm which Aristotle never dreamed of, and his transposition is dictated by a very interesting and earlier biblical one; the same process went on, not from Aristotle to St. Thomas, but from Hellenic concepts to biblical concepts. He himself points out (*Summa Theol.,* II-II,

q. 183, a.1, & ad 3um, a. 4) that there is servitude to sin or servitude to justice, freedom from sin or freedom from justice. Now this little play of thought is inspired by St. Paul (Romans 6:20-22). Addressing himself to Roman Christians, Paul exhorts them: "For when you were slaves to sin you were free as regards justice. . . . But now set free from sin and become slaves to God, you have your fruit unto sanctification and as your end, life everlasting." In an earlier epistle (I Corinthians 7:20-24), Paul made a similar statement, but in a context that takes into account the present situation of his readers, their religious and sociological situation. "Let every man remain in the calling in which he was called. Was thou a slave when called? Let it not trouble thee. But if thou canst become free, make use of it rather [thus the Confraternity version; the "Chicago" Bible has: "Even if you can gain your freedom, make the most of your present condition instead"]. For a slave who has been called in the Lord, is a freedman of the Lord; just as a freeman who has been called is a slave of Christ. You have been bought with a price, do not become the slaves of men. Brethren, in the state in which he was when called, let every man remain with God." Clearly, Paul is transposing the sociological ratios of *slave* and *freeman* to Christian ratios in the same way that Thomas does, and in virtue of this transposition can then refer to those of his readers who are slaves (sociologically) as freemen of the Lord, to those who are freemen (sociologically) as slaves of Christ. The reason why he can thus play with the words is his awareness of the universal condition of all men in reference to Christ: all are in a state of servitude to sin, hence free from justice, or free from sin and slaves to justice.

Thomas's conclusion is clearly implicit in St. Paul and his

whole preaching: the true state of freedom is freedom from sin and servitude to justice. For only in this state can a man come into possession of all the good proper to him, and fulfill the real meaning of his life which corresponds to the deepest aspirations of his freedom and the gift of justice which is the grace of God. On the other hand, he who freely sins, cannot free himself from the wrath of God or the dominion of Satan. This is true servitude. And these are, in the final analysis, and in the eyes of God, the ultimate existential conditions of each and every human being.

Whence comes St. Paul's insight into the existential condition of men? He is, as he himself says, a Hebrew of the Hebrews, and it is from the history of his own people that he contemplates the human condition. Slavery, as such, was not forbidden in the Old Dispensation; in fact, Hebrew has only one word for slave and servant. It was even forbidden that Israelites become slaves; yet there is a persistent search for liberation, a deep conviction that an Israelite should not be enslaved. Their original experience as the People of God, their birth pangs, as it were, from the slavery of Egypt from which God called them, left an indelible mark on their minds and hearts. They realized that a people of God, a chosen people of God, should never be enslaved. Had not God assured them (Leviticus 25:55), "For to me the Israelites belong as servants. They are servants of mine because I brought them out of the land of Egypt. I, the Lord your God."

Yet even after they had been freed, God, once in a while, let them become enslaved again, either in whole or in part. Always because they were unfaithful, because they had sinned against God. In their minds, the connection between sin and slavery grew as, in parallel, the connection between sin and death grew. This conviction is also Christ's: "Every man who commits a sin is a slave" (John 8:34). The parallels: freedom-slavery, justice-sin, life-death are found throughout the New Testament.

Perhaps even more important is the influence of the suffering servant of Isaiah on the New Testament awareness of the Christ. He emptied himself, says St. Paul (Philippians 2:7), "taking the nature of a slave and being made like unto man." Then, the Father for our sakes "made him who knew nothing of sin to be sin, so that in him we might become the justice of God" (2 Corinthians 5:21). The only way in which Christ could conquer sin and death was by accepting an obligation, freely accepting the obligation laid upon him, the command of the Father, and it was in obedience unto death that he won freedom. Notice, in Leviticus, Yahweh has said: "These are my people—this is my servant—because I led them out of the land of captivity." There is no explicit word of a price paid, a redemption. The lord is the Redeemer. He did redeem Israel from Egypt. I have been wondering whether or not a price was paid for that liberation? Was the price paid by Pharaoh, perhaps, symbolically paying with the life of his first-born son? Exodus does explicitly link these two notions together, in God's message to Pharaoh: "Unless you let Israel, my son, free, you shall lose your son." In our own case, there is no doubt that we are freed at a great price, the price being the life blood of Jesus Christ, who gave his life as a ransom for many.

These, then, are some basic considerations of the situation of the Christian "I" in the face of the world, the Church and God today.

In conclusion, let me summarize what has been the burden

The Christian Intellectual in the World

JAMES M. EGAN, O.P.

First of all, I would like briefly to clarify the meaning of the word "intellectual" as I intend to use it. I have in mind any individual who is a Christian, a Catholic primarily, who has been endowed by God with a considerable talent, and has been provided through his environment, his opportunities, with the necessary means of developing it to the extent that his concerns and his whole lifework are largely in the sphere of what we mean by intellectual activity. However, I also wish to keep in mind all those who, through ability and education, should have a deep appreciation of the intellectual values of life, all those who are convinced that there is a unique principle in man, and that this unique principle is his intellect, his capacity to abstract, to universalize, to penetrate the intelligibility of things and at the same time to recognize irrationality when he runs across it. More proximately, of course, I have ourselves in mind, in so far as we are engaged in educational activities on the college level and are in a unique relationship to our students.

Hence, we shall be concerned with the formal apostolate of the intellectual, particularly in the college. I do not need to insist that there is such an apostolate—an apostolate of truth, an apostolate of the intellect, an apostolate of human achievements and human aspirations.

What, then, is asked of the intellectual? And particularly of the Catholic intellectual? I think it is important to realize that what is asked of the intellectual is precisely what is asked of each and every Catholic, at this time, in this place, in this Church of ours. And what is that?

Let us place before our imagination a member of the Church of Christ, one who is responsive to his full obligation as a baptized, confirmed member of the people of God. To the best of his ability, he embraces the concerns of the Church herself, the concerns which, thanks to the initiative of Pope John XXIII, have been made clearer to all of us; this incredible optimist has challenged all of us to a breathless adventure, a stupendous task. He issued this challenge to every one of us with the whole world looking on, thank God. And thank God, again, Pope Paul VI has made it quite clear that he at least intends to take up this challenge of his great predecessor. But then what is this task? It is manifold because each and every baptized and confirmed member lives in a society that is religiously pluralistic, and to a great extent, secularistic, even atheistic. He is a person who is living on the brink of one world in which East and West must come face to face, interpenetrate and learn to know each other and to live together. Hence, the task that Pope John foresaw was fourfold. The first, and undoubtedly the essential task, is to reform the Church itself. This means that everything in the Church must be subjected to investigation and to fearless criticism. Subjected to criticism must be our ways of thinking and acting, our ways of praying and worshipping, our ways of commanding and obeying, and countless other aspects of our lives as Catholics, including our commitment or our lack of commitment to the problems that the world is facing today. This in itself is an enormous task, requiring the generous cooperation of absolutely every member of the people of God.

Pope John felt that this was a preliminary task, because, as it is seriously undertaken, he realized the effect it would have on countless others who glory in the name of Christian, all those in the great Christian tradition who unfortunately have been separated from us for centuries, the great Orthodox Patriarchates and their associated churches, and those closer to us perhaps in one way, yet not nearly as sympathetic and understanding, the great body of non-Catholic Christians. It was Pius XII himself who admitted that what was going on among these Christian bodies, these separated brethren of ours, in their deep thirst for the unity that Christ wanted His Church to have, could be explained only as a moving of the Spirit of God himself. So each of us, as members of the Church of Christ, must become aware of our responsibility in our daily social, economic, political and even prudently religious contacts, to grow in understanding, respect, and love for all Christians.

Of deep concern to the Holy Father was the secular world. The world has found in religion either no inspiration or a positive obstacle to the true greatness of man. This is the world which we and our students, as college graduates, as cultured intellectuals, come into constant contact with. This is the world that must be the object of our deepest concern. Yet out beyond this world, which has contributed so much to making us what we are, are the vast worlds of Mohammedanism, of Hinduism, and of Buddhism, and perhaps other isms, too. John never explicitly, so far as I know, expressed a desire that we make contact with these worlds, although he knew them. Paul VI, shortly after he became Holy Father, did recall to our minds these people who are struggling to emerge from a past and a civilization, which is ancient, revered, precious, rich, and yet has not always stressed the human values, has not always been concerned with human prosperity, with freedom, with intellectual inquiry, with the complete dignity of each human person.

There are vast stirrings in this world, and I do not hesitate to say, as a number of others have said, that the destiny of this one world of ours will depend to a great extent on what happens to these people.

I should like now to communicate to you the conviction I have that the most important effort of the Catholic intellectual, precisely as intellectual, should be devoted to the secular world: that thereby he will also open the way for the most fruitful communication with the Eastern world.

First let me say something of the complex problem the emerging peoples, especially with their religious aspirations, present to us, who are Westerners, Roman Catholics, with a totally different environment and culture. It is my opinion that if the Church becomes seriously and acutely aware of her missionary apostolate to the whole world (and there is more and more evidence that she is becoming so aware), she will see to it that a considerable number of her theologians and scholars, clerical, religious, and lay, devote time and attention to these great religious sectors of mankind. This certainly is a suggestion of Pope Paul himself. And it is undoubtedly essential that we get to know and understand and appreciate the values in their religious traditions. The word of God, which we have received from the Hebrews, which passed through the refinements of Hellenic thought freely used by the fathers of the Church and the Councils, has become so much a part of us that we feel confident the deep meaning of the word of God will have something to say to those of the Oriental religions; yet this is something we must search out and make clear to ourselves first of all.

But there is another aspect, I believe, of this problem of the interrelationship of the East and the West. It is something that has been pointed out by a number of observers who are intimately acquainted with what has been going on in the countries where these religions are dominant. They point out, first of all, that the great religions of Asia and Africa, unlike Judaism or Christianity, have never been subjected to thorough historical criticism. While such criticism might not weaken the deep religious insights of these religions, it might well destroy some of the mythical power they possess for the ordinary believer. Besides, these observers have a feeling that many of the intellectuals and the political leaders are no longer convinced of the truth of their religions. It seems fairly obvious that in the case of Mohammedanism and Bhuddism, and perhaps to a certain extent even in Hinduism, the emphasis on them in the present day, the revival they seem to be undergoing, is intimately linked with the rising nationalism of the peoples of Africa and Asia.

Hence, we of the West are faced with a very special problem. We know that these peoples are looking to us. They do not always trust us. They do not always admire us. They are certainly not eager to embrace the American way of life, the Western view of life, yet they are eager to take from us something that is uniquely ours. And what is this? It is our scientific understanding, our technological know-how. These are the things that they want. Besides they are somewhat influenced, I guess, by our political and social institutions. Again we realize that most of them are far from adopting a completely democratic form of life. It will be principally on the level of scientific penetration and technological know-how that the West will, in the foreseeable future, be influencing the East. It is this very eager acceptation of our science and technology that makes me wonder whether or not the age-old religious views of these nations will be able to survive, much less to dominate and to vivify their lives. Are these people going to turn aside from their traditional religious attitudes and become sheer materialists, eager only for the good things of this life? If this insight is right, then it seems to me that, as Catholic intellectuals, we might very well be able to accomplish two ends at one and the same time.

I have said that we must be deeply concerned about the secularistic and even atheistic trends of thought in the lives of many of our Western contemporaries. The underpinning of this is, to a great extent, the fascination of science—its great accomplishments, its incredible promises for the future.

However, there is considerable tension in our own Western world between the scientific approach and the humanistic approach, and I think here that I am perhaps repeating something that Dr. Thomson has already said. The scientist-novelist, C. P. Snow, has lifted a loud voice of warning. One of his latest reflections on the problem appeared some time last year in the literary supplement of the London *Times*, which recently has been printed in book form with his earlier contributions. Aldous Huxley has made his contribution in a recently published volume on science and literature. *Life*, in another of its fine editorials, quotes an Anglican Bishop to the effect that Western man does not add to the dialogue of the world by being less Western but rather adds to it by giving to it the best he is and has. And I think I can add that the full resources necessary to give to all, and particularly to the Eastern world, the best that we have and are

—these resources are in the hands of the Catholic intellectual.

They must be employed, though, with no air of "triumphalism," but, if I may be permitted an equally crude neologism, a deep sense of "servantism," the spirit so perfectly manifested by Pope John. The editors of *Life* also referred to a notable speech by the profoundly thoughtful Dr. Charles Malik, in which he warned against adding to the materialist delusion of the emerging people, and hardening our own. These wonderful techniques and perfections, said Dr. Malik, are the creations of a whole, distinctive outlook on things: the spirit, namely, of openness to truth, humble submission to facts; the spirit of infinite precision and care of faithful, unbroken transmission from man to man and generation to generation; the spirit of cooperation and law, which believes in free criticism and seeks scientific laws for their own sake, which ever seek out the better and the more true. Even the late President Kennedy made the quotation of the day in the New York *Times,* on October 27, 1963, with these words: "When power leads men toward arrogance, poetry reminds him of his limitations. When power narrows the areas of man's concern, poetry reminds him of the richness and the diversity of his existence. When power corrupts, poetry cleanses."

What does all this mean then for us? Particularly as members of a college community, whether priests, religious, or laity. As Catholic cultured intellectuals, we must never allow ourselves to be drawn either into partisan approval of science as the dominating and domineering element in our future, or of the pretension of the poets and artists to be the only prophets of our day. It is true that both scientists and artists are facing up to the agonizing problems of our time with perhaps much greater courage and frankness than are the philosophers and the theologians, especially the Catholic philosophers and theologians. So while we welcome and join in the great movements that dominate scientific research and artistic accomplishment, we also have to remember that in all things there is an element of objective truth, of universally valid truth, of mysterious truth that shines directly from God's own truth as revealed to us in and by his word. As Catholic intellectuals, this must be our contribution to both the religious and secular world of the West, a deep conviction, an enthusiastic defense of the universal aspects of all reality.

Still, because we are human, and hence limited in our ways of knowing, we can never rest satisfied simply with the universal aspects of reality. We must extend our knowledge and strengthen our insights by facing up to reality in all its concreteness, multiplicity, contingency, irrationality, mystery. Holding on to the guidelines of a perennial philosophy and divine revelation, we must plunge into the maelstrom of human knowing, experiencing and living. Some of us must stand together with the natural scientists in their eager search into the depths and heights of the cosmos and the intriguing phenomena of life. Some of us must accompany the psychologists and the psychiatrists in their attempt to penetrate more deeply into the complexities of human emotion and human conduct. We must be among the social scientists, the historians, the economists, because they too are engaged in the complexity of man's social living. Some of us also, if I may say so, must agonize with the artists and the poets, face up as courageously as many of them do to the seeming absurdity of human life, yet be able to see through it all the hopeful rays of God's loving care.

And not only must we do this ourselves, but we must do it together with our students. Our young people should be assured that they have the right to their contact with everything that is going on, in science, art, philosophy, and theology, anywhere. We can give them the assurance that every man in the sincere pursuit of truth on every level has the right to run the risk of falling into error. He is free to think, to investigate, to do anything, provided he accepts his final obligation to truth. He does not have the right to cling to error, when in the considered and unhindered judgment of his peers (or, in very, very rare cases, in an infallible and openly considered judgment of the Church), it is error. This, I hope, throws some light on the question that every once in a while is agitated among us, whether or not error has rights. Some point out that error is not a person and therefore cannot have rights, which is good. Obviously, this is not putting the problem in the right way. The point is whether or not a person has a right to cling to error. He certainly, as I say, has the right to run the risk of error; he may well fall into error. All men have that right, that possibility. But he has no right to cling to it, and this is not something which is peculiarly Christian, Catholic. Some of you may have read Snow's novel, *The Search,* which is a presentation of the tremendous pressures put on scientific researchers in our days. And if you remember the terrible climax of the whole thing, the man who had climbed up and up through hard work, who was finally in a position to get a very important appointment, was suddenly destroyed. Why? Because he allowed a certain important piece of research—a piece of research in which there was an error—to come out with his approval, although it was done by an assistant. One suspects that the harshness of the consequences in this case was due to the large research grant that was at stake. Certainly, the normal attitude is not to condemn the man who errs, unless he clings to his error. Unfortunately, up to very recently, the attitude of many in the Church was to suppress anything that smacked of the "unorthodox" before it could be brought out in print. The case of Teilhard de Chardin is a sad witness to this policy. Fortunately, there are signs that we are learning that it is as useless to try to suppress ideas we do not like as to boycott movies that supposedly are dangerous. We must hope that such a trend will predominate in the future. The great ideas, the ingenious ideas, the dangerous ideas, the unorthodox ideas will be made available for discussion (among peers, one hopes, although the press makes this difficult) and if they are proven erroneous, the author will accept the verdict, or at least will rigorously review his whole position.

I would like to conclude with a few reflections on what might be called the passion of the Catholic intellectual today. There is no reason to expect that the intellectual can escape the fellowship of the sufferings of Christ or that his greatest pain should be in the area of his intellectual activities. He is a member of a Church (Christ's Church, he is convinced) which for the last few centuries has clung to careful, orthodox ways of thinking, while the secular world has been utterly fearless in its search for knowledge. The lines of communication between these two important spheres have broken down long ago; the developments of the last three centuries have, with some notable exceptions, been outside the Church and, in many cases, used against the Church, so that she has been on the defensive. Such a situation cannot continue and there are many members of the Church who do not intend to let it continue. They are in continuous contact, conversation, communication with all the currents of contemporary thought and achievement. Can they yet feel free? Can they throw off the feeling that there is someone looking over their shoulder? Is there no one in some hidden office waiting to get hold of their manuscript or published work, to go over it with a fine-tooth comb, and come up with all sorts of errors and heresies? The struggle for intellectual freedom within the Church has been engaged, but it has not been won, or, at least, we are not yet sure that it has been won. There may be still much unjust suffering that the intellectual must bear.

There are, however, ways of not undergoing this passion. The first is that of the whiner. There are too many whiners among those who look upon themselves as intellectuals. They are in print, they are on the lecture platforms. They are not satisfied with anybody except themselves. They are continuously complaining, mostly about the hierarchy (above all Pope Paul), about priests and religious; it is rare that they complain about the appalling apathy of the laity to the efforts of truly progressive bishops and priests and religious.

The second way is that of the whisperers, or perhaps, the mimeographers. These are the ones who are very free, audacious even, in their expressions, in hotel rooms during conventions, in the cloister of their classrooms, or in the correspondence which they mimeograph and distribute to a coterie of like-minded whisperers. In these communications, anything goes (at times, it seems, everything is going), but nothing is submitted to criticism. This, I submit, is intellectual cowardice. In fact, such tactics only serve to strengthen any obscurantist attitude on the part of those in authority.

Finally, there is the way of the rebellious, the dissident. There are some with deep Catholic roots, excellent Catholic training, extremely competent in certain intellectual areas, who are asking themselves (agonizingly, I admit) whether they can in conscience remain in the Church. I must confess that I cannot accept such agony as authentic. If the Fathers of Vatican II had shut their minds to the papers and conferences of their "periti," if in their voting the proportions were reversed, then there might be some excuse for agony. Yet even then they would have to answer the question, which they certainly cannot escape answering now: "To whom will you go? Is your loyalty to God and his Christ, is your loyalty to truth served by throwing over your allegiance to the Church of Christ, no matter how difficult it may be, no matter how much suffering it may impose upon you for the moment?" This is the price that the intellectual, the educated Catholic, must pay for the vast transformation that we hope will take place in this Church of ours. Whining, whispering, rebelling are not the answer. These were not the answer of Cardinal Newman or of Teilhard de Chardin. Were they then benighted fools?

The task is enormous. If we are to follow the inspiration of John, the burden will become greater. Even if we are freed of all unjust suspicion and obscurantist restraint, we shall be freed only to face the agony of the world. In the meantime, it might help to realize that the seemingly suspicious, the obscurantists, are suffering an agony of their own. There is only one way for all of us to go—the way of love and loyalty; by love for every member of Christ's mystical body, for each one, in whatsoever way he is sharing the fellowship of Christ's sufferings; loyalty to God, to Christ and to the Church. The order of the last phrase is intentional. In the past, perhaps, we have placed loyalty to the Church first of all, and have not dared to ask whether certain aspects of the Church are not a betrayal of God and Our Lord. The human element in the Church must always stand under the judgment of God and of the Scriptures.

To return now to our own special situation—college teachers in a Catholic college community. There should be in the whole college community an awareness of the urgency of the tasks that we have outlined in this conference, but more, an awareness of the relevance of what we, as Catholics, possess to the accomplishment of these tasks. There is no subject in the curriculum that should be divorced from its relevancy. It need not be an immediate, practical relevancy. If we are convinced that truth, precisely as the grasp of the universal aspects of all things, of order in reality, has relevancy, if we think that the contemplative, the speculative approach to reality has relevancy, then let us prove it. Let us prove it, first of all, in our own lives; let it be communicated to our students, not by exhortations, but by the inescapable evidence of our ways of operating. In this way, we will be able to establish a community that is religiously vital, socially vital, but especially, intellectually vital.

There Has Never Been a Red-haired Saint

Dr. Barry Ulanov

The Russians have a proverb: There has never been a red-haired saint. That's a startling idea. It is true? If it is, all of you who are red-haired should be most unhappy—or challenged. Still, that is my text: There has never been a red-haired saint.

Most people accept the time and place in which they live, unquestioningly. They accept its atmosphere, its way of life, its way of thought, its prejudices, pre-suppositions and values. We may criticize our time at times, we may lament some things about it, bitterly. Some of us may subject it to scrutiny of the most systematically destructive kind, but ultimately, on the whole, we accept what we have inherited, the world into which we are born. We accept and use its language, its clothing, its architecture—even if, as usual, it is not really ours but that of the age before ours. We may rebel against the world and try to change it, but rebellion rarely deals seriously with such things as language, clothing, or architecture, even where rebellion is a concerted attack on a civilization.

No matter how much the communists, for example, attempt to unseat a capitalist economy, they accept their inherited language, their inherited clothing; like us, they accept the architecture, one or two ages removed from them, which they find on their streets. They accept the food, they accept the drink which has come down to them, and all the more, the more successful they are. It is ironic that the communists, who think they are so revolutionary, have been, in fact, more unquestioningly accepting of these things than any other contemporary society. Their arts are all conducted in inherited forms. Their diplomats now wear the best capitalist clothing that communist money can buy. They have been importing Paris design to Moscow.

Rebellion rarely extends to these things. I think this is worthy of close scrutiny on our part.

If the Christian accepts the forms of his age just as easily as other people do, if he accepts its clothing, in the deepest sense of that word and all it signifies, if he becomes completely the product of his own age, can he remain a Christian? If he accepts the creeds, the small creeds, how easy will it be for him to hold on to his large creed? If he accepts the value judgments of a particular time and place, will he also remember the other value judgments which transcend time and place? Isn't it, some of the time, a little like saying "If Baal is the local deity, then he is my God"? We know we must avoid doing that. We have to fight against this attitude in the modern era, and many of us have done so successfully; the Church of Silence is eloquent in its examples of those who will not accept Baal.

There are others, however, who do accept local gods, and among them may be ourselves. It may be that we are so much the product of our time that we don't even realize we are. We may have become too absorbed in it, as some Christians in previous times and places have been absorbed into the trivia of their time, so that we are caught up in things which really are of no importance at all—except in so far as they seduce us from the center of our lives and make us forget our real tradition. What real tradition? The Christian humanist tradition, which is based on text after text, on doctrine after doctrine, on life after life, on saint after saint, all in eccentric rebellion against the easy falling into the concentric spheres of a self-centered, self-satisfied society.

The saints' eccentricity is rarely destructive. Theirs is never a simple rebellion. They are not red-headed hot heads. If saints do destroy anything, it is only so that their destruction may fulfill, that they may remind us of the fact that in every society, in every age, there is a continual and concerted attack on being which must be attacked in turn, an attack on being which comes from accepting existence uncritically and shallowly, and thus not really accepting its essence at all.

Aware of how easy and dangerous it is to accept the superficialities of their time, some Christians turn their attack on the time itself, eager somehow to return to the glories, real or imagined, of the Christian past. But if they do that, then how can they work effectively in their own time? Can they be deeply aware of the glories of past times and still remain very much part of their own time? We know we must use the tools that are ours; we have no others. We cannot travel by another kind of transportation than that which is available to us; we cannot become figures in a medieval tapestry; we cannot move back onto horses. We are stuck, for now at least, with the airplane and the automobile.

How, then, does the Christian make full sense of his own time, without succumbing to the limitations of his own time? We answer quickly: by using the things of his time as tools,

305

as means, not as ends in themselves. That is obvious, we say. But *how* he uses the tools is never obvious, really. He must use them with the attitudes that come out of the Christian humanist tradition. He must use the tools at his disposal with an understanding of the symbolic arts which the Christian humanists have tried to teach us. He must never be content simply to accept, or to reject on the surface level. He must never become a thoughtlessly submissive slave to the value judgments of his own time, or of any other time. He must continually examine and use those things which he has received, use them as Augustine says, use them to such purpose that he may learn to enjoy all that he really is and all that he can become as the result of a full confrontation with himself and with his world, and as full a confrontation as he is allowed of God.

This means that he can never say, in a kind of airy dismissal, "Oh, I cannot accept modern art. I cannot bear modern music. I can't stand modern architecture." These things represent his time, the good and the bad of his time, and as St. Paul said, "the acceptable time is now." He must accept these things as he accepts the time itself, critically, thoughtfully, for many purposes, not the least of them contemplative. The arts represent his time, and in some ways magnificently. Every art in every time offers some magnificences—even the worst of Rococo, or the lowest moment at the end of the nineteenth century; these moments, too, were magnificent when they were used with genius by artists. There are ideas in every time, in every movement, which Christians can, and must, make use of. But the selectivity, the recognition of how to make these ideas, these paints, these textures, these bricks, this vocabulary, these accidentals signify something larger—to do this takes genius, and to

306

appreciate it takes training. It takes training in the Christian humanist tradition of qualified acceptance.

Every single era has had a major contribution to make to mankind. I think this becomes particularly clear to us whenever a major Christian thinker works in a particular time with full use of the tools at his disposal. There is not a period in poetry, there is not a moment in music, or in painting, or in architecture, that cannot be shown, I think, to have given something fresh and valid and lasting to the Christian tradition, if only by enlarging our understanding of our world and its resources. You may not find all eras equally attractive. You may not find each of the same stature as the others. But you cannot name a single period in which there was nothing of quality, not since the time of our Lord—not since the beginning of time, really, but since the coming of Christ our Lord on earth, it seems to me the records have been more complete and the achievement larger, too.

There is no break. The line of continuity is extraordinary, right up to our own day. Turn to the end of the nineteenth century, which is for many the very rock bottom. When else, some say, have men been so totally uninspired? When, some say, was there ever such an absence, such a privation, of quality—and yet did we not get art of quality even then? And Christian art. That is when Paul Claudel became a Christian poet. That is when César Franck sat in a church in Paris, improvising his way, it seems to me, right into the heart of things and making it possible for us to understand how a man can improvise, like a jazz musician, and let the spontaneity of the moment combine with a lifetime of prayer to make music of the highest quality. Both Claudel and Franck, like Yeats, like Strindberg, like Munch, like Mahler, spoke entirely in the accents of their own time. They had no others.

It was at the end of the nineteenth century that Vincent Van Gogh worshipped God and developed three or four religious paintings of overwhelming beauty, penetrating mystery in his terrible mad loneliness, and making it more accessible to all of us. One can go on. There is not a moment when the most dross-filled time would not yield its gold and silver to those to whom time is always alive, to those to whom the investigation of mysteries is never dull, never empty, never a cliché-ridden or shallow activity.

God help us if we allow this to happen, if we allow ourselves to take the center of creation and reduce it to mere peripheral ornament. Huysmans said that the devil, the lord of ugliness, had been permitted to take possession of the architecture and ornaments of Lourdes. After my visit to Lourdes, I felt the same way. And yet in Lourdes, there are groups of people who look like the emaciated figures in some modern paintings, eviscerating examples of suffering and devotion, of solicitude and love, and all around Lourdes, despite its shoddiness, there is a great pulsing excitement and a profound sense of something larger and better, which usually comes only when people go away from a place and produce their poetry, their books, their paintings, their music in solitude, but at Lourdes it comes from the crowds themselves, from people at their last-ditch devoirs, from a tumultuous and endlessly touching mixture of faith and misery. We must recognize there and everywhere, as Huysmans did, that all things, good and bad, do indeed minister to a divine purpose and therefore minister to each other—events, personalities, colors, textures, sounds, metaphors, even literal descriptions of the world around us at its most disagreeable.

The opening line of *Le Soulier de Satin* of Claudel is, it seems to me, apposite: "The gestures are different, but it's the same wind that blows." In our own time there are so many examples—I can only just touch on them, but I do want to touch on them. It seems to me we must, even if there is just time for fragments, for bits and pieces.

I think of the surrealist poet, for instance, Max Jacob, a convert, a Jew and a superb poet. When he was baptized, Pablo Picasso acted as his godfather. Jacob was killed in a concentration camp in 1942. He was a man of holy laughter —there is no man more full of it. Some day people will rediscover Jacob and will see in his poetry that he was taking the nonsense of surrealism, sometimes very engaging nonsense, deliberately formed as nonsense, and giving it further structure, meaning, purpose, and doing so long before he entered the Church because his laughter was from the heart and he was capable of seeing things in true perspective, without pretentiousness, in the great sane proportions of a true wit.

Let me give you another example, in some ways more obvious. St. Cecelia's in Cologne was a church reduced to rubble in the Second World War. Nothing was left but a thirteenth-century statue of Our Lady. The church was stone. The statue was wood. The stone was destroyed and the wood remained, untouched, unharmed, not a splinter lost. The pastor had no money after the war, but he wanted to use his church. So he constructed a small twentieth-century chapel out of some of the smashed stones, and used one large one as an altar base for the thirteenth-century statue. This was St. Cecelia's church, so he made his windows musical windows, with stained glass abstractions of music instruments. But he wanted the Germans to remember that war is a destructive and terrible thing, a discordant thing, so he put below the small stained glass musical window, other windows of clear glass so that people at Mass would see through them out to the wall of rubble surrounding the chapel—which he left there, instead of having it cleared away—and thus be reminded, be reminded over and over again, of the rubble of their own society.

But none of this moves me as much as what he did to get beauty inside. This is God's house. And the pastor has no money. He must have some kind of light. From the ceiling where he had his outlet, he strung six, eight, ten wires—just simple naked wires, each ending in an exposed bulb. He pulled the wires this way and that way, until finally he had a handsome chandelier of looped wires and naked bulbs, all exposed, all without any ornamental enhancement, just as simple, as honest, as can be, and perfectly constructed, exquisitely balanced. To me this is the Christian humanist tradition. This is what it is about. This is how you do it: by seeing the beauty that can be found in using modern materials, with simplicity and honesty. Creating something beautiful not by disguising reality but by revealing it, not by imitating a style of the past but by making a new and unpretentious style out of the ingredients of the present.

When Claudel talks about the churches built in the middle of the nineteenth century which he says have "the interest of a melancholy and guilty confession," he explains negatively what I am trying to say positively: "Their ugliness is the exterior manifestation," he says, "of all our faults, weakness, indigence, timidity in faith and emotion, dryness of heart, contempt for the supernatural, the dominance of conventions and formulas, the exaggeration of individualized and disordered devotions, worldly luxury, avarice, haughtiness, peevishness, pharisaism, and bombast." As a list of nouns, even in translation, that is pretty good. It is worth reading aloud, just to show one how to make words sound.

We have to do what Claudel suggests by negation. We must no longer be peevish, no longer worry about our poverty; as long as we have imagination we are rich. Let us give up the conventions, cease to accept the ugliness and phony ostentation we have inherited, and look to the only inheritance that is permanent, that is always fresh.

I think it is worth repeating in different words what we have heard about the Church's youth because this is, it seems to me, what the Church asks of its thinkers, of its artists, and of its saints. You remember those marvelous lines from Newman's sermon on the second spring: "Yes, my Fathers and Brothers, and if it be God's blessed will, not Saints alone, not Doctors only, not Preachers only shall be ours—but Martyrs, too, shall re-consecrate the soil to God. We know not what is before us, ere we win our own." But this is only the roll call, because "we are engaged in a great, a joyful work," he says, if "the truth is to be spread to any wide extent among this people . . . . how can we hope that trial and trouble shall not accompany its going forth?" The world grows older but the Church is ever young. Trials are nothing. They are no real problems. They are simply the terms of our existence, the textures of our humanity. We need not worry about them and we need not even worry about the conventions which dictate that we shall forever and forever reestablish the Gothic and the Romanesque, and not simply in Church buildings, but in sermons, in our language and in our feeble thought.

Are we incapable of a confidence which is endless, a bold confidence bred of gladness, of joy, of hope, of a certainty that there will be a third spring and a fourth and a thousandth? Can we no longer believe that our prayers will lead wherever we want them to lead, or wherever God wants them to lead? For if we want them to lead where God wants them to lead, there obviously will be no problem. That means, equally obviously, that we must accept ourselves as we find ourselves, in this world, in this time, in this setting, with its and with our imperfections and potentialities, and go on from *here*.

There are people who can guide us, people who will keep us alive in our true tradition, people who will keep us alive to the eternal freshness of that tradition. We must pay attention to them, even if sometimes this means gluing our heads to pages that do not open up quickly or easily. We must read, for example, the work of David Jones, an extraordinary modern poet who started as a water-color artist. He is a Welshman, which means that he is almost unintelligible by birth. And whatever he did not get at birth he has added by hard work, so that now he is really unintelligible. He has written two long poems, book-length poems, *In Parenthesis* and *The Anathemata*—the meaning of the second title, which comes from the Greek, "the devoted things." Jones is a great craftsman. You may have seen some of his work as a letterer, or his illustration for the chapbook edition of T. S. Eliot's Christmas poem, "The Cultivation of Christmas Trees." His drawings and lettering say much, simply, clearly, handsomely. But these poems, these special poems, how much more they say, though not at all simply or clearly. You have to fool yourself into thinking you can understand them until suddenly, by the unction which is ours, I think, when we deal with this kind of art receptively, we do develop something, some small perception, and we do find our way.

In Parenthesis is about the First World War, and it is

comparatively lucid. *The Anathemata* is what it says it is—
about the devoted things, the things of this world, this world,
all worlds. Jones gets his material from Welsh poetry of the
middle ages, especially from the collection of tales called
The Mabinogion. He gets it from the Latin of the Mass and
from the inherited tradition of Britain, the Arthurian legend.
And I think nobody in five hundred or a thousand years,
perhaps, has made so much of the Latin of the Mass as he has
in *The Anathemata.* How those words leap at one on the
page! And if you have trouble and cannot read him in
sequence, that is perfectly all right, too. You don't always
sit down and simply read the Mass through, in sequence, even
in English, even when you are yourself participating in it.
There is something larger involved.

The secret of Jones is that there is an inner order which
one can somehow get at in his great poem, an order of living,
an order of loving, an order of learning, of meditating and
contemplating, an order of artifacting and of artificing, reflected in the order of a work of art. It is an order which is
not disturbed by the calculated disorder which is imposed
over all. It is the same thing you will find in Olivier Messiaen's magnificent music for the organ, his meditations on
the *Nativity,* his *Visions of the Amen,* or his *Ascension* suite.
It is what you will find in the paintings of Alfred Manessier,
whose Christian paintings date, apparently, from the effect
of a Trappist retreat, a series of quiet conversations inter-
spersed with silent private meditations in France in the early
40's, where he discovered for himself a position which he has
called, marvelously well, I think, tragic optimism. Rejecting
the facile optimism of the twentieth century at its most
hedonistic and materialistic, and rejecting with equal certainty and ruthlessness that despairing pessimism which can

never be Christian because despair means lack of hope, Manessier sees the tragedy of man but recognizes too where man's potentialities may lead, to what apotheosis the blessed trivia of this world may be raised.

If you will look at Manessier's paintings you may notice always, over everything, a cruciform structure, whether the painting is sunny or somber, because Manessier takes the world as it is. He is a Christian; he is a Christian humanist. He takes man for what he is and where he is and he recognizes where he is: always within the shadow of the cross. So he uses the symbols of the past as well as the present, the mysteries of the Church as well as the mysteries of the world around us. This is really what I am trying to make clear. We must take the world as it is but recognize that part of what is, is what was, as well as what may be, the making actual not only of what *is* potential but of what *was* potential and what *will be* potential. Both the past and the future are always part of the Christian's present.

There are fearful energies around us, always ready to be translated into words and into actions. We should never be at a loss for words or actions. We have so much material to use. We have the wonders of creation, seen in depth by men who have seen it and who have exclaimed, "Oh, the depth of the riches!" and have then shown some of the depth to us. We have the works of those who have experienced the solaces of redemption and the unveilings of revelation themselves, all of which is more startling than anything ever painted by anybody, more stunning than anything described by anybody, and farther removed from our common prosaic vocabulary than any of us dreams. Redemption is more shocking and stranger than any sounds ever put together by a twelve-tone or electronic composer. Revelation is much bolder than Schoenberg and much more surprising than Jackson Pollack and much more startling than James Joyce or David Jones or Olivier Messiaen or Alfred Manessier.

The Russian proverb about red-haired saints is not bold enough. It should not be "There has never been a red-haired saint." It should be "When will we have a green-haired saint? A purple-haired saint?" Why not? We never know what strange new things may be possible in our ever-changing world. A green-haired saint would be symbolic. Symbolic of what? It would signify, as T. S. Eliot says in "Little Gidding," that

> We shall not cease from exploration
> And the end of all our exploring
> Will be to arrive where we started
> And know the place for the first time.

I have been trying to suggest, with the figures I have dealt with—who are by no means the only figures, and not even necessarily the best figures—how we may go back where we came from, in order to go forward to where we have never been but must go, to go where we are and yet are not to go, where we are not and yet are, to paraphrase both T. S. Eliot in "East Coker" and his source, St. John of the Cross.

It is very important for people to develop a sense of openness and of community and of continuity. It is particularly important that we do these things today. All of us. For several reasons. We must make persons, all kinds of persons, commendable to a world that has lost much of its reverence, including its reverence for persons. If we have been given special graces, our lives hold those graces in trust, for other persons. The world is longing for a sense of community today. We must compassionate that world, and

315

realize that it really wants what Christians have or should have and could have, that in all its impurities the world seeks only purities. This is true. This is God's honest truth. In all its defective, perverted or excessive loves, the world seeks only love.

I think the best summary of all that I can give you is a prayer, a prayer that I say after Mass because it comes from a good time, the eleventh century, which I must confess I noted before I noted the words of the prayer. I like the eleventh century and I like Jean de Fécamp, whose prayer it is, but more important, I like the prayer because I think it speaks so well to our condition. All men, of all times and of all places are brothers, whether they have blond hair or black hair or red hair, long hair, short hair, or no hair or purple hair. We are all one, really one, created by one God, even when we do not act as if we are, or feel as if we are, or look as if we are.

This is no allegory. We are members one of another. There is nothing allegorical about it. It is a fact. And there is no reaching beyond this fact. It covers every level of being, every meaning, every becoming, every place, every time. There is no signification, no matter how many layers of meaning we see, that can be any larger than that.

This is the prayer, which I hope I have translated with some suggestion of the grace that is in the French:

O Sovereign Lord, deign to accept this sacrifice, for your holy Church, for the people you have acquired by your blood. I am only a sinner, and you don't find anything very good in me, but remember that you gave me the responsibility for my brothers. And do not allow my unworthiness to make useless this sacrifice in which you wanted to be the victim, you, our Savior and Redeemer. I offer you, I present

316

to you, O Lord, the insecurity of people, the instability of nations, the anguish of prisoners, the misery of orphans, the needs of travelers, the nakedness of the poor, the despair of the sick, the infirmities of the old, the aspirations of the young, the dreams of young girls, the tears of widows. On all you will have pity O Lord, because you love all who are the work of your hands. Remember what we are, our Father, our God. Do not be angry at us. Allow your love to flow out of your heart and over us. We pray to you, O great God, to look with benevolence on your family, that nobody will find his vow repulsed, his prayer sterile. You yourself tell us the prayers in which you will take pleasure and which you will grant.

Amen.

A Postscript

There is nothing that stands alone but God; everything else comes out of something that has gone before. The Conference in Asheville was the coming together of a number of very different persons from the world of Christian Education. They came from various backgrounds of history and tradition, by God's and man's own fashioning which makes a person what he really is. This group produced the synthesis called the *Conference on Christian Humanism,* a few lectures of which are recorded in this book.

Providence shapes man, and times, and events, without disturbing freedom. It seems Providential that when the great integrating idea of Vatican Council II was being formed in the good mind of Pope John on the other side of the Atlantic, a few educators here in Asheville, North Carolina, like Newman, were thinking of the universal idea of a Catholic college, with a perfect setting, a perfect curriculum, a perfect student-body, and a perfect faculty of master professors.

On this occasion in 1960, there was a wise, scholarly poet, a college president, Sister M. Madeleva, C.S.C., impatient for perfection, who sparked the idea of the *Conference on Christian Humanism* by her provocative questions:

"When are we going to get out of this stratosphere? An ideal Catholic college? An ideal student? A master professor? What are the names of some of these master professors?"

Everyone present named several. Then the conclusion:

"Invite some of these master professors from over the world to Asheville, North Carolina. We will send you some of our college teachers and then we will all go home and be a little more ideal."

Thus was born the *Conference on Christian Humanism,* which brought together about forty persons—master professors and college teachers—over a period of four wonderful summers (1961-1964), with lectures which took 200 hours of tape to record. The Bishop of Raleigh as the host became "the flag pole" around whom gathered this scholarly group at Mount Mary, in the "Land of the Sky", in Asheville, North Carolina.

Throughout the Conferences many professors and teachers expressed the desire for some kind of oral or written record of these lectures, but it was found that transcriptions from tape was an expensive and difficult task. The person transcribing such lectures has to understand perfectly and appreciate thoroughly the lecturer, as well as the lectures given. However, through the help of a New York professional company, this was accomplished at some cost.

The material was discovered to be so rich and voluminous that a selection was necessary but difficult. Providence again came to our rescue in the person of one of our best Christian humanists, Dr. Barry Ulanov, who offered to make a selection and edit the lectures chosen. We are very much indebted to Dr. Ulanov for his laborious editorial work on this book. Without his generosity it would never have been started.

Several publishers showed an interest in the manuscript, but with the exciting follow-up of the Second Vatican Council, and with other various interests and difficulties, publishing of this material was delayed, and some thought that it might be somewhat "dated". It was then proposed by a good friend, Mr. Francis J. Heazel, that the manuscript of selected lectures be printed rather than published. Thus, some of the rich ore mined during the summers of 1961-1964, would be preserved as a landmark of the synthesis of Catholic knowledge and educational disciplines in Catholic thought.

We are indebted to Sister M. Madeleva, C.S.C., (God rest her beautiful soul) for her provocative way of getting things started. We are also indebted to the Reverend William A. Wallace, O.P., who assisted in planning the Conferences and in relating the subjects. Thanks must also be extended to all those master professors whose lectures were selected for this book, and to the hundreds of others who labored and encouraged us to see these talks get into print. Without these, and most especially without the scholarly interest of another great educator, Dr. John W. McDevitt, Supreme Knight of the Knights of Columbus, and a generous donation from the Supreme Board of the Knights of Columbus, out of its Fourth Degree Fund, this book could not have been taken off tape and seen the light of day.

Anything my friend, Bishop John J. Wright of Pittsburgh, attends or is in any way connected with is honored by his presence, wisdom and wit. His Excellency spoke two different summers at the *Conference on Christian Humanism* in Asheville and made a profound contribution and impression on Master Professors and Scholars. He has been most generous in writing the outstanding Introduction to this book.

Though it contains by no means the total lectures of the Conferences, it is a sample of the rich ore which was mined in North Carolina by expert miners and minted into the pure gold of the realm to purchase for us Eternal Life. In thanking God for making the compilation of this volume possible, we would like to also thank those mentioned below —little and big, scholars and homespun people, Christian humanists all—who wanted to see the integration of knowledge brought about, the looking into the souls of each person to find there the uniting principles of the perennial philosophy and theology of the Church.

May we all be united together again in Eternity to come talk about the same subjects, with greater light, greater wisdom, and greater charity because of the Beatific Vision of God.

✝ Vincent S. Waters
Bishop of Raleigh

December 8, 1968,
Feast of the Immaculate Conception

Acknowledgments

We are profoundly grateful to:

Sister M. Madeleva, C.S.C., and members of the "College Planning Workshop for 1959 and 1960."

Dr. Barry Ulanov, the Reverend William A. Wallace, O.P., and to all who planned, executed, and encouraged the Conferences.

The scholarly interest of a great educator, Dr. John W. McDevitt, Supreme Knight of the Knights of Columbus, and a generous donation from the Supreme Board of the Knights of Columbus out of its Fourth Degree Fund, without which help this book could not have been taken off tape and seen the light of day.

The Reverend William F. Frost, Pastor of Sacred Heart Parish, Whiteville, N. C., for the art work used at the Conferences, and for the illustrations on the cover and within this book. He has been most generous of his time and talent.

The Reverend John Brown, Pastor of St. Eugene Parish at Asheville, N. C., for the preparation and furnishing of Mount Mary to receive our Master Professors; to the Reverend William G. Wellein, Director of St. John Vianney Preseminary for the preparation of the Hall to receive our student-guests, and to the Reverend Joseph A. Kerin, Principal of Asheville Catholic High School for the preparation of the high school and the gymnasium for the meetings.

The Asheville Pastors, who so willingly offered hospitality to our overflow of Priest Professors and Priest Students.

The Mother General of the Sisters of Mercy of Belmont, N. C., who cooperated by so generously permitting her Sisters to assist in every way possible in the Conferences.

The Sisters Superior of St. Genevieve of the Pines and St. Joseph Hospital, Asheville, who made space available for additional guests.

Sister M. Stephen, R.S.M., President of Sacred Heart College, Belmont, N. C., the amiable and gracious hostess for the four years of the Conferences. Not only did she welcome and look after the needs of the guests, but enthusiastically arranged trips by cars to various places of interest and scenic mountain beauty, such as Mount Mitchell, with picnic lunches at wayside gardens, visits to the Biltmore Estate, to the home of Thomas Wolfe and to Our Lady of the Hills Diocesan Camp at nearby Hendersonville.

The Very Reverend Charles J. O'Connor, Liturgist, and present Rector of Sacred Heart Cathedral at Raleigh, who arranged with 20th Century Fox for a private showing at the Imperial Theatre, Asheville, of the film, SAINT FRANCIS.

Mr. Francis J. Heazel, Attorney, Asheville, who arranged for tickets and chartered bus to take the professors and students to the Cherokee Reservation for the outdoor pageant, UNTO THESE HILLS, and visit to the INDIAN VILLAGE.

Mrs. Agnes Lux of Richmond, Virginia, our efficient and well-loved Librarian, who took care of the library of books recommended by our master professors, and to Miss Charlotte Ann Field of the Catholic University and Mrs. Paul J. Thayer of Eagle Rock, Virginia, who so capably assisted Mrs. Lux.

Mr. Fritzie Campbell of the Religious Goods Shop at

Richmond, Virginia, who supplied the books for inspection and purchase, as well as the religious articles.

The Sisters of the Visitation at Monte Maria, Richmond, Virginia, who worked so diligently and lovingly in the printing of our beautiful brochures over the four years.

Mr. Ernest Dixon, our jovial chef, whose delicious meals were enjoyed by all; to Mrs. Cordelia Graham, our maid, who assisted so graciously in all domestic work.

The Major and Minor Seminarians who helped to prepare for the Humanist Conferences each year, and especially those who waited on the tables: Messrs. Joseph Gaul, Harry Webb, Charles Williams, and Melvin Wetzel.

The Sisters who assisted Dr. Barry Ulanov in the editing of the tapes selected for this book: Sister M. Annella, R.S.M., Sacred Heart College, Belmont, N. C., Mother Ethel Lunsford, R.C.E., and Mother Helen McCarthy, R.C.E. of St. Genevieve of the Pines, Asheville, and Sister James Eugene, C.S.J., of Brentwood College, Brentwood, N. Y.

The Sisters Adorers of the Most Precious Blood, from the Bishop's Residence, Sister Elaine Marie and Sister M. Benigna, who staffed Mount Mary during the four summers and took such excellent care of the domestic duties of the house for the Bishop and the master professors.

The Bishop's secretary, Miss Mary E. Parish, who recorded the lectures on tape during the four summers and who has worked with enthusiasm to see this book get into print.

Mr. and Mrs. Paul G. Zomberg for their splendid work of proof-reading this book.

Appendix

FOR THE RECORD AND FUTURE RESEARCH
ON THESE CONFERENCES, WE PRESENT THE
ENTIRE PROGRAM OF THE CONFERENCES.
1961—1964

Appendix

STEERING COMMITTEE

Most Reverend Vincent S. Waters, D.D. (host)

Rt. Rev. Msgr. Paul Hanley Furfey

Reverend William A. Wallace, O.P.

Reverend Urban Voll, O.P.

Reverend Benedict M. Ashley, O.P.

Reverend Leo A. Ward, C.S.C.

Reverend Thomas D. Sullivan, S.S.E.

Reverend Charles J. O'Connor

Sister M. Janet, S.C.

Sister M. Madeleva, C.S.C.

Sister M. Stephen, R.S.M.

Sister M. Annella, R.S.M.

Sister M. Theophane, R.S.M.

Dr. Alphonse H. Clemens

Dr. Carl Bauer

Mrs. Anthony Thayer

Dr. Elizabeth Loughran

1961 WORKSHOP PROGRAM

THE AMERICAN CATHOLIC INTELLECTUAL

vs.

THE AMERICAN INTELLECTUAL CATHOLIC
Most Reverend John J. Wright, D.D.
Bishop of Pittsburgh

THE IDEAL OF CATHOLIC EDUCATION AS TRUE HUMANISM

First Week:
Second Week:
Third Week:

MODERN CONCEPTION OF MAN:

Scientific
Irrationalistic
Vitalistic
Communistic
Existentialistic

THOMIST CONCEPTION OF MAN
PHILOSOPHY AND THEOLOGY AS
INTEGRATING FACTORS IN EDUCATION

Reverend Ambrose J. McNicholl, O.P.
San Clemente, Via Labicana, Rome, Italy

THE DEVELOPMENT OF CHRISTIAN HUMANISM
SOURCES AND RESOURCES: THE LITERARY
TRADITIONS OF CHRISTIAN HUMANISM

(Augustine, Boethius, Gregory, Bernard, Thomas, Dante,
Pascal, Shakespeare, John of the Cross, and how they provide a
center and a purpose for a curriculum)

Dr. Barry Ulanov, Barnard College
Columbia University, New York, N. Y.

TEACHING IN THE SPIRIT OF CHRISTIAN HUMANISM

Dr. Frank O'Malley, University of Notre Dame
Notre Dame, Indiana

THE IMPORTANCE OF THE FORM OF TEACHING ON THE DEVELOPMENT OF INTELLECTUAL LIFE

(The Community of Learning)
Dr. Willis D. Nutting, University of Notre Dame
Notre Dame, Indiana

CONFERENCE DIRECTORS FOR 1961

Rt. Rev. Msgr. Paul H. Furfey, Chairman
Catholic University of America
Rev. Leo R. Ward, CSC, Vice Chairman
University of Notre Dame
Very Rev. Charles J. O'Connor, Liturgy
Rector of Sacred Heart Cathedral
Sister M. Stephen, RSM, Hostess
President of Sacred Heart College

1962 WORKSHOP PROGRAM

THE PHILOSOPHY OF SCIENCE

Educational Challenges of the Space Age; Place of Science
in College Curriculum
Galileo and the Inquisition
Newton's Conception of God and Universe
Methodology and Existence of Atoms
Modern Philosophies of Matter
Philosophical Commitments of Physical Scientists
Dialogue Between Science and Theology

Reverend William A. Wallace, O.P., Dover, Mass.
Massachusetts Institute of Technology

SCIENCE AND THE HUMANITIES:
—A New and Urgent Problem

Science and the Humanities in the Renaissance
Science and the Humanities in the 19th Century
Science and the Humanities Today

Dr. Charles DeKoninck, *University of Laval, Quebec, Canada*

THE NEW BIOLOGY

The New Biology; The Education of a Scientist; A More Natural
Approach to Biology and Medicine; Evolution as a Unifying Concept in Biology; Science Education and the Christian Person

Sister Adrian Marie, O.P., *Siena College, Memphis, Tennessee*

PHILOSOPHY OF ART AND COMMUNICATION

Poetry and Knowledge
Poetry and Love
Poetry and Prayer
Art and Nature
Fine Arts in the Hierarchy of Knowledge
Fine Arts in the Curriculum

Reverend Benedict M. Ashley, O.P., *River Forest, Illinois*

THE FINE ARTS

Poets Are to Be Heard
Poetry as a Fine Art
The Poet and the Philosopher
Forming and Informing Poetry
A Poet's Responsibilities
Poets in Particular
The Poet, A Christian Humanist

Sister M. Madeleva, CSC
St. Mary's College, Notre Dame, Indiana

THE MADONNA

In the collections of the North Carolina Museum of Art. Examples
from 13th to the 18th Centuries.

SOME THEMES OF RELIGIOUS ART

In the collections of the North Carolina Museum of Art.

Dr. Justus Bier, *Director*
North Carolina Museum of Art, Raleigh, N. C.

ATLAS OF THE EARLY CHRISTIAN WORLD *and* MEANING OF ICONS

Miss Ade Bethune, *Newport, Rhode Island*

AN ARTIST'S VISION

Rev. Anthony Lauck, CSC, *Head, Department of Art, University
of Notre Dame, Notre Dame, Indiana*

SCRIPTURE AND LITURGY

Rev. Stephen Hartdegen, OFM
Holy Name College, Washington, D. C.

WHAT THE COLLEGE TEACHER AND THE PRIMARY TEACHER HAVE IN COMMON

The Ideals and the Background of Teaching Procedures

Dr. John H. Treanor, *Boston, Mass.*

CONFERENCE DIRECTORS FOR 1962

Rt. Rev. Msgr. Paul H. Furfey
Catholic University of America
Chairman

334

Rev. Leo R. Ward, CSC
University of Notre Dame
Vice Chairman

Rev. Francis Smith
Southern Pines, N. C.

Rev. Charles Hughes
Glenmary Fathers, Glendale, Ohio
Liturgy

Sister M. Stephen, RSM
President of Sacred Heart College, Belmont, N. C.
Hostess

1963 WORKSHOP PROGRAM

MAN AND SOCIETY

First Week:
Second Week:
Third Week:

A study of "The Family",
(The Nature of Man and the Nature of Society).

A Study of "Civil Society".

A Study of "The Economic Order".

LAW—LIBERTY AND SOCIETY

Most Reverend John J. Wright, D.D.
Bishop of Pittsburgh

MATER ET MAGISTRA—The Need for Unity in Thinking on
Problems of Economics, Sociology, and Politics on a World
Wide Scale.

Rt. Rev. Msgr. Peter Pavan
Pontifical University of the Lateran
Rome, Italy

SOCIAL AND POLITICAL PHILOSOPHY

Dr. William Oliver Martin
Department of Philosophy
University of Rhode Island
Kingston, R. I.

NATURAL LAW IN ORIENTAL TRADITIONS

1. A General Survey of Natural Law Concepts in Oriental Traditions
2. Confucian Ethics and Christian Humanism.
3. The "Tao" and the Natural Law

Dr. John Wu
School of Law
Seton Hall University
South Orange, N. J.

THE CATHOLIC FAMILY IN OUR AMERICAN CULTURE

Dr. Alphonse H. Clemens, Director
Marriage Counseling Center
Catholic University of America
Washington, D. C.

SOCIOLOGY OF THE PARISH—Church in the City
CLERGY-LAY RELATIONS

Rev. Joseph H. Fichter, S.J.
Department of Sociology
Loyola University
New Orleans, La.

CULTURAL ANTHROPOLOGY—THE FAMILY IN CROSS CULTURAL PERSPECTIVE

Mrs. Regina F. Herzfeld
Department of Anthropology
Catholic University of America
Washington, D. C.

MANAGEMENT AND LABOR

Rt. Rev. Msgr. George G. Higgins, Director
Department of Social Action
National Catholic Welfare Conference
Washington, D. C.

THE PERSON IN SOCIETY
THE VIRTUE OF PATRIOTISM AND
THE VICE OF NATIONALISM
HUMAN FREEDOM AND AUTHORITY

Dr. Thomas P. Neill
Department of History
St. Louis University
St. Louis, Missouri

THE POPES AND THE SOCIAL ENCYCLICALS

Mrs. Anne Fremantle
New York, N. Y.

INTEGRATION OF THE SCIENCES OF MAN
INTEGRATION OF THE SOCIAL SCIENCES

Rev. William A. Wallace, O.P.
Staff Editor, Philosophy
The New Catholic Encyclopedia
Catholic University of America
Washington, D. C.

INTERRACIAL PROBLEMS IN N. C.

Sister M. Annella, R.S.M.
Department of Sociology
Sacred Heart Junior College
Belmont, North Carolina

JUSTICE AND THE SPIRIT OF SOCIAL RESPONSIBILITY

Brother Leo V. Ryan, CSV
Asst. Sup. General of Clerics of St. Viator
Rome, Italy

CONFERENCE DIRECTORS FOR 1963

Rt. Rev. Msgr. Paul H. Furfey
Catholic University of America

Rev. Leo R. Ward, CSC
University of Notre Dame

Rev. Paul J. Gilvary, S.J.
Liturgy and Music

Sister M. Stephen, RSM
President of Sacred Heart College
Belmont, N. C.
Hostess

1964 WORKSHOP PROGRAM

THE PERSON IN TIME AND ETERNITY
(Education for What?)

First Week:
    (Philosophical accent)
Second Week:
    (Theological accent)
Third Week:
    (Scriptural and
      Theological accent)

A study of "The Person
  in the World"
    (Freedom and Individuality)
A study of "The Christian Person
  in the World"
    (Christian Responsibility)
A study of "The Divine Person—
The Mystical Christ"
    (The Mystical Person in the
    two Worlds)

CHURCH, STATE AND COUNCIL
INDIVIDUAL CONSCIENCE AND PLURALISM
INDIVIDUALISTIC OR GROUP PLURALISM
EDUCATION IN A PLURALIST SOCIETY

Rev. Francis Canavan, S.J.
Associate Editor of "America"
New York, N. Y.

PERSONAL COMMITMENTS OF SCIENTISTS
CATHOLICS AND THE SCIENCE EXPLOSION

Rev. William A. Wallace, O.P.
Staff Editor, Philosophy
The New Catholic Encyclopedia
Catholic Univ. of America
Washington, D. C.

LITERATURE AND PERSONAL VALUES
EXCELLENCE ON THE CATHOLIC CAMPUS
THE COMMON GROUND OF CHRISTIANS
JUSTICE AND MERCY:

THE BIBLICAL TENSION

Dr. Paul van K. Thomson, Director
Liberal Arts Honors Program
Providence College
Providence, R. I.

THE NEEDY ALL OVER THE WORLD
THE PRIMACY OF CONSCIENCE

Miss Eileen Egan, Project Supervisor
Catholic Relief Services, N.C.W.C.
New York, N. Y.

THE PERSONAL PLEROMA OF THE CHRISTIAN

The Christian "I" in the World
The Christian Intellectual in the World
The Christian Apostle in the World

THE MYSTICAL PLEROMA AND THE CHRISTIAN

The Mystical Prophet
The Mystical Priest
The Mystical King

Rev. James M. Egan, O.P.
Director, School of Sacred Theology
St. Mary's College
Notre Dame, Indiana

THE WISDOM OF EVOLUTION
EVOLUTION AND THE FUTURE OF MAN

Rev. Raymond J. Nogar, O.P.
Aquinas Institute of Philosophy
River Forest, Illinois

CHRISTIAN RESPONSIBILITY IN INTERFAITH
    CONTACTS
CHRISTIAN RESPONSIBILITY FOR INTERNATIONAL
    ATTITUDES

Sister Joan, SND
Office of Development
Trinity College, Washington, D. C.

342

HOW JUSTIFY CATHOLIC EDUCATION?
APOSTLES—The End of Catholic Education

    Sister M. Josetta, RSM—Executive Secretary
    Conf. of Major Superiors of Women's Institutes
    Movement for a Better World
    Washington, D. C.

IMPORTANCE AND URGENCY OF EVANGELIZATION
    OF WORLD

    Christ and the Evangelization of the World

ARE WE RESPONSIBLE FOR EVANGELIZATION
    OF WORLD?

    Is it the Whole Church that Must Be Missionary?

ROLE OF OUR SCHOOLS IN EVANGELIZATION
    OF WORLD

    Rev. F. Legrand, Director
    "Christ to the World" magazine
    Rome, Italy

THE MODERN CATHOLIC BIBLICAL MOVEMENT
OLD TESTAMENT PERSPECTIVES—

    The Word in the World

NEW TESTAMENT PERSPECTIVES—

    Christ in the World Today

    Rt. Rev. Msgr. William L. Newton, S.S.D.
    St. Mary's Rectory
    Elyria, Ohio

PRE-CHRISTIAN & NON-CHRISTIAN SOCIAL PRINCIPLES
THE EARLY CHURCH—Slavery, etc.
MEDIEVAL AND RENAISSANCE—Ideas
FROM LOUIS XVI to LEO XIII to PAUL VI

    Mrs. Anne Fremantle
    New York, N. Y.

CONFERENCE DIRECTORS FOR 1964

Rt. Rev. Msgr. Paul H. Furfey
  Catholic University of America
Rev. Leo R. Ward, CSC
  University of Notre Dame
Rev. Cranor Graves and Rev. Declan Gilligan, "Better World
  Movement"
Rev. Walter Sullivan
  Diocese of Raleigh—Liturgy and Music
Sister M. Stephen, RSM
  President of Sacred Heart College
  Belmont, N. C.
  Hostess

EXTRA SPEAKERS FOR THE CONFERENCES

Reverend Riccardo Lombardi, Better World Movement, Rome, Italy
Reverend Peter Minard, O.S.B., Oxford, N. C.
Dr. W. D. Weatherford, Black Mountain, N. C.
Mr. Dale Francis, Huntington, Indiana

SCHOLARS ATTENDING THE CONFERENCES

Very Rev. Msgr. Lawrence P. Cahill, St. John's College, Cleveland, Ohio
Brother Edward Cashin, F.M.S., Marist Brothers Provincialate, Esopus, N. Y.
Reverend Henry Culkin, Jackson Heights, New York, N. Y.
Reverend Richard J. Dombro, S.M., University of Dayton, Dayton, Ohio
Reverend Florance M. Gillis, S. J., College of Holy Cross, Worcester, Mass.
Reverend Christopher Huntington, Pius X Seminary, Uniondale, N. Y.
Brother D. John, F.S.C., Elkins Park, Pa.
Reverend Joseph Jurasko, O.P., Barry College, Miami, Florida
Reverend Paul R. Milde, O.S.B., Belmont Abbey College, Belmont, N. C.
Reverend John Oetgen, O.S.B., Belmont Abbey College, Belmont, N. C.
Brother Placidius, O.S.B., Belmont Abbey College, Belmont, N. C.
Reverend Joseph Quigley, Amherst College, Amherst, Mass.
Reverend Edmund Rhodes, S.M., University of Dayton, Dayton, Ohio
Reverend William A. Scott, S.J., LeMoyne College, Syracuse, N. Y.
Reverend Thomas D. Sullivan, SSE., St. Michael's College, Winooski, Vt.

Dominican Sisters of Sinsinawa, Wisconsin:

Sister M. Melchior, O.P., Edgewood College, Madison, Wisc.
Sister Mary Grace, O.P., Edgewood College, Madison, Wisc.
Sister M. Matthias, O.P., Edgewood College, Madison, Wisc.
Sister M. Esther, O.P., Edgewood College, Madison, Wisc.
Sister M. Elaine, O.P., Edgewood College, Madison, Wisc.
Sister Mary Brandon, O.P., Rosary College, River Forest, Ill.
Sister Mary Colum, O.P., Rosary College, River Forest, Ill.
Sister M. Aurelia, O.P., Rosary College, River Forest, Ill.
Sister Albertus Magnus, O.P., Rosary College, River Forest, Ill.

Dominican Sisters of Adrian, Michigan:

Sister Robert Louise, O.P., Barry College, Miami, Florida
Sister Thomas Aquin, O.P., Barry College, Miami, Florida

Dominican Sisters of 3rd Order of St. Dominic, Amityville, N. Y.:

Sister M. Doreen, O.P., Molloy Catholic College, Rockville Centre, N. Y.
Sister M. Marlene, O.P., Molloy Catholic College, Rockville Centre, N. Y.

Sisters of St. Joseph of Cleveland, Ohio:

Sister Mary Xavier, CSJ, St. John's College, Cleveland
Sister Immaculata, CSJ, St. John's College, Cleveland
Sister M. Celine, CSJ, St. John's College, Cleveland

Sisters of St. Joseph of Salina, Kansas:

Sister M. Eloise, CSJ, Marymount College, Salina
Sister M. Monica, CSJ, Marymount College, Salina
Sister M. Leonida, CSJ, Marymount College, Salina
Sister Mary Mark, CSJ, Marymount College, Salina

Sisters of St. Joseph, Brentwood, N. Y.:

Sister Mary Germaine, CSJ, Brentwood College, Brentwood
Sister James Eugene, CSJ, Brentwood College, Brentwood

Sister of St. Joseph of Springfield, Mass.:

Sister James Mary, CSJ, College of the Elms, Chicopee, Mass.
Sister John Martha, CSJ, College of the Elms, Chicopee, Mass.
Sister Ignatius Loyola, CSJ, College of the Elms, Chicopee, Mass.

Sisters of St. Joseph of Carondelet, Latham, New York:

Sister Elizabeth Catherine, CSJ, College of St. Rose, Albany, N. Y.

Sisters of Charity of St. Augustine, West Richfield, Ohio:

Sister M. Maureen, CSA, Mt. Augustine

Franciscan Sisters of Immaculate Conception, Little Falls, Minn.:
Sister Mary Anastasia, OSF, St. Clare College, Little Falls
Sister Mary Kathleen, OSF, St. Clare College, Little Falls

Sisters of St. Francis of Mary Immaculate, Joliet, Ill.:
Sister M. Beatrice, OSF, College of St. Francis, Joliet
Sister Veronica, OSF, College of St. Francis, Joliet
Sister M. Seraphim, OSF, College of St. Francis, Joliet
Sister M. Elvira, OSF, College of St. Francis, Joliet

Sisters of St. Benedict of Atchison, Kansas:
Sister M. Juanita, O.S.B., Mt. St. Scholastica College, Atchison

Sisters of St. Benedict of Chicago, Illinois:
Sister M. Mercedes, O.S.B., St. Scholastica School, Chicago

Benedictine Sisters of Diocesan Jurisdiction, San Antonio, Fla.:
Sister Caroline, O.S.B., St. Leo College, San Antonio
Sister Mary Grace, O.S.B., St. Leo College, San Antonio
Sister M. Celine, O.S.B., Holy Name Priory, San Antonio

Sisters of St. Benedict of Erie, Pennsylvania:
Sister Mary David, O.S.B., Erie, Penna.
Sister Lois Marie, O.S.B., Erie, Penna.

Religious of the Sacred Heart of Mary of Tarrytown, N. Y.:
Mother M. Brendan, RSHM, Marymount College, Tarrytown
Sister M. Gerard, RSHM, Marymount College, Tarrytown
Mother M. Jogues, RSHM, Marymount College, Tarrytown

Sisters of Charity of Mother Seton, Greensburg, Penna.:
Sister Harold Ann, S.C., Seton Hill College, Greensburg
Sister Teresa Martin, S.C., Seton Hill College, Greensburg
Sister Sara Louise, S.C., Seton Hill College, Greensburg
Sister Richard Ann, S.C., Seton Hill College, Greensburg

Sisters of Charity of Cincinnati:
Sister M. Janet, S.C., Mt. St. Joseph, Ohio

Sisters of Charity of Nazareth, Kentucky:
Sister George Cecilia, SCN, Academy of Our Lady of Nazareth, Wakefield, Mass.
Sister Winifred Ann, SCN, Frankfort, Ky.
Sister Mary Pauletta, SCN, Nazareth College, Nazareth
Sister Jeanne D'Arc, SCN, Nazareth College, Nazareth

Congregation of the Maryknoll, Sisters of St. Dominic:
Sister Rose Michele, Maryknoll Teachers College, New York
Sister Marie Joan, Maryknoll Teachers College, New York

Sisters of Mercy of Union in the United States, Dallas, Penna.:
Sister Mary Assumpta, RSM, Mt. Aloysius Jr. College, Cresson, Pa.
Sister M. Thaddeau, RSM, Mt. Aloysius Jr. College, Cresson, Pa.

Sisters of Mercy of Erie, Pennsylvania:
Sister Mary Brigid, RSM, Mercyhurst College, Erie
Sister Mary Matthew, RSM, Mercyhurst College, Erie
Sister M. Loretto, RSM, Mercyhurst College, Erie

Sisters of Mercy of Belmont, North Carolina:
Mother Mary Benignus, RSM, Sacred Heart College, Belmont, N. C.
Mother Mary James, RSM, Sacred Heart College, Belmont, N. C.
Sister M. Theophane, RSM, Sacred Heart College, Belmont, N. C.
Sister M. Christine, RSM, Sacred Heart College, Belmont, N. C.
Sister M. Annella, RSM, Sacred Heart College, Belmont, N. C.
Sister M. Stephen, RSM, Sacred Heart College, Belmont, N. C.

Sisters of St. Casimir of Chicago, Ill.:
Sister M. Agnesine, SSC, St. Casimir Jr. College, Chicago
Sister M. Simplicita, SSC, St. Casimir Jr. College, Chicago

Ursuline Nuns of the Congregation of Paris, Cincinnati, Ohio:
Sister Mary James, OSU, Ursuline Jr. College, Cincinnati
Sister Elizabeth, OSU, Ursuline Jr. College, Cincinnati

Ursuline Nuns of the Congregation of Paris, Cleveland, Ohio:
Sister Miriam Lynch, OSU, Ursuline College for Women, Cleveland
Sister Michael Francis, OSU, Ursuline College for Women, Cleveland

Sisters of Blessed Sacrament for Indians and Colored People, Cornwells Heights, Pa.:
Sister Francis Mary, SBS, Blessed Sacrament College, Cornwells Heights
Sister M. Ignacita, SBS, Blessed Sacrament College, Cornwells Heights

Sisters of Notre Dame de Namur, Baltimore, Md.:
Sister Berchmans Julia, SND, Trinity College, Washington, D. C.

Mission Helpers of the Sacred Heart, Towson, Maryland:
Sister M. Rosalia, MHSH, Sacred Heart Convent, Towson
Sister Marie, MHSH, Columbia, South Carolina

Religious of Christian Education of Milton, Mass.:

Mother Margaret Potts, RCE, St. Genevieve of the Pines Academy, Asheville, N. C.

Mother Ethel Lunsford, RCE, St. Genevieve of the Pines Academy, Asheville, N. C.

Mother Helen McCarthy, RCE, St. Genevieve of the Pines Academy, Asheville, N. C.

Mrs. Theresa M. Armstrong, Parry Sound, Ontario, Canada
Dr. Carl Bauer, Catholic University, Washington, D. C.
Miss Ella V. Cleary, Morehead Rehabilitation School, Butner, N. C.
Miss Charlotte Ann Field, Catholic University, Washington, D. C.
Miss Frances P. Herlehy, Brooklyn, N. Y.
Miss Caroline E. Schutzinger, Univ. of Detroit, Detroit, Michigan
Miss Ruth Thome, University of Detroit, Detroit, Michigan

GUESTS ATTENDING CONFERENCES

Most Reverend Paul J. Hallinan, Archbishop of Atlanta
Rt. Rev. Msgr. Ferotto, Rome
Reverend Adrian Cervia, Better World Movement, Rome
Reverend Stanley Kusman, S.M., Better World Movement, U.S.A.
Reverend Leo A. O'Connor, S.J., Pittsburgh, Penna.
Reverend Cuthbert Allen, O.S.B., Belmont Abbey College, Belmont, N. C.
Reverend Richard F. Allen, Diocese of Raleigh
Reverend Henri Blanc, Diocese of Raleigh
Reverend John M. Breunig, Diocese of Raleigh
Reverend Jesse L. Creel, Diocese of Raleigh
Reverend Howard Lane, Diocese of Raleigh
Rt. Rev. Msgr. George E. Lynch, Diocese of Raleigh
Rt. Rev. Msgr. James E. McSweeney, Diocese of Raleigh
Reverend Francis R. Moeslein, Diocese of Raleigh
Reverend Charles Mulholland, Diocese of Raleigh
Reverend Roderick B. O'Connor, Diocese of Raleigh
Rt. Rev. Msgr. F. John Roueche, Diocese of Raleigh
Reverend Donald Staib, Diocese of Raleigh
Sister Mary Patricia, R.S.M., St. Joseph Hospital, Asheville, N. C.
Sister Mary Lawrence, R.S.M., St. Joseph Hospital, Asheville, N. C.
Sister Rosaria, R.S.M., St. Joseph Hospital, Asheville, N. C.
Mother Quinn, R.C.E., St. Genevieve of the Pines, Asheville, N. C.
Sister Mary Anthony, O.L.M., Our Lady of Mercy Convent, Charleston, S. C.

Sister M. Benedictus, CSC, St. Mary's College, Notre Dame, Indiana

Sister Bertrande Meyers, Marrilac College, Normandy, Mo.

Sister Mary Michael, Medical Missionaries, Philadelphia, Pa.

Sister Francis Regina, S.C., Sisters of Charity of Cincinnati, Cincinnati, Ohio

Sister M. Cecelia, S.C., Sisters of Charity of Cincinnati, Cincinnati, Ohio

Sister M. Madonna, MHSH, Mission Helpers of Sacred Heart, Statesville, N. C.

Mrs. T. Frank Driscoll, Roanoke, Va.

Mrs. Justus Bier, Raleigh, N. C.

Mr. and Mrs. Francis J. Heazel, Asheville, N. C.

Mrs. Osborne A. McKegney, New York City, N. Y.

Miss Elizabeth Nugent, New York City, N. Y.

Mrs. Willis D. Nutting, Notre Dame, Ind.

Mr. Louis Palanca, Grand Forks, N. D.

We request of those who read this book, prayers for the following who have gone to God since the Conferences:

Reverend James Mark Egan, O.P.

Reverend Raymond J. Nogar, O.P.

Reverend Howard Lane

Sister M. Madeleva, C.S.C.

Dr. Charles de Koninck

Miss Ella Cleary

Sister Mary Grace, O.P.

Most Reverend Paul J. Hallinan

The Workshop participants are grateful to your Excellency for having put out the Flag-pole at Asheville.

They promise a remembrance in prayer during the coming year.

The Flag Pole